Port Royal, Jamaica

♦

Michael Pawson

and

David Buisseret

The University of the West Indies Press
Barbados • Jamaica • Trinidad and Tobago

The University of the West Indies Press
1A Aqueduct Flats   Mona
Kingston 7   Jamaica   WI

©1974 by Oxford University Press

©2000 by Michael Pawson and David Buisseret
All rights reserved. Published 2000

04 03 02 01 00   5 4 3 2 1

CATALOGUING IN PUBLICATION DATA

Pawson, Michael.
Port Royal/Michael Pawson and David Buisseret. – 2nd ed.
p. : ill.; cm.

Includes bibliographical references and index.

ISBN 13: 978-9-7664-0072-9

1. Port Royal (Jamaica) – History. 2. Jamaica – History.
I. Buisseret, David. II. Title
F1895.P6P38   2000   972.92 dc-20

Book design by Carol Lehman
Typeset at the University of Texas at Arlington
Cover design by Robert Harris

For Margaret and Patricia

Preface to the First Edition (1974)

Michael Pawson and I first met in 1968 when he was reading for a part-time BA degree at the University of the West Indies, and I was teaching there. In his spare time - he was by profession an accountant with the Jamaica Omnibus Services - he had become very interested in the history of Port Royal, largely as a result of diving on the sunken city. I too had become interested in Port Royal's history, from another angle; it seemed to me, as a newcomer to Caribbean history, that previous authors had greatly underestimated the quantity and quality of written evidence bearing on the town.

Our collaboration therefore ensued, and this book has resulted from it. Of course, we were obliged to take a great deal of advice along the way, much of it from colleagues at the University. Professor Hall criticized the first plan for us, and Mr. Ken Ingram, university librarian, provided us with some very useful references to manuscripts in England and North America. The chapter on Port Royal's geography owes much to the late Professor Tom Goreau, and the medical section was helpfully vetted by Dr. Hal Dyer, head of the University Health Service. Bill Claypole, research student from Canada, opened up many new areas of investigation in the course of his Ph.D. dissertation on 'The merchants of Port Royal'. The final draft was read and corrected by those two unsparing critics, Rod Cave of the Library School and John Ingledew of the Department of English.

We also received valuable help from persons outside the University. The staff of the Institute of Jamaica were nearly always helpful, and we enjoyed good and mutually profitable relations with the archaeologists working at Port Royal, Robert Marx and Phil Mayes. Finally, the chapter on naval affairs was vetted with profit by Commander W.E. May, of London. All in all, this is a book which owes a great deal to a large number of people. We hope that they and others will enjoy reading the results of our collaboration, though we recognize that it is in certain respects imperfect.

Easter 1974   DAVID BUISSERET
                     Mona, Jamaica

                     MICHAEL PAWSON
                     Wellsford, New Zealand

Preface to the Second Edition (2000)

Twenty-five years after we first published *Port Royal, Jamaica,* Michael Pawson and I were delighted to be asked to undertake a new edition of it, this time in Jamaica, and including accounts of much work that has been done in the intervening years. Most of the persons mentioned in our first preface are still alive, and many have continued to exchange ideas about our theme. It has not tempted many new scholars, but we have greatly profited by the help and advice of Jean and Oliver Cox, particularly from the architectural point of view. The book was widely reviewed, and many of those reviews have been helpful in rewriting certain sections.

The new information has been incorporated into the appropriate chapters, but we thought it helpful here briefly to summarize the nature of the changes. One of the few historians directly to address early Port Royal was Nuala Zahediah, in two articles in 1986 on the Spanish contraband trade and on Port Royal's role in the early economic development of Jamaica (see the bibliography for full references). Much of the argument in the collaborative work *Atlantic Port Cities*, of 1991, also concerned Port Royal, setting its history into a wider context. The architects and archaeologists have been particularly active in revising our ideas about the city. In their unpublished reports on 'Seventeenth-century Port Royal, its urban form and architectural character' (1992) and 'The naval hospitals of Port Royal, Jamaica' (1995), both deposited at the National Library of Jamaica, Jean and Oliver Cox brought a new precision to the interpretation of both historical documents and archaeological evidence.

Among the archaeologists, the successor to those enumerated in chapter 11 was Professor D. L. Hamilton, from the Department of Anthropology at Texas A & M University. Between 1981 and 1990 he and his students worked yearly at Port Royal, publishing their findings in the Texas-based *INA* (Institute of Nautical Archaeology) *Newsletter.* Hamilton's students included in their assessments not only their recent finds, but also those of such previous archaeologists as Anthony Priddy, Philip Mayes and Robert Marx, thus drawing together a huge volume of work.

From about 1986 onwards, there was a remarkable conservation complex and museum in the Old Naval Hospital at Port Royal; here, under the supervision of Jamaican archaeologists Anthony Aarons and Roderick Ebanks, much material could for some years be viewed, often with the help of Richard McClure, artefacts officer of the Jamaica National Heritage Trust. However, this extensive and costly facility was vulnerable both to rough weather and to cutbacks in government spending, and it has for some years operated only at a greatly reduced level.

All in all, we have come to know early Port Royal considerably better thanks to this great variety of research. Our hope is that we have successfully incorporated the new knowledge into our old account.

Summer, 1999   DAVID BUISSERET
University of Texas at Arlington

MICHAEL PAWSON
Queensland, Australia

Contents

List of figures	x
List of appendices	xi
Abbreviations	xii
Introduction: the sources	xiv
1 The geography of Port Royal	1
2 The coming of the English: Fort Cromwell 1655-1660	7
3 The consolidation of English power: privateering 1657-1680	25
4 The consolidation of English power: the fortifications	49
5 The consolidation of English power: the navy 1668-1692	57
6 The economic development of Port Royal in the seventeenth century	85
7 The topography of Port Royal 1660-1692	109
8 Everyday life at Port Royal before the earthquake	135
9 The earthquake and the passing of commercial primacy 1692-1722	165
10 Port Royal as a naval station 1692-1900	173
11 Archaeological investigations at Port Royal	203
12 Port Royal today	211
Conclusion	215
Appendices	219
Bibliography	234
Index	241

List of Figures

1. The formation of the Palisadoes spit — 1
2. Aerial photograph of the Palisadoes spit (Jack Tyndale-Biscoe) — 2
3. The site of Port Royal about 1655 — 3
4. Port Royal after the earthquake — 4
5. Present shoreline at Port Royal — 4
6. Aerial photograph of Port Royal (Jack Tyndale-Biscoe) — 5
7. The development of the Point to 1660 — 15
8. Map of the Point about 1666 (Public Record Office, London) — 50
9. Position and shape of Fort James — 51
10. The fortifications of Port Royal about 1690 — 53
11. Sequence of naval vessels at Port Royal to 1692 — 59
12. The younger van de Velde, H.M.S. *Phoenix* (National Maritime Museum) — 61
13. Model of H.M.S. *Mordaunt* (National Maritime Museum) — 66
14. The younger van de Velde, H.M.S. *Drake* (National Maritime Museum) — 71
15. The loss of H.M.S. *Norwich* in 1682 — 76
16. Tonnage of vessels arriving at Port Royal, 1670-1692 — 88
17. Edward Barlow, *The Cadiz Merchant* (National Maritime Museum) — 95
18. John Fletcher's land, New Street, 1692 (drawing by Oliver Cox after the excavation of Anthony Priddy, 1972) — 110
19. Street plan of Port Royal before 1692 — 111
20. Edward Barlow, View of Port Royal (National Maritime Museum) — 113
21. Detailed plan of part of Port Royal before 1692 — 114
22. William Hack, Plan of Port Royal (British Library) — 118
23. John Taylor, Plan of Port Royal (National Library of Jamaica) — 121
24. The yards of houses at Port Royal (drawing by Oliver Cox, following the excavation of Anthony Priddy, 1972) — 128
25. Comb case from Port Royal, dated 1673 (National Library of Jamaica) — 143
26. Tombstone of Lewis Galdy at Port Royal (photo by Buisseret) — 167
27. Christian Lilly, 'The profil or elevation of Fort Charles ... 1699' (Public Record Office) — 170
28. Christian Lilly, 'The Ichnography of the Town of Port Royall', c. 1700 (Public Record Office) — 175

29. Anon., Sketch of the dockyard in 1735 (Library of Congress)	180
30. The dockyard in 1739	180
31. The work of the 1720s by Fort Charles	181
32. The dockyard in 1770	184
33. Leading-marks for the South Channel (Hydrographic Office, Taunton)	186
34. The dockyard in 1799	187
35. Anon., Port Royal from the Apostles' Battery (National Library of Jamaica)	188
36. Archibald Campbell, 'Plan of the town and works of Port Royal, 1782' (British Library)	189
37. Anon., H.M.S. *Raccoon* returning to Port Royal (National Library of Jamaica)	192
38. Anon., H.M.S. *Shark* at Port Royal (National Library of Jamaica)	192
39. Anon., H.M.S. *Hercule* at Port Royal (National Library of Jamaica)	193
40. The dockyard in 1900	194
41. Joseph Kidd, View of Port Royal about 1830 (National Library of Jamaica)	195
42. Photograph of the dockyard about 1865 (National Library of Jamaica)	196
43. Anon., Watercolour of the dockyard about 1865 (National Library of Jamaica)	196
44. Albert Huie, The eastern end of Port Royal (National Library of Jamaica)	197
45. Adolphe Duperly, Naval vessels at Port Royal about 1855 (National Library of Jamaica)	199
46. Areas of archaeological investigation	206
47. Surviving sites of interest	213

LIST OF APPENDICES

1. Privateers frequenting Port Royal 1659-60	219
2. An account of the private ships of war belonging to Jamaica in 1663	220
3. The sites of the Anglican churches before 1692	221
4. List of craftsmen and tradesmen in Port Royal before 1692	223
5. A list of Port Royal taverns	232
6. Anglican ministers and churchwardens at Port Royal before 1692	233

ABBREVIATIONS

Blathwayt Papers	The correspondence of William Blathwayt, preserved at Williamsburg
B.M.	British Library, containing:
	Add. MSS. Additional Manuscripts
	Egerton Egerton Manuscripts
	Harleian Harleian Manuscripts
	Sloane Sloane Manuscripts
C.S.P.	*Calendar of State Papers, America and the West Indies*
Coventry Papers	The correspondence of Henry Coventry, Secretary of State between 1671 and 1680, preserved at Longleat House
N.L.J.	National Library of Jamaica
I.R.O.	Island Record Office, Spanish Town
Interesting Tracts	*Interesting Tracts relating to the island of Jamaica* (Spanish Town, 1800)
J.H.R.	*The Jamaican Historical Review*
J.H.A.	*Journals of the House of Assembly of Jamaica* (14 vols., Kingston, 1811-29)
J.C.H.	*The Journal of Caribbean History*
N.G. card	One of the file-cards prepared and circulated by the National Geographic Society during the 1959 Link-National Geographic Society-Smithsonian Institution Expedition (see chapter 11)
P.R.O.	Public Record Office, containing:
	Adm. Admiralty records
	C. Chancery records
	C.O. Colonial Office records
Taylor MS.	'Multum in parvo or parvum in multo', by John Taylor, gent., an account of his travels in America, preserved at the National Library of Jamaica
Thurloe	*A collection of the state papers of John Thurloe*, ed. Thomas Birch (7 vols., London, 1742)
U.W.I.	University of the West Indies

Note All dates before 1752 are Old Style, except that the year is taken to begin on 1 January.

Introduction: The Sources

Port Royal is today a singularly unspectacular little town. Many a casual visitor, aware perhaps of its extraordinary past, must have been disappointed to find so few apparent relics of it. Until recently, indeed, it was also believed that the documentary evidence bearing on Port Royal's seventeenth-century history was equally scanty. In general, the view held was that of Edward Long, who wrote that with the 1692 earthquake 'fell the glory of Port Royal, and with it all the publick records'.[1]

Such a view is radically mistaken; in fact, the history of Port Royal is better documented than that of most English towns of comparable size for that period. In Jamaica itself there are primarily the Archives and Island Record Office both at Spanish Town. The Jamaica Archives has a remarkable series of plat-books, patents, and inventories, and the Island Record Office the deeds and wills; these all run from the time of English occupation. In Kingston there are the National Library of Jamaica, formerly the West India Reference Library of the Institute of Jamaica, and the library of the University of the West Indies. At the former may be found an excellent range of printed documents, as well as a small but select collection of manuscripts. The most important of the latter for our purposes has been the 'Taylor manuscript', which was acquired recently and contains a full if rather imaginative account of seventeenth-century Port Royal. The library of U.W.I. has been chiefly useful to us through its extensive collection of microfilm, reproducing documents held in many overseas depositories.

In England, most of our material was in the Public Record Office and the British Museum. At the P.R.O., the papers of Thomas Brailsford, deposited in the Chancery series, offered fresh information about the operations of an individual merchant, and the Customs returns (C.O. 142/13) allowed a fairly full reconstitution of the course of trade during the 1680s. It would have been desirable to have read in full many of the documents listed in the *Calendar of State Papers*, but neither of the authors could ever spend long in London; we were therefore forced to rely on the *Calendar of State Papers* and on photocopies of the more important documents from it. The P.R.O. has many other series which it would have been desirable to examine; the eighteenth-century Admiralty logs, for instance, or the port books (E 190). These we regretfully passed by, indicating in our text where we felt that research would be fruitful.

The Department of Manuscripts at the British Library has a good deal of material concerning seventeenth-century Jamaica, much of it acquired among the papers of governors. By far the most important document for our purposes was Additional Manuscript 12423, the so-called D'Oyley's journal. This has very rarely been used in the past, but contains much information about the early years of the English settlement. The first part of this document has been edited and published in *The Jamaican Historical Review* (x [1973] 33-112 and xi [1978] 62-117), but we have thought it better in our notes, to refer readers back to the original manuscript. To complete the survey of London archives, we should mention the library of the Royal Society, which contains the valuable letter of George Ellwood.

Outside London, most material came from the Coventry Papers, preserved at Longleat House. Volumes 74 and 75 of this collection contain a wide selection of letters to Henry Coventry from officials and others at Port Royal. At Oxford the Bodleian Library contains the Rawlinson Papers, bequeathed by Dr. Richard Rawlinson in the eighteenth century. In this collection are various papers of Samuel Pepys, including for instance the log of H.M.S. *Boneta* during her stay at Port Royal. At Cambridge too, useful information was found among the Pepysian Manuscripts, preserved at Magdalene College. In general, though, we were unsuccessful in our attempts to track down material relating to Jamaica which Pepys must have possessed.[2]

We were also unsuccessful in our attempts to discover more than a few of the early English maps of Port Royal. We know from various references that maps were sent back to England at certain stages of the town's growth, but most of these can no longer be found. It is not likely that they were destroyed, as they would have been agreeable to look at and of obvious interest, particularly from a military point of view. We have to confess, though, that we did not make a systematic search for families whose forebears had held high office in Jamaica; it is quite possible that such an investigation would be fruitful.

Outside Jamaica and England, material was found only in the United States. The Library of Congress has an interesting early map of the Port Royal dockyard (see figure 29), and at Colonial Williamsburg are preserved the Blathwayt Papers. These contain letters from a great variety of persons resident in seventeenth-century Jamaica, and are a source which does not appear to have been much used until now.[3]

As will become apparent from chapter 1, much evidence bearing on Port Royal's history is still buried beneath the land and under the sea off the spit. We have tried in chapter 11 to summarize such evidence as has so far been recovered from archaeological investigations, but it is as yet relatively slight; the sources of Port Royal's history are still primarily written sources, scattered among the archives of three different countries.

NOTES

[1] Edward Long. *A history of Jamaica* (3 vols., London, 1774) ii. 143. See also G. W. Bridges, *The annals of Jamaica* (2 vols., London, 1827-8), i. 309: 'one loss was irrecoverable, and is still severely felt; that of all the official papers public and records of the island, whose history is thereby rendered so obscure and incomplete'.

[2] In spite of the help both of the curators of the relevant collections, and of Sir Arthur Bryant.

[3] On these papers see L. J. Cappon, 'The Blathwayt Papers of Colonial Williamsburg, Inc.', *The William and Mary Quarterly*, iv. 3 (1947), 321-31.

CHAPTER ONE

The Geography of Port Royal

The history of Port Royal begins high up in the mountains behind Kingston, at the sources of those rivers whose torrential, gravel-laden waters spill out into the Caribbean Sea to the east of the Liguanea Plain. From here the prevailing south-easterly winds and strong westerly current carry the sedimentary waters towards the cays off Kingston (figure 1). These cays, which are the surface projections of an extensive shelf, tend to slow down the easterly current, and so cause the river-water to deposit its burden of sands and gravels.

The whole Palisadoes spit should probably be envisaged as a series of cays connected in this way by precipitations of sandy detritus. Figure 2 makes the process graphically clear, for at each of the major outcrops of land, and particularly from Plumb Point, a considerable build-up of sandy beach is visible. To the effect of the south-easterly

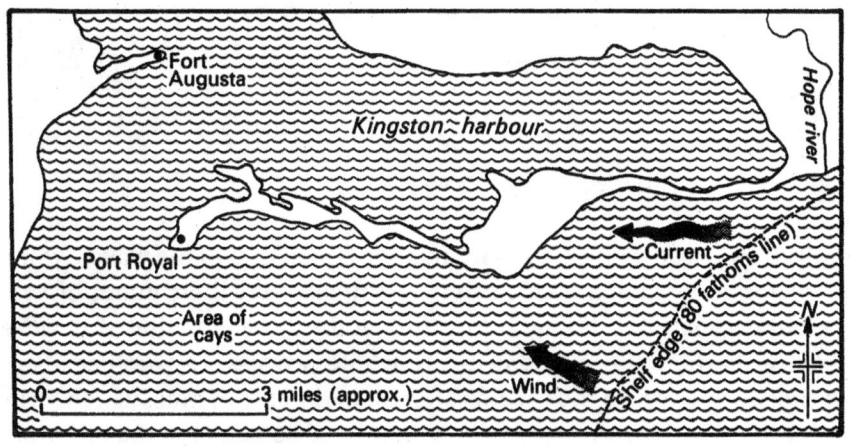

Figure 1 The formation of the Palisadoes spit

Figure 2 Aerial photograph of the Palisadoes spit

wind and west-tending current must be added that of the waves, which breaking on the exposed beach continually add their quota of sedimentary material. Some authorities, indeed, believe that this wave-action is the main element in the whole process, in part because it tends to encourage the precipitation of carbonate of lime, which forms a hard rock - the so-called beach rock - and so cements the other material together.[1]

Be that as it may, it is certain that the Palisadoes spit has formed a more or less continuous line for at least the last 400 years, in spite of the fact that for at least 100 feet below ground-level it is composed of unconsolidated materials: sands, gravels, silts, and so forth. It is only below this level that bores begin to reach solid limestone rock. When the English came to Jamaica in 1655 the shape of the tip of the peninsula seems to have been something like figure 3.

The centre of the 'cay' was at about point 'A', and the cay was separated from the rest of the spit by perhaps 100 yards of shallow water. The water off this broken peninsula was very deep, reaching 30 feet at most points only a few yards from the shore. Accretion had taken place not only on the south side of the spit, but also on the north side, probably as a result of eddies swirling round the point and then doubling back along the edge of the land.

Needless to say, land formed in this way from unconsolidated material is extremely vulnerable, particularly given the very steep slope at the water's edge. So it was that when there was an earthquake in 1692, much of this northern section of the spit slipped into the sea. It is probable that this submarine landslide occurred partly because there had developed a 'fluidized layer' at some point; that is why, in the way characteristic of landslides of this kind, the whole land seems to have slipped downwards, rather than toppled outwards; such an interpretation of what happened has been closely vindicated by the fact that the lines of the original streets do not seem to have changed position very far.

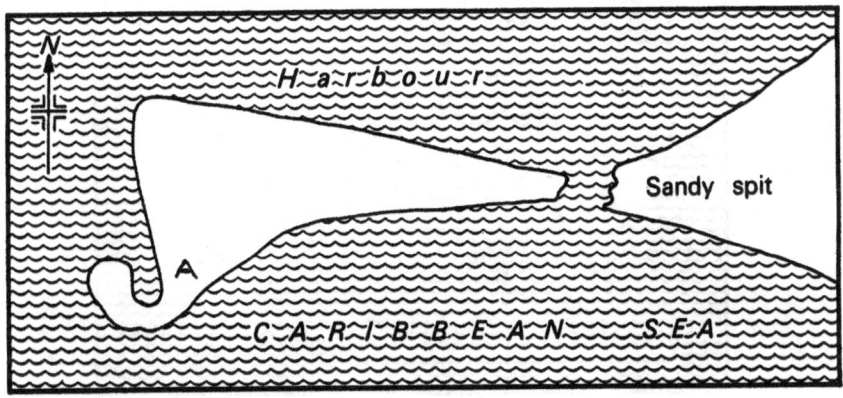

Figure 3 The site of Port Royal about 1655

The human and economic consequences of the landslide will be discussed in chapter 11; its geographical result was further to isolate the Port Royal cay from the rest of the spit, and greatly to reduce the area of the land. Immediately after the earthquake the site of Port Royal was marked by a small island, known as 'Port Royal cay' (figure 4). For several decades this Port Royal cay remained detached from the mainland. Maps of 1704, 1718, and 1728 show the intervening stretch of

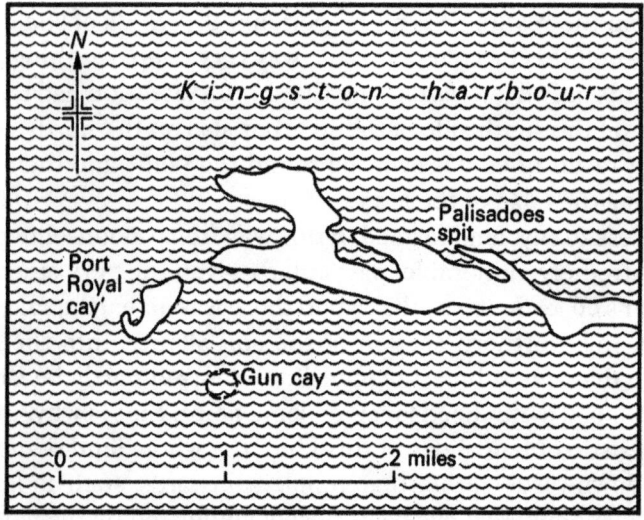

Figure 4   Port Royal after the earthquake

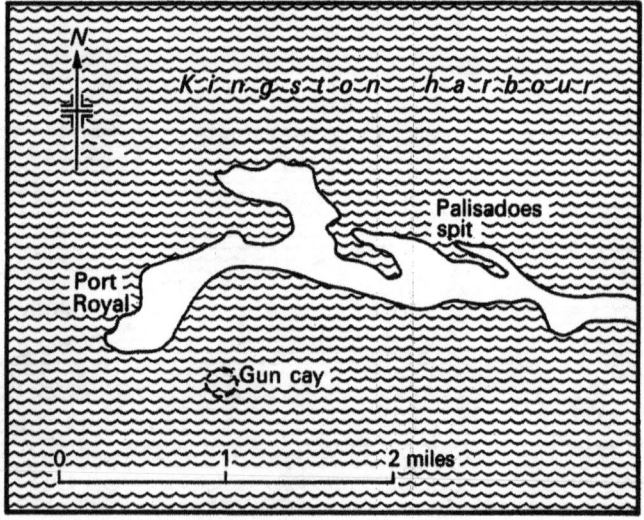

Figure 5   Present shoreline at Port Royal

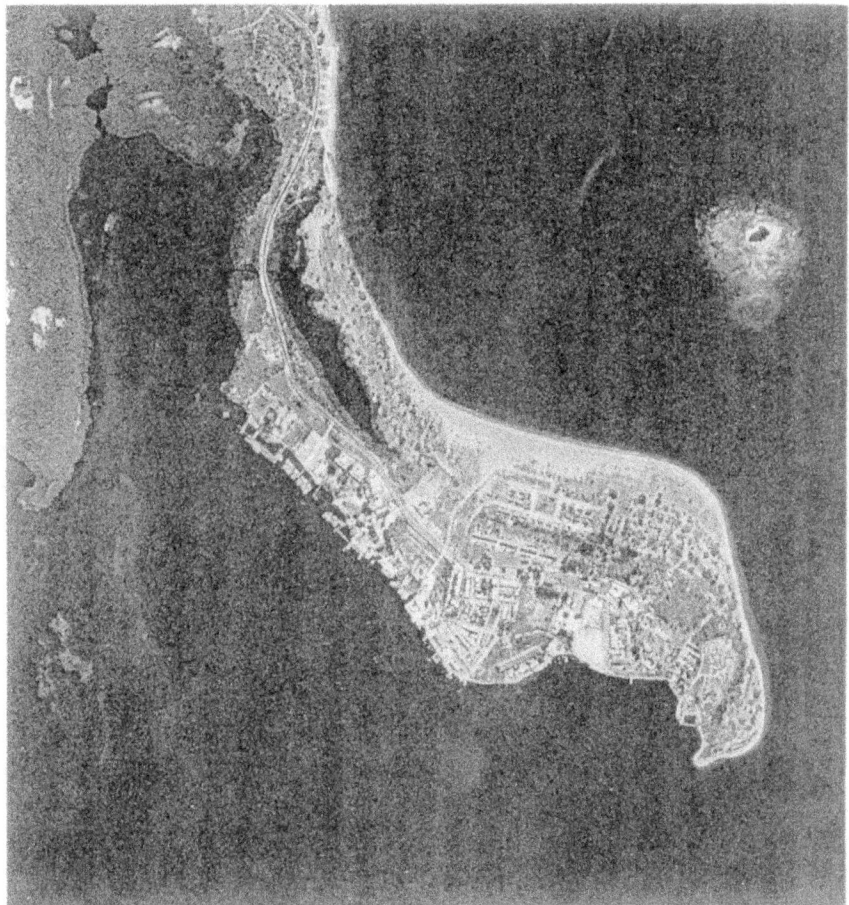

Figure 6 Aerial photograph of Port Royal

water as receding, however, and by 1772 (and probably a decade or two earlier) Port Royal was once again united to the peninsula. This natural process had been accelerated by the sinking of old vessels filled with stones into the gap. During these years, too, the cay was gaining ground to the west and to the south, until by 1900 the spit had assumed more or less its present shape (figure 5).

There has been very little coastal movement on the north side since 1692, no doubt because the mass of debris in the harbour has inhibited the passage of the gravel-laden waters. To the south and west, however, the growth has been spectacular, each decade adding its contribution. Figure 6 reveals the striated layers which bear testimony to this process. Needless to say, all this land remains 'new', totally unconsolidated, and very vulnerable to any fresh earthquake. A considerable strip on the south side fell into the sea during the severe tremors of 1907, and it is to be anticipated that future earthquakes will see similar losses. Indeed, one authority has gone so far as to affirm in conversation that the present condition of the southern and western shoreline at Port Royal is very similar to that of the northern coastline before 1692.

Whatever the truth of the matter, it is clear that the whole Palisadoes peninsula has always been at the mercy of natural disasters. A severe hurricane may cut the road, which was not constructed until the 1930s, at any several vulnerable points, and an earthquake of even moderate intensity could easily lead to further losses at the points of accretion off the spit. If ever there were an example of a historic phenomenon depending on the accidents of nature, it is Port Royal, whose history is incomprehensible without a firm grasp of its geography.

The first people to visit the future site of Port Royal were no doubt Taino Indians, who would have put in there during their fishing expeditions.[2] In the sixteenth century these Tainos were greatly reduced in number by the Spaniards, but their conquerors seem to have made scarcely more use of the spit than the Tainos had done. The main Spanish naval base was in Old Harbour Bay, and they used the Palisadoes point, or perhaps we should say the westernmost of the series of cays, merely for careening; indeed, they gave that little island the name of *cayo de carena*.[3] At the most, they may have erected one or two wooden huts to shelter the crews of boats on the careen; the point was virtually bare when the English came.[4]

NOTES

[1] On the geology of the spit, see T. Goreau and Kevin Burke, 'Pleistocene and holocene geology of the island shelf near Kingston, Jamaica', *Marine Geology*, iv (1966), 207-25.
[2] And who perhaps even settled there; see Robert F. Marx, *Pirate Port* (London, 1968), pp. 23-4 and 101.
[3] See Frank Cundall and Joseph Pietersz, *Jamaica under the Spaniards* (Kingston, 1919), p. 55.
[4] Taylor MS., p. 491.

CHAPTER TWO

The Coming of the English: Fort Cromwell 1655–1660

It was on 10 May 1655 that the English fleet, carrying an army which had just been ignominiously repulsed from Santo Domingo, sailed into what is now Kingston Harbour. They met, of course, with no resistance from *cayo de carena*, and were able to brush aside the Spanish militia at Passage Fort, where they landed with a view to attacking Spanish Town.[1] The invading forces greatly outnumbered those of the defence, and very soon all open resistance had ended, and the capture of Jamaica was apparently complete. Although the English had to fight hard and sometimes desperately against the guerrilla forces still under the leadership of Don Cristoval Arnaldo Ysassi,[2] the capture of the island had in part fulfilled the aspirations of Cromwell's 'Western Design'.[3]

It rapidly became clear to the English that if they were to protect their fleet and the base at Passage Fort, they would have to fortify *cayo de carena*, which they mistakenly called 'Cagway', taking the name of Passage Fort (*Caguaya*) to be that of the cay.[4] Barely a month after the landing, General Robert Venables wrote that 'there must some block houses be erected at the harbour's mouth, were our men able to work at such hard labour'.[5] His doubts about the army's ability to perform this task were based on its sufferings from dysentery, fevers, and shortage of provisions; little work could be expected from men who 'for these seventeen days have had but three biskets of bread a man, neither officer nor soldier, and sometime little or no meat for two to three days together'.[6]

The shortage of bread and other provisions was due to the late arrival of supply-ships, and to the refusal of the fleet to help with its provisions. Though the *William* and the *Recovery* arrived on 19 May,[7] nine days after the landing, 'the bread they brought', according to Venables and Butler, 'is so inconsiderable that it will but serve the army

22 days at half allowance'.⁸ In a further letter, Venables complains that the two ships brought 'some biscuit which we extremely want, but the fleet claim it as theirs, and then we starve'.⁹ Cattle had been abundant at the time of the landing, but wholesale slaughter by the troops soon drove the remainder deep into the woods, where guerrillas operated. In spite of the famine, Venables had to forbid his men to follow them: 'the men being sometimes slain by stragling, I ordered that no private soldier should henceforward go forth to kill cows alone'.¹⁰

Despite such difficulties and shortages, the fortifying of Cagway, or 'the Point' as it was also called, started in early July. Simon de Casseres wrote to Thurloe in September 1655 about Captain 'Hewes [Hughes]. . ., whom I left in the same point of the harbour fortifying'; he added that 'the fortification of the harbour cannot be made strong without it be made of stone and lime which may be easily made within two miles'.¹¹ This was useful and accurate information, for directly across the harbour mouth from Cagway lay the Port Henderson hills, rich in limestone and also the site of an abandoned Spanish lime-kiln.

From July to December 1655 the work at the fort was carried on slowly and unenthusiastically. Captain Hughes was in command of the labour force, which by November had mounted nine or ten guns.¹² Writing from on board the flagship *Torrington* in 'the port of Jamaica' in January 1656, Vice-Admiral William Goodson made this rather unfavourable report:¹³

> We have been at work about building a fort for the securing of the harbour; when it is built it will be but mean, and is yet but half-built. However, we are resolved to set to it heart and hand and finish it if possible; there is in it all the battering guns brought out of England and all those taken at St. Martha; mounted 20 guns.¹⁴

On 14 January 1656, orders were issued to Colonel Humphrey to 'march with his regiment to Captain Hughes' fforte',¹⁵ and for the accomodation of this reinforcement 100 tents were provided 'with all things necessary and belonging to them'. Humphrey's regiment had arrived the previous October, and had been garrisoned at Spanish Town until being sent to the Point. However, 'they proved altogether, notwithstanding any encouragement we could give them, useless'.¹⁶ Some of the regiment filtered back to Spanish Town, and the numbers of those at work on the fort were constantly reduced by death, so that seamen from the fleet had to be pressed into service.¹⁷

In March 1656, the resident supervisor at the fort was changed. Captain Martin Van Alphan of Colonel Humphrey's regiment replaced Captain Hughes, who returned to 'the Towne' (as Spanish Town was called), where he supervised the repair of eighty empty hogsheads to be used for carrying lime to the Point. Two men, Thomas Gibbons and a workman, were employed full time in preparing lime, for which they were provided with regular weekly provisions.[18] In April 1656, Captain Van Alphan was joined by Nicholas Keene 'fyre master', who in 1657, when the first recorded grants of land were made on the Point, was given the additional responsibility of Surveyor. From April onwards Keene and Van Alphan shared the duty of overseeing progress on the fort, the former in charge of 'those artificers and workemen on the fort',[19] and the latter responsible for those soldiers of Humphrey's regiment who still remained on the Point.

In March 1656 it had been proposed to build a round stone tower within the squarish area of the fort,[20] and with this in view a quantity of stone was unloaded onto the adjacent beach, presumably after being quarried from the Port Henderson hills. There were constant problems, for masons were few and lime even scarcer; an appeal to the army for more men brought only the reply that none could be spared. In spite of all these difficulties, the tower by the end of April 1656 was five feet high, and the 'grand fort' was 'almost finished'.[21] At this stage it was not in fact very grand, since it consisted merely of a rectangular surround in the centre of which was the round stone tower; the gun-platforms on the perimeter were simply banks of board and sand broken by open sally-ports, and Fort Cromwell retained this shape until 1662.[22]

Credit for such progress as was made seems to have been due to the excellent spirit of co-operation which existed between Commissioners Sedgwick and Goodson. Both were determined that the fortification of the Point should go forward at all costs, in order to provide a stable base for the embryonic colony. When the army faltered, Goodson brought in his seamen, while Sedgwick, despite pressing administrative duties, kept a watch on progress at the fort by actually living close by. From the time of his arrival on the *Marmaduke* in October 1655 until his death in May 1656 he lived constantly on board, anchored close in to the cay. This was not to the taste of William Godfrey, *Marmaduke's* captain, who complained that he had 'remained in harbour ever since he had arrived, conceiving it merely for the accommodation of commissioner Sedgwick who hath continued always on board'.[23]

The activity of the English on the Point was closely watched by the Spaniards. On 3 April 1656 Ysassi himself observed from a vantage-point on Port Henderson hill 'eighteen vessels riding in the harbour' and 'about eighteen houses on the point of *cayo de carena*, and on the inner harbour seven thatched huts'.[24] He added that he 'did not see the little fort on the point to carry artillery because it must be low'. An undated Spanish manuscript map of 1655-6 shows twenty 'casas de cayo carena' and also the fort, which is an idealized concept since it is shaped like an eight-pointed star, instead of the rather pedestrian square of reality.[25]

Curiously enough, we search in vain for any mention in D'Oyley's journal of 'houses' on the Point at this period. It may be, though, that he was concerned only with what he called '*state*' expenditure, and that the houses, rude as they must have been, were private ventures. A succession of officers had been stationed at the Point during the building of the fort, and they may well have constructed for themselves quarters more comfortable and permanent than the tents of the private soldiers. Furthermore, from immediately after the arrival of the force in May 1655 the Point had been used to careen ships, both of Goodson's fleet and visiting supply-vessels; a certain quantity of stores would have been kept there to help in this, if only to avoid the constant fetching and carrying from the main storehouse across the water at Passage Fort.

Events on the mainland in fact had a direct bearing on the rate of progress at the Point. When Sedgwick arrived in October 1655, he was accompanied by four merchant ships carrying almost a thousand tons of stores. As there was no suitable place to receive these supplies, and as the army were by now 'a people in such condition as they had rather die than work',[26] Goodson's seamen set about constructing storehouses, and in about eight days built at Passage Fort a storehouse 100 feet long and 25 feet wide. This was apparently built within the perimeter of the Spanish breastwork, and became the nucleus of a base described in these words by Ysassi, writing to the duke of Albuquerque, viceroy of Mexico, in 1657:

> On the seashore there is an enclosure of entrenchments of fascine and earth, eight feet thick with a few loopholes and two redoubts for clearing the outlying country . . . in the middle of this fortification there are three stores; when there are provisions and munition in them, a guard of 90 men goes into this port.[27]

Work went on at Passage Fort from January 1656 onwards,[28] and from November 1655 other soldiers and workmen were busy in Spanish Town itself, building a palisade around the whole town.[29]

During the latter part of 1656, then, there was a period of consolidation, both on the Point and on the mainland. The early shortage of supplies had considerably eased, with the frequent arrival of merchant ships, and the regiments themselves had been persuaded to adopt a policy of 'plant or starve'; most of the men had fallen in with this, and areas of permanent settlement were emerging.[30] On the Point these months saw constant improvements to Fort Cromwell - first mentioned by this name in our documents in October 1656 - and a semi-permanent force of 31 civilian artisans and 52 soldiers was constantly engaged there.[31]

Captain Harrington of Colonel Barrington's regiment had meanwhile become 'governor of the fort' at Passage Fort,[32] and there too around the military base private building seems to have started, for George and John Evans, as early as April 1656, received from D'Oyley 'a sutler's lycence to sell all manner of provision and liquer usually bought and sold'.[33] Meanwhile, too, the palisade around Spanish Town had been finished, and within that town five men and a woman (Christian [sic] Rust, wife of Ensign Rust) were also granted 'sutlers' licences'.[34] In short, by the end of 1656 civil as well as military institutions were well established at the three sites.

In the middle of the following year, Commissioner William Brayne (14 December 1656 to 2 September 1657) summarized the emerging importance of the Point when he wrote that 'There is the faire beginning of a town upon the poynt of this harbour . . . there I intend all our stourehouses and trade shall be, which will soone make it a flourishing place.'[35] By his orders, the first public buildings were erected on the Point, at the expense of 'His Highness [Cromwell] and the Commonwealth of England'.[36] They comprised a dwelling-house with two out-houses 'for the use of the commander-in-cheife', and construction was undertaken in three phases.

First, the frames for all three buildings were made and erected by Thomas Keyes, carpenter, at a cost of £40. The dimensions of the dwelling-house were 38 feet in length and 20 feet in breadth, while the two out-houses each measured 20 feet by 14 feet. The second phase was the responsibility of another carpenter, Richard Brock,[37] who fitted wooden boarding to the frames, both inside and out, put in the flooring and partitions, made doors and windows, and attended to the 'settinge on the lockes, and severall other things for furnishing the said house', for which he was paid £31 and 'in brandy tenne gallons, in bread 672 pounds'. The roofing was made of wooden shingles from old condemned staves 'belonging to severall shipps', and the work cost £8. Finally, there was built 'a fence with palisadoes round about the yard of the said house'.[38] In this phase the seamen were used for 'fetching of twelve hundred of palisadoe nails and poles, and for the cutting and fitting of the palisadoes and setting them up, and making the fence around', all at a cost of eighteen gallons of brandy. A pair of double gates gave access to the buildings through the fence; the whole structure must have looked rather like the stockaded strongholds built by Europeans in North America at this time. All the materials were transported to the Point from 'the other side of the water', out of the state storehouse at Passage Fort, and included nails of various sizes, pitch, tar and resin, together with pine, deal and cedar planking of various thicknesses, supplemented by local purchases of cotton-tree boards at a cost of 11/2 $d.$ per foot. The hardware 'as lockes, keyes, hindges, bolts, staples etc. were make at ye stat's forge by smiths in that pay and service'.[39]

About this time too a state storehouse was built on the Point. We do not know its exact size, but it was certainly larger than the commander-in-chief's house, and more substantially built, of board and brick; at least 6,400 feet of board and 21,900 nails were brought from Passage Fort storehouse and used in its construction. The bricklayer, John Durant, received £16. 10$s.$ 0$d.$ for his part in the work, while the lime, at a cost of twenty gallons of brandy, was made at Spanish Town and shipped across the harbour.[40]

The private dwellings recorded by mid-1657 were all on ground allotted by Governor Brayne, who unfortunately did not record such grants. However, after his death in September 1657 D'Oyley once again assumed command, and he noted in his journal all subsequent grants. The first of these was dated 5 September 1657, only three days after Brayne's death, and ordered Mr. Nicolas Keene (surveyor) to 'set forth unto Nicholas Alexander and Quartermaster Morris sixty foote of land in Cagway'.[41] By the end of that month, D'Oyley was spending most of his time on the Point, and found it necessary to make arrangements for the defence of Spanish Town during his long absences: 'whereas the multiplicity of the affairs of the sea doth oftentimes require me to stay longe at Cagway for the better management thereof, I doe therefore in my absence from the towne of St. Jago de la Vega hereby appoint you, Major Thomas Fairfax, from time to time to look to the security of the said towne . . .'.[42]

With the virtually permanent removal of D'Oyley to the Point, the expansion of the hamlet began in earnest, and three months later, at the beginning of January 1658, the 'church or market house' was under construction, built in part of oak planks.[43] Early the following month D'Oyley authorized the payment of 'tenne pounds upon accompt' towards the cost of building a house and forge upon the Point 'for the state's smith', thereby ensuring that those building houses or refitting ships would not be held up for want of metal parts. The brickmaking industry, at this period under the control of a certain Bartholomew Harvey, remained on the mainland, for the Point contained no deposits of clay among its scrub and sand. Harvey, no doubt in order to supervise the sale of his bricks, obtained a grant of 60 feet of land on the Point 'near the sea or harbour side where he should make choice'.[44]

By August 1658 there were at least three rows of houses already established on the Point, for during this month Nicholas Keene was ordered to 'set forthe unto Robert Thetford sixty foote of land near unto Robert Jeffries' house in the middle row'.[45] Apart from these private houses there were also Fort Cromwell, the commander-in-chief's house, the state storehouse, and the state forge. However, the emerging town was undefended and vulnerable at its eastern end, and about this time Major Richard Stevens began 'the building of a fort on the easternmost end of Point Cagway', designed to remedy this defect. Stevens' fort was in fact little more than a line of palisades running across the peninsula from north to south; however, these were probably well and stoutly constructed, and sufficed to keep out marauders, while honest citizens could come and go by a gate in the middle of them. Eventually, of course, this line of 'pallisadoes' gave its name to the whole strip, and at one time to the airport there.[46]

By the end of 1658 the church or market house must have been largely finished, and Richard Brock was again employed, this time to begin work on the court house. Like the church, this seems to have contained a great quantity of oak.[47] Meanwhile more plots of land were being taken up by private individuals, and by the middle of 1659 it was no longer possible easily to obtain land directly on the harbour side. Many of the plots were by then taken by private individuals, and others were assigned to various naval ships. Each of these seems to have had its own parcel of land, probably as close as possible to its anchorage, and here no doubt guns, yards, sails and stores were laid up while the ship was on the careen. Some of these plots even had little houses on them, as emerges from the grant made to Captain Langford of land 'between the state's storehouse, and that that was the *Indian's* house'.⁴⁸ By 1660 D'Oyley had begun attaching covenants to grants, requiring that a house be built on the land within a specified time (on one occasion three months), as otherwise the allotment would be cancelled.⁴⁹ One curious feature of the growth of the town is that the streets took a long time to receive names. As late as September 1659 we find plots being identified as being 'beyond Mr. Darrell's house in Mr. Workeman's rowe', or 'sixty foote square of land in the rowe Marshall Webbing's house stands in'.⁵⁰

Mr. Nicholas Keene, 'Fyremaster and surveyor of point Cagway', was undoubtedly the man who laid out the plan of the town, probably in consultation with Brayne and then D'Oyley. He continued these duties until 17 December 1661, when he surveyed for Captain Samuel Barry '100 foot square of land in some convenient place or more upon point Cagway'.⁵¹ Unfortunately for Keene, a certain John Man, merchant, during a visit to England petitioned the king for the office of surveyor, stressing the fact that he had 'for many years studied mathematics, and practised the art of surveying land, and that he understood that a gentleman totally ignorant of mathematics intended to petition for the office'.⁵² In January 1661, Man was granted the office of surveyor-general in Jamaica, but he seems to have been chiefly taken up with a general survey of the island,⁵³ while Keene continued to supervise grants at the Point.

Between April 1656 and the end of 1657, little work had been done at Fort Cromwell other than routine repairs and maintenance. But in February 1658 Christopher Myngs arrived from England, bringing £2,572. 17s. 11d. 'from His Highness the Lord Protector', and instructions that it 'shall be employed and laid out for the use of and carryinge on the worke of fortification of this island of Jamaica'.⁵⁴ To this purpose it was promptly applied; part was spent in finishing Fort Henry at Spanish Town, part went on the eastern defences at the Point, and the rest was used in improving Fort Cromwell. Some of the sand and board platforms were replaced by stone works, and Captain Van Alphan's company was increased to 104 men; to this force was also added a further 92 men under Ensign Soames and 21 men under Lieutenant Jotherill.⁵⁵ The soldiers were accommodated in a tent, made by Nicholas Keene from the old mainsail of the *Hector*. As in the years 1655-6, seamen were also used, though in smaller numbers, and possibly in order to take advantage of their special skill (in moving guns and heavy equipment, for instance). While ships were refitting some of their crew would be sent across to help; Captain Lloyd of the *Diamond* was thus in 1659 ordered to 'send sixteen of his men to Fort Cromwell to relieve the *Hector's* men at worke there'.[56]

Throughout 1658 and 1659 work on the renovation of Fort Cromwell was extensive and intense. To ensure an uninterrupted supply of lime, stone, wood, and water, a shallop, a galliot, a hoy, and two 'perriagoes'[57] were specially allotted and continually employed to carry such items across from the mainland. The guns of the fort were also properly mounted on carriages, which would seem to have been locally made, since the storehouse issued 'two cwt. of flatt iron to shoo the carriages at Fort Cromwell'.[58]

The stone tower in the centre of the fort now served also as the prison, where Provost-Marshal Weblinge detained malefactors. Here was confined on 14 January 1660 a certain Peter Swayne, a pirate, who 'meeting with a shallop at sea belonging to —— Hines of the island of Barbadoes did feloniously robb and plunder the same and hath disposed and converted the goods thereout taken to his owne use'.[59] Weblinge was ordered to 'take the body of the said Peter Swayne into your custody and him safely keepe in the tower untill he shall be released or condemned by law'.

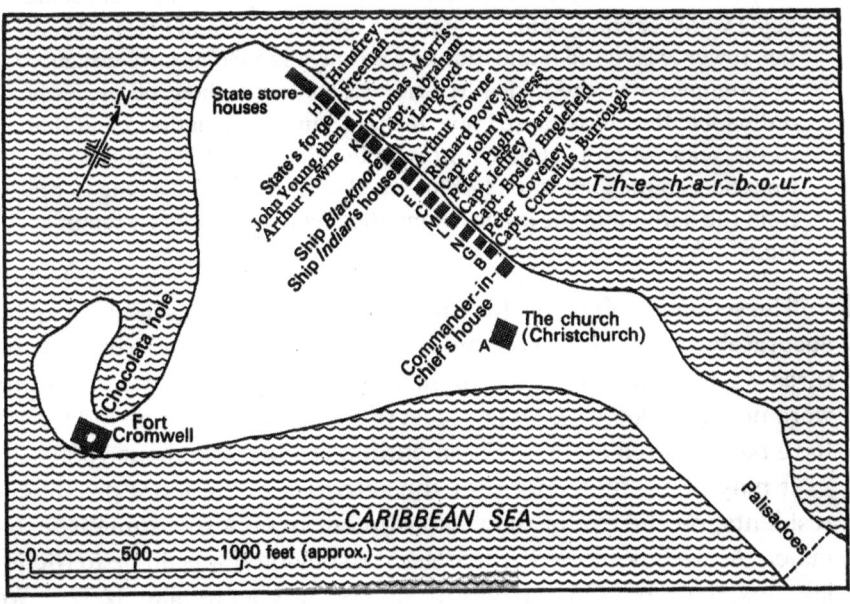

Figure 7 The development of the Point to 1660

Meanwhile the town continued to grow. At the end of 1659 Captain Cornelius Burrough completed his private storehouse,⁶⁰ and local production of bricks was so far unable to meet demand that 'ships ordered [to Jamaica had to] be ballasted with bricks'.⁶¹ In August 1660 news reached the Point of the restoration of Charles II, which had taken place the previous May; D'Oyley must have changed Fort Cromwell's name to Fort Charles fairly soon after this news, though the first mention of the new name occurs in his journal only the following November.⁶²

In September 1660 the state of affairs on the Point was described by Captain (later Sir) Thomas Lynch:

> [the town is] . . . seated on the extreme end of the pointe, containing in itt about 200 houses, all buylt by the English, with some publique houses, and that wherein the lieutenant generall constantly dwells, and the houses where all the stores for fleete and army were kept.
>
> This is the place where all merchants, strangers and saylers reside as being the seate of trade and the most healthy place in the island, whither resort all the men of warre that frequent the pointe, which makes houses soe deare that an ordinary house in this towne is worth £40 or £60 per annum.
>
> Uppon the utmost angle of the pointe to seaward is a round tower buylt of lyme and stone in which is mounted 15 peices of ordinance, some being whole cannon, demy cannon and demy culverin of brasse. About this tower is layd the foundation of a strong and regular forte designed to circumference and flanck itt, and will contayne about 60 pieces of ordinance. Butt itt is raysed noe further than to the platform and that to the seaward only, although itt may have cost £2000. About a mile from here to the land was a fort intended to be buylt, and a lyne to run from the harbour to the sea to defend the towne against any attempt by land . . .⁶³

The sequence of establishment of the public buildings has been quite accurately determined in the preceding pages, but for the private structures we can make only approximations, since so many land-grants were not recorded by D'Oyley. Most of the grants which he did record have been plotted on figure 7, an outline of the town about 1660.

It may be useful to run over the activities of the more prominent residents, on the eve of the establishment of civil government in Jamaica. As we have seen, the first grant to be noted was made to Nicholas Alexander and Quartermaster Morris on 5 September 1657.⁶⁴ We do not know who Alexander was, but he may well have been a civilian artisan from Saint Christopher's or Nevis; Morris was the quartermaster of D'Oyley's regiment and, in addition to his military duties, supervised the delivery of building materials to the site of the church, probably at 'A' on figure 7.

In October 1658 Captain Cornelius Burrough, steward-general appointed by Admiral Penn 'in room of John Carter, since deceased', was already building a timber house on the Point, though the first grant made to him is not recorded by D'Oyley until 14 September 1659.[65] This plot, '138 foote in lengthe and 110 foote in breadthe', was 'next the harbourside between the house of the commander-in-chiefe and the house of Mr Peter Coveney'; it may well have been situated at 'B'.

Captain John Wilgresse, like Captain Burrough, was also building a wooden house in the latter part of 1658, purchasing the boards from the state's storehouse. Curiously, D'Oyley makes no mention of any grant of land to him, but a patent registered in November 1661[66] states, *inter alia,* that he owned land to the east of Arthur Towne, bordering on the harbour-side, approximately at 'C'. Captain Wilgresse (sometimes spelt Wilgeeffts or Willgris) was, even by the standards of the day, a wilful and vehement character. On 13 June 1656 he resigned his command of the naval ship *Falmouth* 'rather than face a court-martial for drunkenness and swearing',[67] but somehow regained his captain's commission, for between 1660 and 1671, the year of his death, he commanded a whole sequence of ships: *Beare* 1660, *Hector* 1664, *East India Merchant* 1664, *Beare* 1665, *Marmaduke* 1665, *House de Swyte* 1666, *Welcome* 1670, and *Assistance* in 1671.[68]

Arthur Towne, gentleman, on 10 June 1659 received a plot of land measuring 'one hundred and fifty foote in breadthe by the harbourside, between Commissary Povey his lands and house, and the land taken up for the ship *Blackmore's* use'.[69] This site was at about 'D'; Towne is mentioned in November 1655 as 'council secretary',[70] and was evidently a civilian. His wife was called Elizabeth, and they had a daughter of the same name, who married Lieutenant-Colonel William Ivy.[71] Towne also owned property on the mainland, which he left to his wife, for on 11 August 1665 a certain 'Charles Whitfield, merchant, bought of widow Elizabeth Towne 182 acres of meadowland for £200 sterling'.[72] The Towne plot on the Point was slightly enlarged by a patent of November 1661, and then after Arthur's death his daughter and her husband Lieutenant-Colonel Ivy sold it in February 1665 to Mr. Thomas Clark, 'sayle-maker', for £45.[73] By the following month the Ivys had moved in order to live in Clarendon; they must surely have been almost the first of a long sequence of inhabitants of the Point who established themselves eventually in the hinterland.

The 'Commissary Povey' mentioned in Towne's original grant is Richard Povey. His grant does not appear in D'Oyley's journal, and so it was probably made some time between December 1656 and September 1657, when General Brayne was commander-in-chief. This land 'by the harbourside' was probably at 'E'. Richard Povey became island secretary and commissary and steward-general of stores in Jamaica on 10 January 1661, presumably superseding Cornelius Burrough as steward-general, and was also appointed a member of the Council.[74] He was a junior member of a merchant dynasty which had connections in many parts of the West Indies, and which was able to reach the ear of Cromwell himself. To sketch in only the most obvious elements in these connections, Richard had a brother William, Barbados factor for a third (and elder) brother Thomas, who was a London merchant in partnership with Martin Noell, one of Cromwell's 'merchant-advisers'.[75]

Another enterprising early inhabitant of the Point was Captain Abraham Langford, who on 14 July 1659 received a small plot of land ('F') 'betweene the state's forge and that that was the *Indian's* house'.[76] He was in some sense the precursor of the naval officer, Reginald Wilson (see below), for he was called upon from time to time to survey naval ships 'and report upon their fitness for doing service in the island'.[77] Langford made an abortive expedition against Tortuga in January 1663, and then became governor of Petit Goave at the western end of Hispaniola. By 1664 he was in England, petitioning the king (unsuccessfully) for the governorship of Tortuga and the coasts of Hispaniola.[78] A contemporary giving an opinion on 'the present design upon Tortugas',[79] wrote of Langford that he:

> speaks no French, nor does he understand it; he is a man of no wisdom, his interest in Jamaica and person is despicable, his fortune forlorn, his honesty questionable. Fears lest all his contrivance [i.e., the petition to the King] amounts to no more than a desire to repay out of the King's purse debts he has contracted by his debonnaire life and defrauding, as 'tis said, his principal. Denies not he is a good seaman and skilled in those parts, but so opiniative he will boast of much more than he knows and seems resolute to ignore nothing.

In contrast to both Langford and Povey, Mr. Peter Coveney seems to have been a quiet and retiring man. He held land close by that of Cornelius Burrough ('G'), but seldom appears in the records. In October 1662, though, he and John Walker were directed to decide all disputes as to quality in respect of the money value of sugar, cocoa, and tobacco, respectively 3*d*., 4*d*., and 3*d*. per pound; the practice of permitting produce to 'pass' as money reflected the shortage of specie at this date, and followed the pattern already set in 'Barbadoes and other plantations'.[80] Coveney was 'lately deceased' by 26 October 1666.[81]

About point 'H' was the '60 square foote of land by the seaside, between the state's storehouse and state's forge on pointe Cagway, by the harbour side, for Humfrey Freeman', granted by D'Oyley on 15 June 1659.[82] Freeman also acquired land in Saint Catherine's parish, where he patented 627 acres in 1670.[83] In early summer of 1672 he married the widow of Captain John Noy,[84] who also in 1670 had patented a large tract of 5,868 acres in Saint Catherine, described as 'wast land by the sea side, most part covered with salt water etc'.[85] By 1678 Mrs. Freeman too was dead, and a part of the former Noy estate passed on to her daughters.[86]

The plot marked 'J' was described as '60 foote in lengthe, 30 foote in breadthe between the smith's house [i.e. the state forge] and Captain Langford's, next the harbour side'. It was granted on 5 April 1660 to John Younge, who was the carpenter of the frigate *Hound*. Unfortunately for Younge, he was never able to enjoy possession, for, failing 'to build upon the same in two months, upon which consideration the general gave it to him',[87] it was re-granted, to Arthur Towne. In general, the land grants of 1660 normally involved humbler men than had been the case up until then. Younge is one example of this tendency; another is Thomas Morris, cooper, who in June 1660 received land 'by the seaside between Captain Langford and John Younge, where the ketche's house stands'.[88] This grant is significant for another reason; it looks as if the naval ships, which until 1659 or so had enjoyed a priority in obtaining land for storing their tackle at the Point, were now being ousted, since Morris's grant covered the ground 'where the ketche's house stands', at about 'K' on the map.

Along the harbour-side ('L') 'between the land of Mr. Pugh and Captain Englefield', Captain Jeffrey Dare was 'ordered to have 110 foote in lengthe and upwards to the street, and 3 score foote along the harbour side'.[89] Dare was captain of the state's ship *Beare,* which was ordered home by General Brayne 'being a very unuseful ship here'.[90] She carried as cargo, with Brayne's permission, thirty tons of the dye-wood called fustick from Lieutenant-Colonel Archbould's property on the mainland, and other commodities consigned by 'some officer'. In these early years of Jamaica's settlement by the English, a great deal of 'civilian' cargo was carried, with or without the knowledge of the Admiralty, by naval vessels, some of whose officers were closely concerned with various commercial ventures. As we shall see in chapter 5, this practice of loading up with merchandise led on at least one occasion to the loss of a naval vessel.

The land to west ('M') of Captain Dare was owned by Mr. Peter Pugh, for whom no grant appears in D'Oyley's journal. He was a rather obscure figure until in November 1662 when he was 'appointed Deputy Commissary and Steward-General, upon Secretary Povey's motion';[91] he had previously been assigned the post of auditor-general by Brayne in January 1657[92] and earlier in that same month was referred to as 'Treasurer'. By 1663, he was undertaking more and more work for the governor and Council, work which ranged from 'bringing in an abstract of the tenths and fifteenths . . . due from the records of the Admiralty Court' to contracting (with others) 'with a carpenter for rebuilding the bridge at Passage Fort, and report [ing] on the best means of levying the same on boatmen, alehouse-keepers and merchants'.[93] He progressed further, and in June 1664 was sworn in as secretary of the Council.[94]

Perhaps commercial opportunities came his way more easily after that; certainly, after his resignation in November 1664 he turned to commerce, and is referred to in a deed of April 1666 as 'merchant of Port Royal'. By the end of that year, though, he was dead, and three 'merchants resident in Jamaica', William Beeston, Joachim Hayn, and John Belfield, were empowered to recover from his estate debts due to Ralph Standish and William Jaques of London, merchants.[95]

Directly to the east of Captain Dare's land ('N') lay that of Captain Epsley Englefield, a military man who in December 1662 is mentioned as an officer in the 5th regiment of militia 'raised by order of His Excellency Thomas, Lord Windsor'.[96] Other than this, he seems not to have been a man of public affairs. He died some time before 1665, and his land at the Point was sold to Charles Whitfield, merchant, 'by the Provost-Marshall of this island to satisfy an execution upon a judgement'.[97] Before his death, Captain Englefield had rented part of his holding to a certain Mr. Robert Coolkeith, while the other part was occupied by a tavern called 'The Three Tunns'.

The earliest residents on the Point, then, seem to have been either soldiers or sailors or civilians attached to the administration, men like Towne and Povey. There do not seem to have been many who were simply merchants there at the start; no doubt the supply-vessels from

England and New England[98] lay off the Point until they had disposed of their cargoes, and then sailed away for more. Some of the early townsmen, as we have seen, turned merchant like Povey or Pugh, and the classic example of this development is provided by Captain Cornelius Burrough and one of his storehouse assistants, Captain William Dallyson. The latter was well connected in England, for his cousin was Robert Blackhorne, secretary to the Admiralty commissioners. In February 1659 Dallyson wrote to Blackhorne in these terms:

> [he] is bound for New England on an undertaking he hopes will prove satisfactory, to put off certain goods and bring back those [we] stand in need of, the General [D'Oyley] having freely given him leave. Has interwoven his fortunes in this undertaking with Mr Burrough, and Captain Myng and others have examined the business and well approve of it, part being to buy plank and board to finish our fort in this point.[99]

In fact, Dallyson does not seem to have had any 'fortune' to speak of,[100] and Captain Burrough was almost certainly the major partner in this venture. Writing to Blackhorne a little after Dallyson's departure, Burrough remarked that 'Captains Myng and Lloyd, with whom [we] consulted, said it was a warrantable business and an opening of trade between New England and Jamaica';[101] evidently the pattern of trade between the regions was not as yet by any means established.

We get a clue as to the probable nature of the 'certain goods' to be put off in New England from one of the transactions of Mr. John Loving, one of the few exceptions to the general rule about early residents in that he was an independent merchant. On 7 September 1657 he was awaiting a survey report and certificate by Cornelius Burrough and William Dallyson on tobacco he had purchased. Such a certificate was necessary in order to take advantage of the right to import it into England duty-free; eight days later the issue of the certificate was authorized, and it covered the following commodities:

> ... five thousand four hundred and seventy-nine pounds of tobacco, five hundred and twenty-two hide and eighty skins, thirty-two tunns and a halfe and four hundred and twenty-three pounds of fustick. Lignum vitae, three-fourths of a tunne, and fifty-four sticks of ebany, to be of the growth of this island of Jamaica.[102]

This cargo, which was shipped aboard the *Martyn* of Southampton, contains as yet no mention of sugar, the export commodity which, as we shall see, began to outstrip all others in the later 1670s.

In most other ways, though, the period around 1660 sees the Point soon to become Port Royal, well prepared to expand in the decades to come. The last Spanish governor had left the island that spring, and the hold of the English on the hinterland was now secure. Plantations began to develop with surprising rapidity, laying the foundation for a thriving export trade. Already in 1659 Christopher Myngs had made a successful raid on the Spanish Main, from which 'not a man on the island but can say hath reaped a benefit';[103] one way and another, Port Royal was well placed soon to exceed in wealth and notoriety the more ancient cities of Spanish America.

NOTES

[1] The previous English expeditions of Sir Anthony Shirley (1596), Christopher Newport (1603), and Captain William Jackson (1643) had all come this same way; had the Spaniards had sufficient resources they surely would have learned from this, and fortified *cayo de carena*.

[2] The five years' resistance by the Spaniards and their Negro allies has been well described by S. A. G. Taylor in *The Western Design* (Kingston, 1965). For a contribution to the naval history of the conquest, see John F. Battick (ed.), 'Richard Rooth's sea journal of the Western Design', in *Jamaica Journal*, v. 4 (1971), 3-22.

[3] This does not seem the place to go into the motives behind this venture; they are well analysed in a number of works, including particularly A. P. Newton's *The colonizing activities of the English puritans* (Oxford, 1914).

[4] Cundall and Pietersz, *Jamaica under the Spaniards*, pp. 15-16.

[5] Thurloe, iii. 514, Venables to Thurloe, 13 June 1655.

[6] *Narrative of General Venables*, ed. C. G. Firth (London, 1900), p. 41, letter of Captain Daniel How dated 4 June 1655.

[7] Thurloe, iv. 28.

[8] Thurloe, iii. 510.

[9] *Narrative of General Venables*, p. xxxiii.

[10] Ibid., p. 39.

[11] Thurloe, iv. 61; Captain Hughes was probably the officer noted in the *Narrative of General Venables* as commanding the artillery-train (pp. xxviii and 122).

[12] C.S.P. 1675-6, 236 of 14 November 1655.

[13] Thurloe, iv. 459.

[14] Towards the end of 1655 Goodson had sacked the town of Santa Marta in what is now Colombia; C.S.P. 1675-6, 236 of 14 November 1655.

[15] B.M. Add. MSS. 12423, fo. 4r.

[16] Thurloe, iv. 601, Sedgwick and Goodson to Cromwell, 12 March 1656.

[17] Thurloe, iv. 605, Sedgwick to Thurloe, 12 March 1656.

[18] B.M. Add. Mss. 12423, fo. 13r.

[19] Ibid., fo. 12r

[20] Thurloe, iv. 650 Sedgwick to Thurloe, 12 March 1656.

[21] Thurloe, iv. 749, Sedgwick to Thurloe, 30 April 1656.

[22] *Interesting Tracts*, pp. 277-8.

[23] C.S.P. 1675-6, 256 of 30 April 1656.

[24] See 'Two Spanish documents of 1656', ed. J. L. Pietersz and H. P. Jacobs in *J.H.R.*, ii. 2 (1952), 24, Ysassi to don Francisco de Proenza, 3 April 1656.

[25] Cundall and Pietersz, *Jamaica under the Spaniards*, Map III.

[26] Thurloe, iv. 153, Sedgwick to Cromwell, 5 November 1655.

[27] Cundall and Pietersz, *Jamaica under the Spaniards*, p. 58.

[28] B.M. Add. MSS. 12423, fo. 6r.

[29] Ibid., fo. 2v.
[30] On this development see W. A. Claypole, 'Land settlement and agricultural development in the Liguanea plain 1655-1700', unpublished M.A. dissertation, U.W.I., 1970.
[31] B.M. Add. MSS. 12423, fo. 31r.
[32] Ibid., fo. 28r.
[33] Ibid., fo. 122r.
[34] B.M. Add. MSS. 12423 fo. 122r.
[35] Thurloe, vi. 391, Brayne to Thurloe, 9 July 1657.
[36] B.M. Add. MSS.12423, fo. 38r and 42v.
[37] Ibid., fo. 42v.
[38] Ibid., fo. 42v.
[39] Ibid., fo. 43v.
[40] Ibid., fo. 42v.
[41] Ibid., fo. 36r.
[42] Ibid., fo. 37v.
[43] Ibid., fo. 39r.
[44] Ibid., fo. 56r.
[45] Ibid., fo. 54v.
[46] Ibid., fo. 55r.
[47] Ibid., fo. 58r.
[48] B.M. Add. MSS. 12423, fo. 67r; the *Indian* was a fourth-rate ship which left Jamaica in 1658.
[49] Ibid., fo. 93r and 99v.
[50] Ibid., fo. 72r.
[51] Ibid., fo. 108r.
[52] *C.S.P.* 1675-6, 360 of 18 December 1660.
[53] B.M. Add. MSS. 12423, fo. 108r. Man called his survey 'A new description of the island of Jamaica'; see B.M. Add. MSS. 16371. i.
[54] Ibid., fo. 45r and *C.S.P.* 1675-6, 296 of 26 February 1658.
[55] B.M. Add. MSS. 12423, fo. 71r.
[56] Ibid., fo. 79r.
[57] These were small, shallow-draught coastal vessels with oars as well as sails.
[58] B.M. Add. MSS. 12423, fo. 76r.
[59] Ibid., fo. 80v.
[60] Ibid., fo. 86v.
[61] *C.S.P.* 1574-1660, 55 of 30 November 1660.
[62] B.M. Add. MSS. 12423, fo. 98r.
[63] *C.S.P.* 1574-1660, 57 of November (?) 1660; Lynch's 31-page report.
[64] B.M. Add. MSS. 12423, fo. 36r.
[65] *C.S.P.* 1675-6, 278 of 6 January 1657.
[66] Jamaica Archives, Patents, liber I, vol. 19.
[67] *C.S.P.* 1675-6, 252 of 13 March 1656.
[68] *Catalogue of Pepysian manuscripts*, i. 256 etc.
[69] B.M. Add. MSS. 12423, fo. 63r.
[70] Ibid., fo. 2v.
[71] I.R.O. Deeds, liber I, fo. 18v.
[72] Ibid., fo. 13r.
[73] Ibid., fo. 18v.
[74] *C.S.P.* 1661-8. 4 of 10 January 1661.
[75] See Newton, *Colonizing activities of the English puritans*, pp. 325-6.
[76] B.M. Add. MSS. 12423, fo. 67r.
[77] *C.S.P.* 1574-1660, 26 (ii) of 26 July 1660.
[78] *C.S.P.* 1661-8, 820 of 1664 (?).
[79] *C.S.P.* 1661-8. 819 of 3 October 1664. The Council minutes of August 1661 describe him as a 'promoter of mutiny'; N.L.J. MST 60, p. 22.
[80] *C.S.P.* 1661-8, 374 of 10 October 1662.
[81] I.R.O. Deeds, liber I, fo. 26.
[82] B.M. Add. MSS. 12423, fo. 80r.
[83] *C.S.P.* 1669-74, 270 of 23 September 1670.

[84] I.R.O. Deeds, liber IV, fo. 368.
[85] *C.S.P.* 1669-74, 270 of 23 September 1670; this tract was near Naggo Head, in the Hellshire Hills.
[86] I.R.O. Deeds, liber IV, fo. 368.
[87] B.M. Add. MSS. 12423, fo. 93v.
[88] Ibid., fo. 91v.
[89] Ibid., fo. 94r.
[90] Thurloe, vi. 235.
[91] *C.S.P.* 1661-8, 388 of 19 November 1662.
[92] *C.S.P.* 1675-6, 280 of 27 January 1657.
[93] *C.S.P.* 1661-8, 446 of 28 April 1663.
[94] Ibid., 746 of 25 June 1664.
[95] I.R.O. Deeds, liber I, fo. 45.
[96] *C.S.P.* 1661-8, 397 of December (?) 1662.
[97] I.R.O. Deeds, liber I, fo. 16.
[98] *C.S.P.* 1675-6, 293 fo 2 February 1658.
[99] Ibid., 313 of 2 February 1659.
[100] I.R.O. Deeds, liber I, fo. 16.
[101] *C.S.P.* 1675-6, 315 of 23 April 1659.
[102] B.M. Add. MSS. 12423, fo. 36v.
[103] *C.S.P.* 1675-6, 319 of 9 June 1659.

CHAPTER THREE

The Consolidation of English Power: Privateering 1657–1680

Jamaica lay in the very heart of the Spanish Caribbean, ideally situated to wage maritime warfare upon Spanish trade-routes and colonies. However, by the same token she herself would be highly vulnerable, if ever the English lost command of the sea, and this was what seemed to be happening about 1657. The great invasion-fleet of 30 warships had rapidly melted away, as the vessels became unseaworthy and had to be sent back to England; by 1656 there were fewer than ten left,[1] and Governor D'Oyley greatly apprehended a Spanish counter-attack against which he would have been virtually defenceless, for the Spaniards could count on greatly outnumbering the English, if only they could mobilize and transport their forces.

In this desperate situation a desperate expedient suggested itself. D'Oyley knew that on the northern shores of Hispaniola were groups of English and French pirates, 'the brethren of the coast', who used this wild land as a base from which to plunder Spanish ships.[2] Their most considerable base was on the island of Tortuga, conveniently situated alongside the Windward Passage between Cuba and what is now Haiti. Tortuga was well fortified, but did not have the same potential as the Point either for victualling or for the disposal of prizes. D'Oyley was therefore able in 1657 to begin luring away some of the buccaneers of Tortuga. He counted on gaining naval protection and some revenue[3] from them, while they acquired a superlative harbour, which was increasingly well defended, a good market for their loot, and better facilities both for repairing their ships and for stocking them for future voyages.[4]

We have no documents dealing with D'Oyley's earliest negotiations with the buccaneers, but by 1659, for instance, he was concerned about the prize ship *Angell Gabriell,* a 'good ship and cannot be sold here for her worth'.[5] D'Oyley's solution for this was to order Cornelius Burrough,

Privateering 25

steward-general, 'to deliver possession thereof to Captain Povey, commander of the ketch, with all her rigging, and to victual her company as other of the fleete here'. In other words, the *Angell Gabriell* was incorporated into the English force. Other prizes were sold back to privateers. In that same May of 1659, for instance, the *New Garden* of Flushing was sold to 'monsieur Lepene' for £300.[6] The Frenchman renamed her the *Bonaventure* and also bought her cargo of 110 hides and ten barrels of 'rozin'; the latter he sold back to the state at £3 per barrel, for which he was paid in 'cacao nutts calculated at 4 1/2d. per lb.'.[7] Lepene sailed from the Point on 17 September 1659, bearing D'Oyley's 'commission', as the letter of marque was commonly called.

Another privateer who eventually took one of D'Oyley's commissions was Captain Maurice Williams, who achieved wide notoriety in the 1660s. In May 1659 he bought at the Point 'by inch of candle' (that is, to the last bidder before the marked inch burned out) the Spanish prize *Rabba Bispa* for £120.[8] This ship had in fact been captured and brought in by the state's ship[9] *Diamond*, one of the few remaining seaworthy frigates, and put up for sale by the state. Williams renamed her the *Jamaica* and immediately acquired a privateering commission; as the vessel was short of guns, he bought five cannon from the state storehouse on the Point. She was also short of men, and D'Oyley, in a remarkable demonstration of his support for privateering, signed his consent to a proclamation 'that such seamen aboard the *Marston Moor* frigott that will go along with the aforesaid captain Maurice Williams may have liberty to go on board the said *Jamaica* frigott at their pleasure'.[10]

In acting like this, D'Oyley was surely stretching to a wonderful degree his discretionary powers as governor. In fact, he was a man of action who did not care overmuch about legal niceties. The whole system for the disposal of prizes was an example of this, for the prize courts erected by D'Oyley never received the approval of the Admiralty commissioners in England.[11] He based their foundation, in 1657, on the instructions sent to the commissioners for the expeditionary force in October 1655. These stated, *inter alia,* that 'all prizes [were] to be preserved for the public service, a perfect account kept, and to be disposed of for carrying on the present service'. The function of prize officer was performed after April 1659 by Captain Povey;[12] this appointment by D'Oyley apparently confirmed a previous one by earlier commissioners.

The process of the prize courts in D'Oyley's time was simple and rapid. When it was brought into the harbour, the prize was received by

Povey, and evidence was collected by commissioners appointed by D'Oyley. In the case of the *Susannah*, in September 1657, for instance, the commissioners were Cornelius Burrough, William James, Peter Pugh, and John Browne.[13] Once the vessel had been declared prize it was publicly sold 'by inch of candle'.

When Thomas, seventh baron Windsor, succeeded D'Oyley in August 1662, the new governor was able to set up formally established vice-admiralty courts. From this time onwards the Jamaican courts boasted the same officials as their counterparts in England: judge, advocate, proctor, registrar, and marshal. However, the procedure remained essentially the same as in D'Oyley's time, and the latter never incurred any censure for the institution of his informal prize courts.[14]

In the two or three latter years of D'Oyley's government, privateering was becoming so attractive to the colonists that merchant-ships as well as plantations were suffering from a shortage of labour. D'Oyley was therefore compelled publicly to order 'any private men of warre fitted out here at Jamaica not to take in anywhere they find seamen or landmen, upon penalty of haveing their owne shipp made prize'.[15] It is unlikely that proclamations of this kind had much effect, and by the middle of 1660 D'Oyley was keenly apprehensive about the situation in which no naval vessels remained, and the island's safety was dependent upon the dubious loyalty of the privateering fleet.[16]

The problem was not only that the privateers might not be able or willing to defend the island against a full-scale Spanish assault, but also that they were sometimes disinclined to distinguish between an enemy vessel and an English one, when the chance of a prize offered itself. D'Oyley did his best to counter this by sending instructions to Captain John Lloyd, commander of the frigate *Diamond*, that when on patrol he should intercept and examine the commissions of 'divers rovers or private men of warre att sea, who daily commit insolencies on the bodies and goods of the allies and considerably of our nation'. Those who could not produce commissions issued either from the High Court of Admiralty in England or from D'Oyley himself were to report to the Point within three months to obtain lawful commissions, 'or they shall be looked upon as pirates and robbers . . . and dealt with accordingly'.[17] On at least one occasion D'Oyley acted upon this warning, for on 23 January 1661 Captain Thomas Wilkes, commander of H.M.S. *Convertine*, was ordered to receive on board George Freeborne, Robert Martyn, Wm. Foxery, Roger Tayler, and Jeremy Medlicoate (in irons), all for robbery and piracy.[18]

In spite of these undesirable side-effects, D'Oyley's resolve to call upon the buccaneers had by the end of his governorship proved to be a resounding success. Although the privateers were never called upon to repulse a direct attempt by the Spaniards to recapture the island, they were a formidable deterrent, and took part in the operations which by 1660 had finally rid the island of Spaniards and their sympathizers.[19] They also conducted harassing operations on Spanish shipping which kept the Spanish forces committed to the defence of their own territories, as well as supporting naval attacks on the Main such as that on Santa Marta in 1655 and on Coro and Cumana in 1659.

The whole Western Design had been a policy of the Interregnum - even if it was in effect a continuation of earlier trends - and with the restoration of Charles II in May 1660 it was to be expected that peace with Spain would soon come. In February 1661, in fact, D'Oyley received not only a commission recognizing him as governor, but also news that an armistice had been made with Spain;[20] he thereupon published a proclamation commanding the cessation of all acts of hostility against the king of Spain, and ordering all captains of ships of war then abroad to return to Port Royal (as it was by then) with all speed for further orders.[21]

The reaction at Port Royal to this proclamation is easy to imagine; in a letter of the following month to 'his kinsman, Sec. Nicolas', D'Oyley remarks that he has 'already, by the order for cessation, sufficiently enraged the populacy, who live only upon spoil and depredations'.[22] In fact the privateers appear entirely to have ignored his proclamation; D'Oyley was anxious to return to England, and the following August Windsor was named as his successor. The new governor arrived a year later, in August 1662, with instructions to reverse the policy of the past seven years, and 'to obtain and preserve good correspondence and free commerce with the plantations belonging to the king of Spain'.[23] If this plan did not succeed, an additional instruction permitted him 'to settle such trade by force'.

Windsor seems to have made a genuine attempt to promote trade between Jamaica and the islands of Puerto Rico and Santo Domingo, but he had to contend not only with opposition from Port Royal, but also with the unrelenting hostility of the Spanish governors. Very soon hostilities broke out again, this time in the shape of devastating raids on Santiago de Cuba and Campeche. The first of these raids was led by Captain Christopher Myngs in the frigate *Centurion,* supported by 'eleven other ships and about 1300 men'.[24] This venture surpassed expectations, for the town was taken and the fort defending it was blown up. In the absence of the fleet, Windsor called in 'all commissions for privateers and endeavoured to reduce them to certain orderly rules, giving them commissions to take Spaniards and bring them to Jamaica'.[25] He also, as we have seen, established regular vice-admiralty courts before leaving for England late in October.

The operation of the court in disposing of the prizes captured at Santiago de Cuba has been described by Dr. Helen Crump.[26] Its first meeting took place on the eve of the fleet's departure for Cuba, but it was of course on its return that it became really busy. In all, seven ships and barques had been taken, and the court met on 29 October before William Michell, who was a doctor of civil law and judge of the Admiralty. Normally the court met at Port Royal, though some of their sessions might be held in Spanish Town. Petitions and particular claims were brought by Captain Myngs of the *Centurion*, Captain Swart of the *Griffin*, and other officers and commanders. At this first session of the court the main facts were established, and enquiry was made concerning the owners of the prizes; as these naturally failed to appear, a first default was entered.

The court met next on 3 November, and the registrar, Charles Hadres, began the proceedings by moving on behalf of the king that sentence might be passed on the prizes lying in Port Royal Harbour. Thereupon motions were issued on the petitions and the defendants were again cited to appear; as nobody came forward, the second default was recorded. Meanwhile Captain Myngs reported that he had agreed to share the proceeds of the prizes equally between the naval and the privateering vessels, and a board was constituted to look into the claims of the privateers; the members of this body were Myngs, with Edward Pinhorne and three other merchants. Evidence having been heard concerning the number of vessels captured, the proceeding closed with a third summons to the defendants, which of course again went unanswered. Thereupon the court proceeded to the decree, condemning all the vessels captured at Santiago de Cuba as lawful prize,[27] reserving the admiral's tenths. After these had been paid to the judge of the Admiralty, the prize commissioners divided the rest according to custom.[28] Six of the prizes were then sold by inch of candle, but the seventh was given to Robert Avis, a freeholder of Port Royal, for it had never left Santiago and had to be salvaged, a feat which he accomplished 'through a great deale of labour and charge'. The sale of the ships realized £390. 10s. 0d., and that of their cargoes of sugar and molasses brought the total up to £729. 7s. 6d. Out of this the deputy-governor, Sir Charles Lyttelton, took £72. 18s. 6d. for the Lord Admiral, £200 for the king's share for the *Centurion*, and £105. 4s. 6d. for the *Griffin;* these sums included the fifteenths due to the king on all prizes. What was left was then divided among the privateers.

The success of the raid on Santiago encouraged the Council of Jamaica late in 1662 to plan another venture, this time 'to leeward, on the coasts of Cuba, Honduras, and the bay of Campeache'.[29] Myngs again led the attack, and was once more supported by privateering vessels. With twelve ships and fifteen or sixteen hundred men, he captured and sacked the town of Campeche; the booty allegedly amounted to 150,000 pieces of eight.[30] The Spaniards naturally made a bitter complaint to the English court, and Lyttelton received orders directly from Charles that no more such assaults should be undertaken.[31] These orders did not, however, give any instructions about the future of the privateers; plainly the English government could hardly be expected to disarm so redoubtable a host.

Lyttelton himself was not likely to call in the privateers, when he was receiving grants like the one of August 1663, which allowed him £1,000 towards his expenses in Jamaica, 'to be by him received and retained out of prizes and prize goods without account'.[32] No wonder we find him reporting to England the following October that he 'finds that the war with privateers was not to be taken off by the king's instructions, so has not thought it his duty to call them in'.[33] In any case, it would have been next to impossible to persuade the privateers to give up their lucrative pursuits, especially when their presence at Port Royal and activities in the Caribbean were warmly regarded not only by the Port Royal merchants, but also by the deputy-governor and the Council. By the end of 1663, there were 22 full-time privateering craft using Port Royal's facilities.[34]

Lyttelton soon tired of Jamaica, and asked leave to return to England on the grounds of health and for other personal reasons. He sailed on 2 May 1664, and on 4 June his successor, Sir Thomas Modyford, expressly instructed to prohibit the granting of letters of marque,[35] stepped ashore from the *Marmaduke* to begin a six-year governorship notorious for its support of privateering. Some of the reasons for this apparent paradox emerge from a letter written during the interval between Lyttelton's departure and Modyford's arrival, by Lieutenant-Colonel Thomas Lynch, president of the Council, to Secretary Sir Henry Bennett.[36] Lynch was not in favour of a serious attempt to 'call in' the privateers, for 'naked orders to restrain them or call them in will teach them only to keep out of this port [Port Royal] and force them (it may be) to prey on us as well as the Spaniards'. Lynch went on to point out that it would be no good demanding that they return to Port Royal unless this request were backed by 'five or six men-of-war', for 'if they want [for] English commissions, [they] can have French and Portugal papers, and if with them they take anything, they are sure of a good reception at New Netherlands or Tortugas'.

Modyford seemed to have good intentions at the start, for immediately upon his arrival he called a meeting of the Council and repealed all privateering commissions, a move which led one commentator to remark that 'the privateers are a little discouraged by the peace'.[37] In fact they need not have worried, for scarcely two weeks later Modyford informed Bennett[38] that he 'thought it more prudent to do by degrees and moderation what he had resolved to execute suddenly and severely, hoping to gain them [the privateers] off more safely by fair means and reduce them to planting, to accomplish which he must somewhat dispense with the strictness of his instructions' (i.e., those prohibiting the granting of letters of marque). Subsequent events were to show that in Modyford the privateers had found their most enthusiastic patron.

In spite of his continuing remonstrances against the evils of privateering, and declarations that he desired as earnestly as anyone in England a trade with the Spanish territories, Modyford never ceased to permit Spanish prizes to be brought into Port Royal. Quite unashamedly, he wrote to Bennett in February 1665 that 'the Spanish prizes have been inventoried and sold, but it is suspected that those of Morrice and Bernard Nichols have been miserably plundered, and the interested parties will find but a slender account in the Admiralty'.[39] In general, he was prepared to tolerate commissions granted by previous governors until they expired, but after that he regarded their holders as pirates, and sometimes took steps to bring them in.[40] Sometimes too, though, having captured a pirate of this kind he was willing to let him go again if he would accept Modyford's terms. Such a case occurred on 6 February 1665,[41] when:

> about fourteen pirates were tried and condemned to death under the statute of Henry 8 ... and finding so moderate a sense touching privateers and the great occasions His Majesty might have for them, and having shown the law and force, [I] changed my copy, pardoned all the pirates but three which [I] have reprieved, and declared publicly that commissions would be granted against the Dutch.

The following April, he wrote in similar vein that 'upon my gentleness towards them, the privateers come in apace and cheerfully offer life and fortune for His Majesty's service'.[42]

What greatly helped Modyford in his forward policy was the fact that in 1664 an informal war had broken out between England and Holland; the two countries formally declared hostilities open in March 1665. With commissions against the Dutch to be had for the asking, Modyford organized and despatched an expedition under Lieutenant-Colonel Edward Morgan, the deputy governor, comprising ten ships and some 500 men, 'chiefly reformed privateers', to fall upon the Dutch fleet trading at Saint Christopher's, capture Eustatia, Saba, and Curaçao, and on their homeward voyage call in at Tortuga. All this, he wrote, 'is prepared by the honest privateers at the old rate of "no purchase no pay"'.[43]

Unfortunately Edward Morgan died just before the Dutch surrendered Eustatia, and the privateers' subsequent attack on Saba did not net them much booty. Morgan's successor was a certain Colonel Theodore Cary, whom Modyford described as 'a man of too easy disposition'; Cary was certainly unable to persuade his companions to press forward the attack against Curaçao, though he himself attributed this failure to the problems inherent in leading a force 'whose plunder is their pay, and obedience guided by their wills'.[44] The expedition having failed to live up to its promise, Modyford acted quickly as the privateers straggled back to Port Royal. Feeling it imperative to regain their confidence, he 'sent for the leading men of the privateers, whom he had obliged by not questioning them, and caused Major Byndloss to hold a correspondence with the old privateer, Captain Mansfield, and to appoint a rendezvous at Blew Fields Bay, where it its calculated will be no less than 600 privateers, and they will forward the design of Curaçao'.[45]

Modyford knew, however, as well as any privateer in the Caribbean, that the richest pickings were to be had not from sorties against the Dutch, but from their old adversaries the Spaniards. When the Council of Jamaica met at Spanish Town on 22 February 1666, it therefore passed a resolution containing no fewer than twelve reasons why it was to the interest of the island to grant letters of marque against the Spaniards.[46] It was unanimously concluded 'that the granting of the said commissions did extraordinarily conduce to the strengthening, preservation, enriching and advancing the settlement of this island'. Meanwhile, in a further attempt to induce anti-Spanish feeling, Modyford was reporting to England case after case of Spanish depredations against

English shipping and seamen. This policy was effective; on 1 March 1666 'his Grace' gave the governor 'latitude to grant or not to grant commissions against the Spaniards'.[47]

Almost at once the Port Royal privateers amalgamated their forces, chose Mansfield as their captain, and departed in force to capture Curaçao. This attempt proved as abortive as the earlier expedition, for 'the private soldiers aboard the admiral were against it, averring publicly that there was more profit with less hazard to be gotten against the Spaniard, which was their only interest'.[48] Two of the fleet rapidly departed for Tortuga, and the remaining four joined up with two French rovers and sailed off to attack Providence, contrary to any of Modyford's orders. The latter as usual was quick to excuse their conduct:

> on the 12th inst. [June 1666] arrived Captain Mansfield and one other ship, and complains that the disobedience of several officers and soldiers was the cause of their not proceeding on the design of Curaçao; in the meantime the old fellow was resolved (as he tells me) never to see my face again until he has done some service to His Majesty, and therefore with 200 men which were all were left him, and about 80 of them French, he resolved to attempt the island of Providence . . . [I] have yet only reproved Mansfield for doing it without orders, and really [I] dare not go further than rebukes without His Majesty's express orders, lest [I] should drive them from that allegiance which they make great profession of now more than ever.[49]

So the farce continued, with Modyford granting commissions against the Spaniards, and the English Crown either remaining silent or, if the state of negotiations with Spain demanded it, sending him some token rebuke. On one occasion Modyford was ordered by the King to restore a Spanish vessel captured and brought in to Port Royal; this order provoked from Modyford a long self-justifying letter to Lord Arlington,[50] explaining that he used his power to grant commissions only as a last resort to save not only the loss of Jamaica of the privateering force, but also to save Port Royal itself, for:

> looking on their weak condition, the chief merchants gone from Port Royal, no credit given to privateers for victualling etc. and rumours of war with the French often repeated, he issued a declaration of his intentions to grant commissions against the Spaniard. His Lordship cannot imagine what a universal change there was on the faces of men and things, ships repairing, great resort of workmen and labourers to Port Royal, many returning, many debtors released out of prison, and

the ships from the Curaçao voyage, not daring to come in for fear of creditors, brought in and fitted out again.

Needless to say, much of this distress was the work of Modyford's fertile brain; the journal of Captain Beeston, which covers these years, mentions only that privateers were continually 'going in and out' and frequently bringing prizes.[51]

This privateering continued throughout 1667, in disregard of those negotiations between Spain and England which on 13 May 1667 resulted in the signing of the first Treaty of Madrid.[52] This treaty made the English valuable commercial concessions, and in theory now made the privateers' attempt to 'force' trade with the Spanish Indies redundant. However, so far from privateering diminishing, it was now approaching its apogee. So was the power of Modyford; by the beginning of 1668 he had established a large and powerful privateering force, based on Port Royal, and had engineered the appointment of his brother, Sir James Modyford, as chief judge of the Court of Admiralty in Jamaica. It now remained only for Henry Morgan to emerge, and complete the trio which was to wreak such havoc on the Spaniards in the West Indies, and to stupefy the chanceries of Europe by the audacity of their attacks.

The 'old fellow' Captain Mansfield having died, Henry Morgan was commissioned by Modyford about February 1668 'to draw together the English privateers, and take prisoners of the Spanish nation, whereby he might inform of the intentions of that enemy to invade Jamaica'.[53] On the pretence of capturing Spanish prisoners (though it hardly needed ten ships and 500 men), Morgan led his expedition first to Porto Principe in Cuba, where he learned that considerable Spanish forces were expected to rendezvous at Havana from Porto Bello, Cartagena, Vera Cruz, and Campeche, presumably to attack Jamaica. Having sent this information to Modyford, Morgan sailed in May 1668 to Porto Bello. Anchoring some 40 leagues to leeward, he transferred his men to canoes and at 3 a.m. on 26 June landed at Porto Bello itself. 'Seeing that they could not refresh themselves in quiet', they were 'forced' to assault the castle. This and the other two major forts were quickly captured, and the town itself soon fell. The president of Panama with (according to Morgan) a force of 3,000 men attempted to retake the town, but was beaten off by the buccaneers. Finally, a ransom of 100,000 pieces of eight was accepted for the return of the town and castles, and the expedition re-embarked and sailed for Port Royal.[54]

Esquemeling agrees in principle with Morgan's account, except that he mentions that the expedition returned to Jamaica via Cuba, where Morgan:

> sought out a place wherein with all quiet and repose he might make the dividend of the spoil they had got. They found in ready money 250,000 pieces of eight besides all other merchandizes, as cloth, linen, silks and other goods. With this rich booty they sailed again thence to their common place of rendezvous, Jamaica. Being arrived, they passed here some time in all sorts of vices and debauchery, according to their common manner of doing, spending with huge prodigality what others had gained with no small labour and toil.[55]

The arrival of Morgan and the fleet meant another business boom for the residents of Port Royal. Sir James Modyford, writing to his agent in London, Sir Andrew King, complained that he was unfortunately so short of ready cash that he missed the opportunity to buy cheaply from the buccaneers:

> to let you have ye enclosed relation concerning ye privatiers' expedition to Porto Principe and Porto Bello; for ye latter place I am confident they brought more plunder in jewells, gold and silver standard than twice ye value of ye ransome they had for ye place, and I might have bought what I would almost att 40s. per ounce gold, and silver from 2s. 6d. to 3s. per ounce, but I was not in cash here. Some goes now for Old, and more for New England.[56]

Early in 1669, Morgan's career almost came to an abrupt end, when the *Oxford* blew up while he was on board holding a Council of War concerning a proposed attack on Cartagena.[57] Modyford, meanwhile, was as anxious as Morgan to launch another attack on the Spaniards, and sent deposition after deposition to England in an effort to get outright permission to deploy the privateers again.[58] Each of these documents followed a similar pattern, setting out the despicable actions of the Spaniards, their boasts about not giving any quarter either to Englishmen or to Jamaicans, and their alleged declaration of war 'by beat of drum' in Cartagena. The secretary of state, Lord Arlington, informed Modyford that 'His Majesty's pleasure is, that in what state soever the privateers are at the receipt of this letter [it was dated at Whitehall, 12 June 1670], he keep them so till we have a final answer from Spain, with this condition only, that he obliges them to forebear all hostilities at land.'[59]

Fortunately for Modyford, his opportunity and excuse to attack the Main again was provided by the Spaniards themselves. In June 1670 they made an attack on the north coast of Jamaica, setting fire to several houses, killing some of the inhabitants and capturing others. On 2 July 1670, Modyford therefore gave Morgan a commission appointing him 'commander-in-chief of all the ships fitted or to be fitted for the defence of this island, and to use his best endeavours to surprise, take, sink, disperse or destroy the enemy's vessels, and, in case he finds it feasible, to land and attack St. Jago or any other place'.[60] In a further letter containing additional instructions, Modyford told Morgan that the expedition would be 'on the old pleasing account of no purchase no pay', and that he granted Morgan full power to grant commissions to those that did not have them and might wish to join the fleet.[61]

Modyford then wrote to England to justify his actions, while Morgan and his buccaneers sailed to their rendezvous at the Ile-à-Vache (off what is now Haiti). From this base detachments of the fleet were sent to patrol south Cuban waters and also to watch the coasts of the Main, so as to gain intelligence of Spanish shipping movements. Morgan's plan for a great attack on one of the Spanish possessions, which as we shall see was not put into effect until December 1670, was well known on the streets of Port Royal in the preceding August. In that month Edward Stanton, a prominent and influential merchant, wrote to Colonel Thomas Lynch in England remarking that 'our fleet, though gone out, will not be ready for their design for months'.[62]

By 18 December 1670 all was ready for the great design. Modyford's letter to Arlington of that date confirms that Morgan had assembled a force of thirty-six ships and about 1,800 men at the Ile-à-Vache ready for the attack, but, continues Modyford:

> [I] have despatched to the admiral [Morgan] before the first of these expresses arrived, a copy of the articles of peace with Spain,[63] intimating that though [I] had them from private hands and no orders to call him in yet, yet thought fit to let him see them . . . and to do nothing that might prevent the accomplishment of His Majesty's peaceable intentions; but the vessel returned with [my] letters, having missed him [Morgan] at his old rendezvous. However, [I have] returned her to the Main with strict instructions to find the admiral out.[64]

We can never know, of course, what instructions Modyford in fact gave the captain of the vessel 'seeking' Morgan, though we may guess that he was privately recommended not to find him; Modyford was plainly concerned chiefly to safeguard his position once his treachery was revealed.

The attack on Panama which followed has become legendary. It was a brilliant operation, intelligently conceived and led, and Morgan cannot be denied the 'glory' of that day. His report of the expedition states that the plunder only amounted to £30,000 and that this was divided among the buccaneers when they retraced their steps and arrived back at Chagres.[65] There were, however, those in the company who thought otherwise; as Esquemeling puts it:

> every company, and every particular person therein included, received their portion of what was got, or rather what part thereof captain Morgan was pleased to give them ... for they judged it impossible that no greater share should belong to them than two hundred pieces of eight per capita, for so many valuable booties and robberies they had obtained.[66]

Morgan seems to have left Chagres rather hurriedly leaving most of the fleet behind; followed by three or four vessels belonging to his closest companions, he arrived at Port Royal in April 1671, to the acclamation of the colonists. None of them was as yet aware of the conclusion of the second treaty of Madrid, signed in July 1670 and ratified in August 1671. It does not seem possible that this omission on the part of Charles II's government can have been accidental; knowing Modyford as they did, they surely counted on him to bring off one final *coup* before the curtain came down.[67]

Morgan had not failed them, but the scandal which the sack of Panama gave to the diplomats of Europe meant that Sir Thomas Modyford's conduct could no longer be excused. In fact, even before the ships had returned from Panama the king had (on 4 January 1671) signed a revocation of his commission and appointed in his place Sir Thomas Lynch. In a letter of private instruction, the king required of Lynch that:

> As soon as he has taken possession of that government and the fortress [Fort Charles] so as not to apprehend any ill consequences thereupon, he cause the person of Sir Thomas Modyford to be made prisoner and sent home under a strong guard, [because] he hath contrary to the King's express commands made many depredations and hostilities against the subjects of His Majesty's good brother the Catholic King.[68]

Privateering 37

We shall shortly see how Lynch set about this difficult task, but before continuing that narrative it may be well to look at some of the consequences of Modyford's six years of encouragement to privateers. To start with, it does not seem as if the public revenue benefited to a significant extent from the buccaneers' exploits. Modyford's accounts of the revenue and expenditure of the island[69] from 4 June 1664 to 25 June 1671, and particularly the account headed 'fifteenths of prizes for accompt of His Majesty', show surprisingly little income from this source. This particular account appears to start under the date of 20 August 1665, and to close on 17 November 1667, if in fact the years are successive. This total revenue due to the king amounts to £858. 18s. 3d. (though it is in fact given as £860. 9s. 11d.), which seems very little in view of the privateers' activity at that time. The sworn statement made before Sir Thomas Lynch by Modyford's book-keeper, Cary Helyar, that 'the account of fifteenths doth agree with the records of the Admiralty court' can only raise more doubts about the accuracy and honesty not only of the island accounts but also of the proceedings of that court. Even more interesting might have been Helyar's explanation of the absence of any revenue whatsoever from this source in the period from 1668 to 1671.

It is pretty clear, then, that the Crown, as represented in its public accounts, did not reap much of the harvest from Porto Bello and Panama, to name only the richest prizes. What is not so easy is to say exactly where the loot went. As we have seen above, much went out again almost at once, to 'Old and New England', where it no doubt helped pay for the men and materials needed for establishing Jamaican plantations. When we come, in chapter 6, to examine the economic relationships at Port Royal, and particularly those between London merchants and their attorneys, and between Port Royal merchants and planters, we shall see that a model of this kind is by no means unrealistic. The merchant buys pirated gold and silver (and no doubt other goods) cheaply, sends them to his representative in the metropolis, has them sold at a considerable profit, and is thus enabled both to buy more goods for sale in Port Royal, and to finance the equipment of plantations in the Jamaican hinterland. Meanwhile the buccaneer's money normally re-enters circulation in Port Royal fairly rapidly, in payment for the wide variety of services available there,[70] though some of the leading privateers, like Henry Morgan himself, would have received and saved enough to set themselves up as planters.

It is one thing to construct a crude model of this kind, and quite another to find the examples necessary to test and refine it. The best we can do is to take one or two examples of the relationship between privateers, merchants, and planters, as illustrations of the general structure. One of Morgan's boon companions was a certain Captain Lawrence Prince, who was in fact a lieutenant-colonel in the attack on Panama. By 1672, no doubt using his share of the Panama loot, Prince had become a considerable landowner on the Liguanea plain,[71] which at that time was being rapidly opened up for cultivation.[72] Morgan himself looked further afield for his investment; it was in the parish of Saint Mary that he built up the estate to which he gave the name of Llanrumney, and he had other widely scattered land-holdings.[73]

Many of Port Royal's inhabitants had investments in privateering. Robert Hardson, for instance, 'chyrurgeon', was confident that he could repay an outstanding mortgage 'at or upon the return of the fleet of Jamaica, now being under the command of admiral Henry Morgan', by a payment of '440 ounces of merchantable silver plate'.[74] Merchants like Anthony Swymmer, who represented his father's Bristol firm in Port Royal, constantly bought prize ships. Sometimes these were condemned, not under letters of marque, but because they had violated the Navigation Acts. On 5 February 1673, for instance, Mr. Charles Atkinson prosecuted against the *Primrose*, 'now riding at anchor in Port Royal harbour, William Westone master, burthen about 25 tunns'; this ship, valued at £150, was duly condemned and when offered for sale was bought by Swymmer.[75] Other resident merchants had more direct interests in privateering. On 14 January 1670, for instance, Peter Quadman bought for £37. 3s. 0d. from George Jacobson the pink *Sacrifice of Abraham* 'now out in His Majesty's fleet for Jamaica, admiral Henry Morgan commander-in-chief'.[76] One way and another, nearly all the propertied inhabitants of Port Royal seem to have had an interest in privateering.

However, Port Royal was not Jamaica, and the interests of its inhabitants were not necessarily those of the island as a whole. The agricultural development of the hinterland, often initiated by the merchants themselves, led to the emergence of an increasingly powerful 'planting' interest, which looked with distaste upon buccaneering, not only because it made trade hazardous but also because it lured men away from agricultural work. One of the earliest representatives of this planter group was John Styles, who first came to Jamaica in 1665 and owned land in the parish of Saint John.[77] Styles seems to have been very outspoken in his attacks on privateering, for during Modyford's governorship he was actually brought to trial 'for words spoken at the session house'.[78] In January 1669 he wrote at length to secretary Sir William Morris, complaining *inter alia:*

> That the trade [of Jamaica] now consists principally in plate, money, jewels and other things brought in by privateers . . . in colonel D'Oyley's time . . . there was a considerable army of young lusty men under command and pay, but now almost all are gone, or dead, or out for privateers [of which] about 800 are out on that employment. Questions if there be need of their help whether they would afford any, when they have none or so little interest upon land that they value it not; gold and gain is their only god they worship . . . the settlement of Jamaica will never be in a better condition without a speedy supply from England of Christian planters, not merchants.[79]

Such sentiments as these cut directly across the policies both of Modyford and of the merchant class of Port Royal; Styles was fined £500 and was for a time imprisoned for his 'words'.[80] However, he was a very determined advocate for his cause, and again in 1670 was harping on the evil effects of privateering; even if commissions are withheld, he says, 'yet they [the buccaneers] go forth with let-passes, which is all one as to consuming men of this place, who from enquiries . . . still decrease in all parts except Port Royal'.[81] No doubt Styles was representative of a growing body of feeling in the island, not only among the planters but also perhaps among the merchants, some of whom may have seen more profit in peaceful trade, now that the Spanish prohibition had been breached by the agreement of 1667. When Lynch came out in June 1671, then, he found a considerable body of opinion favourable to his instructions to remove Sir Thomas and reverse his policies. However, the buccaneering habit died hard, as we shall see; for the next two decades the ghost of the privateers continued to haunt Jamaican politics with its rivalries and temptations.

As we have seen, it was expected that Lynch might encounter some resistance in securing the person of Sir Thomas, even though the latter 'has not in him or any the least appearance of any disposition to resist the King's authority'.[82] A severe attack of gout in fact incapacitated Lynch upon his arrival in the island, and after that he had to wait a while both for suitable transport to be available and, it may be surmised, for the mood of the island to be gauged. However, Modyford's son Charles had been put in the Tower of London in the middle of May as security for his father's conduct, and when this news reached Jamaica, some time early in August, Lynch could wait no longer; inveigling Modyford aboard H.M.S. *Assistance*, he made the royal wishes known. Morgan was ill at the time and nobody else made any attempt to rescue the ex-governor, who within a few days was transferred to the *Jamaica Merchant* (Captain Joseph Knapman), which sailed for England on 22 August 1671.[83]

Many of the buccaneers had not in fact returned to Port Royal, 'fearing His Majesty's displeasure for their past irregular actions'. Lynch now offered royal pardons to all who would come in, and this policy was so successful that by December 1671 he was able to report that 'there are but three privateers out, one captain Diego, and Yhallahs and Martin';[84] the former had been a member of the Panama fleet and all three were being sought by H.M.S. *Welcome* and *Assistance*. With Modyford safely in the Tower, Lynch was able to attend to Morgan himself, who was also sent back to England as a prisoner, on H.M.S. *Welcome* in April 1672.[85] In fact, Morgan had by then been deserted by most of those of his old comrades-in-arms who were still about; Lawrence Prince, for example, was made one of Lynch's lieutenants.[86] Perhaps the great buccaneer himself was not loth to return to England, for he must have realized that no great harm would come to him, and this was a good opportunity to change his allegiance from his pirates to the Crown.

Lynch now applied himself in earnest to the task of rooting out all privateers and pirates, wherever they might be based, who were a threat to the peace of the Caribbean. Those that declined to accept the king's pardon were declared pirates, and there followed exchanges of correspondence between Lynch and the Spanish authorities in Cuba in an attempt to hound these pirates from the seas. As we shall see in chapter 5, the naval forces at Lynch's disposal were inadequate for this task, but pirates were caught from time to time. Captain Witherborn, indeed, was captured, tried for piracy, and condemned to death at Port Royal before Morgan had gone;[87] both sailed together on H.M.S. *Welcome*, to rather different fates.

From this time onwards, no Jamaican governor could connive at privateering in the way that Modyford had done. However, during the 1670s there were a good many more or less surreptitious pirates operating out of Port Royal, and these continued until about 1680 to receive underhand encouragement from Morgan, who in November 1674 was appointed lieutenant-governor and knighted.[88] Sir Henry Morgan returned to Jamaica in March 1675, just ahead of the new governor,

Lord Vaughan, with whom he was soon at loggerheads.[89] Their rivalry had its petty aspect, as on the occasion when Vaughan wrote to Morgan requesting him to vacate the King's House at Port Royal - where the deputy governor in fact normally resided - as he Vaughan wished to live there himself. But it was based on the much more serious problem that Vaughan suspected that Morgan was still secretly encouraging his old friends the privateers. Nor was this merely suspicion, for Morgan appears actually to have written a letter on one occasion, encouraging one Captain John Edmunds, who was then operating under a French commission, to come into Port Royal.[90] Vaughan meanwhile was waging a fierce war on the privateers, for as he wrote to the Lords of Trade and Plantations:

> The only enemy to planting is privateering, which I have by all means possible endeavoured to restrain and prevent . . . sand had gone so far in reducing them that most of them were on the point of coming in and betaking themselves to another course of life, when the covetousness and unfaithfulness of some people obstructed my design.[91]

These 'people' were surely Morgan and his brother-in-law Robert Byndloss, both commissioners of the admiralty court. Vaughan went so far in May 1676 as to write to Secretary Sir Joseph Williamson in these terms; 'I find Sir Henry, contrary to his duty and trust, endeavours to set up privateering, and has obstructed all my designs and purposes for the reducing of those that do use the curse of life'.[92] In the same letter he accused Morgan of recommending some of the English privateers to the French government in Tortuga for commissions, and of putting a power of attorney into Byndloss's hands to receive tenths for the king of France. Vaughan suspected much, but could prove little, for 'during all this time there was no public commissions given against the Spaniards, nor privateering publicly countenanced, but many times things came in by stealth'.[93]

There is little doubt that Vaughan's suspicions were well founded, and that Morgan and Byndloss favoured not only privateers, but also interlopers, and especially those who discharged cargoes of slaves in certain remote bays. In July 1676 matters came to a head, when Vaughan brought charges against Morgan and Byndloss before the Council of Jamaica. Morgan he accused of corresponding with known privateers, using the governor's name, while Byndloss was attacked for complicity and for corresponding with Monsieur d'Ogeron, governor of Tortuga, with a view to holding the Frenchman's power of attorney to collect the king of France's tenths from such French privateers as slipped unnoticed into Port Royal Harbour.[94] In spite of a good deal of correspondence between England and Jamaica on this subject, Vaughan was eventually unsuccessful in upholding his accusations, and his two adversaries went unscathed.

The mutual distrust between Vaughan and Morgan continued until the former left the island in March 1678; despite the warning which Vaughan had given Whitehall to dismiss Morgan from all public offices,[95] Sir Henry remained as deputy governor under the earl of Carlisle. During this governorship privateering saw a certain resurgence, not because of Carlisle's deliberate policy, but because he was engrossed by his quest for personal enrichment and by his quarrel with the House of Assembly.[96] In fact, Carlisle was obliged to revert in some degree to the old policy of relying on privateers for protection, in the face of the French threat: '... about 1200 privateers abroad, but some have come in since my arrival, and more hoped for from the encouragement I have given them to stay; they have generally French commissions ... If a war with France, this island will stand in need of their assistance, for we have not above four thousand whites able to bear arms, a secret not fit to be made public.'[97] During Carlisle's administration, then, there was a slackening of hostility towards privateering, and men like Coxen, Sharp, Essex, Allison, Row and Maggott came into Port Royal and were allowed to leave in order, as it was hoped, to resume their attacks on the Spaniards.[98]

With the departure of Carlisle in May 1680, Sir Henry Morgan as lieutenant-governor again determined policy, but by this time his attitude had changed, and he showed himself to be resolutely hostile to privateering. He even went so far as personally to organize vessels which chased and captured various pirates, who were then tried, convicted and executed.[99] By the time that Sir Thomas Lynch returned for his second spell as governor, in May 1682, large-scale privateering was virtually at an end; it was therefore rather ironic that at this stage Sir Henry and Byndloss were suspended form the Council and from all commands (October 1682).[100]

Morgan's final change of heart reflected a general shifting in attitudes in Jamaica. As the island became increasingly reliant for her prosperity on the export of sugar, piracy under whatever name it masqueraded came to be seen merely as a dangerous impediment to trade; a majority even of the inhabitants of Port Royal probably concurred in this view by 1680. The next 20 years therefore saw the emergence of different patterns of piratical activity. First there was a tendency to follow the example set by Harris, Cox, and Sharp in crossing the isthmus to the Pacific and then attacking Spanish shipping up and down the South Sea coast. After that, as pressure was increasingly exerted both by French and by English governors, many of the pirates moved their bases completely out of the Caribbean, and frequented instead the ports of the Carolinas, where until 1685 they enjoyed a certain immunity.[101]

In 1687 James II offered a pardon to all buccaneers who would give up their calling; a similar proclamation came from the French the following year, and after that time the incidence of piracy markedly dropped. As we shall see in chapter 5, this period was also marked by the appearance in the Caribbean of much larger and more efficient naval forces, which would have made the presence of any considerable number of pirates very hazardous. In short, towards the end of the century the great days of the privateers in the West Indies came to an end, overtaken both by economic development and by refinements in the art of naval warfare.

CONCLUSION

Their Port Royal operations fall into three distinct phases. The first lasted from D'Oyley's appeal to Tortuga in 1657 until Modyford's dismissal in 1671; this was the heyday of privateering, when it played a crucial role in the struggle against Spain, and when its profits were commensurate with this. The second phase might be described as one of 'surreptitious piracy', and lasted from 1671 until Morgan's lieutenant-governorship of 1680. There were probably still fortunes to be made from it at Port Royal in these years, but our evidence of this activity is naturally negligible. The third phase set in after 1680, and was one of frank decline, when pirates were regarded simply as a nuisance.

All the same, the sad and rather sordid tales of the pirates after 1680 should not blind us to their remarkable contribution during the first period. As we shall see, Port Royal came to be heavily fortified, and in the 1680s became the base for an increasingly powerful naval fleet. Without the protection of the buccaneers between 1657 and 1671, however, the fortifications of Port Royal might well have fallen, or might have come to defend an island so ravaged as to be almost valueless. Without the buccaneers, too, the naval base would probably have been lost before the Admiralty became powerful enough to man it. All in all, Long was not far wrong when in 1774 he wrote that 'it is to the bucaniers we owe the possession of Jamaica to this hour'.[102]

NOTES

1. The running-down of the fleet is more fully described in chapter 5.
2. The best work on the origins and progress of these pirates is C. H. Haring, *The buccaneers in the West Indies in the 17th century* (London, 1910). Privateers were legally distinct from pirates, because the former had 'letters of marque' empowering them to capture the vessels of certain specified nationalities.
3. See below for the operation of this system.
4. The privateers received no stipend, of course, and lived on what they captured; hence the traditional 'no purchase, no pay'.
5. B.M. Add. MSS. 12423, fo. 61v.
6. Ibid.
7. B.M. Add. MSS. 12423, fo. 74v.
8. Ibid., fo. 61v.
9. This designation 'state's ship' was used during the Commonwealth.
10. B.M. Add. MSS. 12423, fo. 63v.
11. Much of this section on prize courts is based on the work of Helen J. Crump, *Colonial admiralty jurisdiction in the seventeenth century* (London, 1931).
12. B.M. Add. MSS. 12423, fo. 61v.
13. Crump, *Colonial admiralty jurisdiction*, p. 101.
14. In fact, the commissioners of the Admiralty had been unwilling at the time to advise him about the legality of his prize courts: *C.S.P.* 1574-1660, p. 467.
15. B.M. Add. MSS. 12423, fo. 64r.
16. *C.S.P.* 1574-1660, p. 485, D'Oyley to commissioners of the Admiralty, 26 July 1660.
17. B.M. Add. MSS. 12423, fo. 67r.
18. Ibid., fo. 101r.
19. These operations have been described by D. J. Buisseret in 'Edward D'Oyley, 1617-1675', *Jamaica Journal* (1971).
20. *C.S.P.* 1661-8, 17 of 5 February 1661, D'Oyley to all governors etc.
21. A partial list of 'privateers frequenting the Point' at this time is given in Appendix 1.
22. *C.S.P.* 1661-8, 61 of March (?) 1661.
23. On the various changes in English policy, see A. P. Thornton, *West-India policy under the Restoration* (Oxford, 1956).
24. There is a good account of this expedition in *Interesting Tracts*, p. 277.
25. *C.S.P.* 1661-8, 379 of 20 October 1662.
26. In *Colonial admiralty jurisdiction*, pp. 107-9.
27. This was the crucial stage in the process, for once vessels had been adjudged lawful prize, the future owners could receive certificates of ownership under Admiralty seal.
28. The commissioners were now Captain Myngs, John Man, Epinatus Crosse, Robert Castells, John Loving, Edward Pinhorne, and William Beeston; Crosse, Pinhorne, Loving, and Beeston were merchants of Port Royal.
29. *C.S.P.* 1661-8, 379 of 15 October 1662
30. Haring, *The buccaneers in the West Indies*, p. 108.
31. *C.S.P.* 1661-8, 443 of 23 April 1663.
32. Ibid., 535 of 19 August 1663.
33. Ibid., 566 of 15 October 1663.
34. See Appendix 2; this list, from B.M. Add. MSS. 11410, fo. 10, is rather fuller than the one quoted by Haring, *The buccaneers in the West Indies*, p. 273.
35. *C.S.P.* 1661-8, of 18 February 1664.
36. Ibid., 744 of 25 May 1664.
37. Ibid., 762 of 26 June 1664.
38. Ibid., 767 of 30 June 1664.
39. Ibid., 942 of 20 February 1665.
40. Ibid., 942 of 20 February 1665.
41. Ibid.
42. *C.S.P.* 1661-8, 976 of 12 April 1665.
43. Ibid., 979 of 20 April 1665.
44. Ibid., 1088 of November 1665.
45. Ibid., 1085 of 16 November 1665.

[46] Ibid., 1138 of 22 February 1666.
[47] Ibid., 1144 of 1 March 1666.
[48] Ibid., 1213 of 8 June 1666.
[49] Ibid., 1216 of 16 June 1666.
[50] Ibid., 1264 of 21 August 1666.
[51] *Interesting Tracts*, pp. 285-6.
[52] On these (very complicated) negotiations see Keith Feiling, *British foreign policy 1601-1672* (London, 1930), pp. 228-34.
[53] *C.S.P.* 1661-8, 1838 of 7 September 1668.
[54] Ibid.
[55] John Esquemeling, *The buccaneers of America* (London, 1911), p. 149.
[56] A. P. Thornton, 'The Modyfords and Morgan', in *J.H.R.*, ii. 2 (1952), 48.
[57] See chapter 5 for details of this catastrophe.
[58] *C.S.P.* 1669-74, 162 172, 182, and 206 between March and June of 1670.
[59] Ibid., 194 of 12 June 1670.
[60] Ibid., 211 of 2 July 1670.
[61] Ibid., 212 of 2 July 1670.
[62] Ibid., 240 of 25 August 1670.
[63] Concluded by Godolphin in July 1670; see Feiling, *British foreign policy*, p. 326.
[64] *C.S.P.* 1669-74, 359 of 18 December 1670.
[65] *C.S.P.* 1669-74, 504 of 20 April 1671; Morgan's full account.
[66] *The buccaneers of America*, pp. 237-8.
[67] This at any rate is the opinion of A. P. Thortnon, whose *West-India policy* minutely traces the correspondence on the matter (pp. 114-23).
[68] *C.S.P.* 1669-74, 405 of January(?) 1671.
[69] P.R.O. C.O. 138/1.
[70] D'Oyley himself maintained that most of the loot was dissipated in the taverns; B.M. Add. MSS. 11410, fo. 14.
[71] I.R.O., Deeds, liber I, p. 129.
[72] See Claypole, 'Land settlement and agricultural development in the Liguanea plain 1655-1700'.
[73] On his purchases of land see the excellent section in E. A. Cruikshank's *The life of Sir Henry Morgan* (Toronto, 1935), pp. 346-8.
[74] See chapter 6 for more details of his activity.
[75] I.R.O., Deeds, liber III, p. 244.
[76] I.R.O., Deeds, liber I, p. 91.
[77] *C.S.P.* 1669-74, 270 of 23 September 1670, 'The survey of the island of Jamaica'.
[78] Ibid., 138 of 4 January 1670.
[79] Ibid., 7 of 14 January 1669.
[80] Ibid., 138 of 4 January 1670.
[81] Ibid.
[82] Thus Lynch, surprised, to Lord Arlington; *C.S.P.* 1669-74, 580 of 2 July 1671.
[83] Modyford reached the Tower in November 1671; on the circumstances of his arrest see Thornton, *West-India policy*, p. 122.
[84] *C.S.P.* 1669-74, 697 of 17 December 1671.
[85] Ibid., 794 of 4 April 1672.
[86] Ibid., 967 of 17 December 1671.
[87] *C.S.P.* 1669-74, 785 of 20 March 1672.
[88] On the circumstances of this see Cruikshank, *The life of Sir Henry Morgan*, pp. 224-5.
[89] Vaughan had been appointed to succeed Lynch because the latter wished to return to England for personal reasons; see Frank Cundall, *The governors of Jamaica in the seventeenth century* (London, 1936), p. 46.
[90] *C.S.P.* 1675-6, 657 of 25 August 1675.
[91] Ibid., 863 of 4 April 1676.
[92] Ibid., 912 of 2 May 1676.
[93] According to Captain Beeston, *Interesting Tracts*, p. 291.
[94] *C.S.P.* 1675-6, 998 of 24 July 1676.
[95] Ibid., 566 of 18 May 1675.

[96] On which the fullest treatment is to be found in Agnes Whitson's *The constitutional development of Jamaica, 1664-1729* (Manchester, 1929).
[97] *C.S.P.* 1667-80, 815 of 24 October 1678.
[98] See Haring, *The buccaneers in the West Indies,* pp. 223-6.
[99] *C.S.P.* 1681-5, 16 of 1 February 1681 and 158 of 2 July 1681.
[100] On the occasion for this see Cruikshank, *The life of Sir Henry Morgan,* pp. 361-9.
[101] *C.S.P.* 1685-8, 363, 364, 639, and 1164; August 1685 to March 1687.
[102] Long, *A history of Jamaica,* i. 300.

CHAPTER FOUR

The Consolidation of English Power: The Fortifications

By 1660, as we have seen in chapter 2, the nascent town at the Point was protected by Fort Cromwell at its western end, and by a line of palisades along the peninsula at the eastern end. Fort Cromwell was, however, a very crude structure, consisting of a round tower with an unfinished square platform around it; palisades, while useful against casual robbers, would not withstand serious attack.

So the next 30 years saw a constant effort to improve the town's defences, which would be crucially important if ever there sailed against Jamaica a hostile fleet too large to be stopped by the English naval forces, whether regular or irregular. The history of the fortifications is thus central to an understanding of the strategic situation of Port Royal. It is also important to any study of the expansion of the town, for Port Royal's eventual shape, like that of most other large 'European' towns of the period, was largely determined by the line of its fortifications.

Fort Cromwell, politically rechristened 'Fort Charles' in 1662,[1] received most of the attention during the 1660s. In November 1662 about 40 men were hired to finish the platforms around the tower, and by the end of December they had completed the 'platform in the half-moon towards the sea', and had mounted in it one whole cannon and three demi-cannons.[2] Early the next year H.M.S. *Greatguest* brought carriages and equipment for the guns in the fort,[3] and during 1664 there was continued expenditure on Fort Charles. About this time the earliest plan, of a tower in the centre of a square, seems to have been abandoned, and a more elaborate plan was adopted, with demi-bastions in the east and west, and a sort of redan to the north.[4] Between 1664 and 1666 work went ahead on this modified scheme, and by 1667 it was completed. The central tower was now used only as a magazine, and about 36 guns were mounted on the ramparts which surrounded it (figure 8).[5]

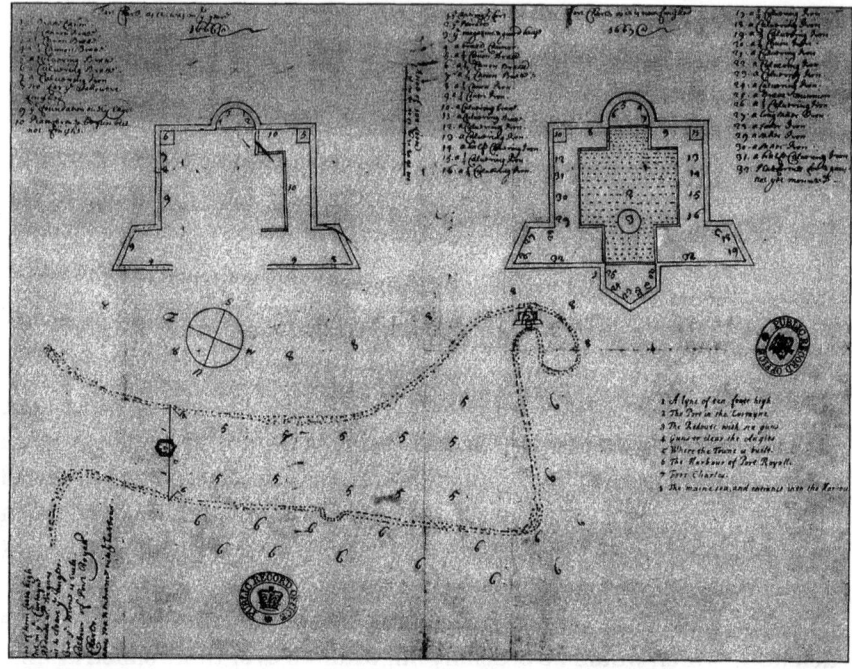

Figure 8 Map of the Point about 1666 (Public Record Office, London)

It had at first been intended to build on Gun Cay as well, for as a report of about 1662 says, '. . . on a small island a little to the eastward of the Point are eight pieces of ordnance and a fort design'd, but little done at itt as yet'.[6] However, this project seems to have been abandoned, probably because it was realized that Gun Cay is too exposed for any extensive structure to survive in storms.[7] At the other end of the Point there was a need to replace the palisades with something more substantial, and about 1665 a line of masonry was constructed, with gun-ports in it and a central tower holding six guns.[8] According to one account, this tower was at first called 'the Landward fort'.[9] The completion of this line meant that Port Royal was reasonably well-protected at its eastern and western extremities.

But the central area, and especially the harbour, remained very vulnerable, as the author of 'The present state of Jamaica' observed in August 1671: 'There needs two platforms and a fort at Bonham's Point to make the harbour secure.'[10] Nine months later the Council was thinking in larger terms: '[with Fort Charles], a platform at Bonham's Point, a slight one at the prison, and one at the breastwork to seaward, will secure the harbour against a considerable force'.[11] The proposal for a platform at Bonham's Point was the most urgent of these projects, and received 'a very liberal contribution from . . . planters'. So Colonel Theodore Cary, captain of Fort Charles, was authorized to oversee the work and to make all the contracts necessary for the supply of lime, stones and other materials.[12] In spite of opposition from their owners, 200 slaves[13] were allocated to Cary for this work, which began in April 1673.[14] By August of that year, the platforms were completed not only at Fort James, flanking the harbour, but also at 'Prison Point', which is perhaps to be identified with the southern end of the palisadoes line;[15] Sir Henry Morgan wrote to the king at that time, requesting guns for these new batteries.[16] We cannot tell what the platform at Prison Point looked like, but we know at least that one of the platforms at Fort James was a westward-facing obtuse angle, whose superstructure was built of brick.[17] It presumably looked something like this (figure 9):

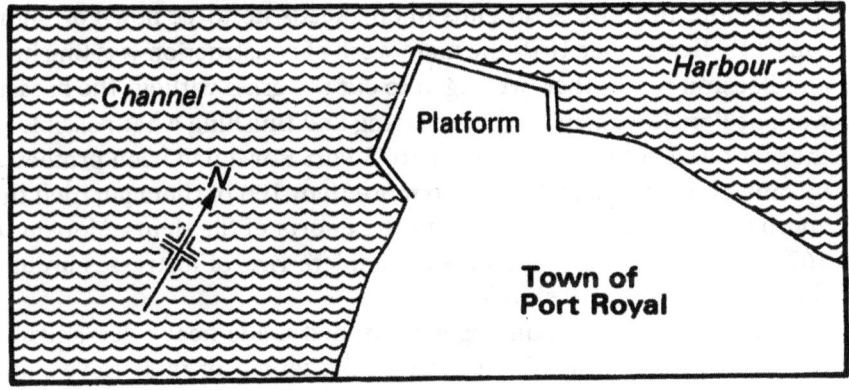

Figure 9 Position and shape of Fort James

Sir Henry Morgan was a great enthusiast for defensive works, and in April 1678, during one of his periods as lieutenant-governor, he called a council and, as he says, 'took with me some of the gentlemen to view the forts'.[18] No doubt he persuaded them that the existing defences were inadequate, for three weeks later we find him writing to Coventry that 'very extraordinary things will be done for the reputation and strength of Port Royal'.[19] This time the effort was concentrated on the eastern defences, and on the central area to the south of the town. New lines of stone were laid at the 'prison', which developed into Fort Rupert, mounting 22 guns and guarding the south-eastern approaches to the Point.[20] A whole new fort was constructed at the northern end of the palisadoes line, and called 'Fort Carlisle' in honour of the new governor, who arrived in July 1678.[21] In addition, Fort James was strengthened by the addition of a new stone platform.[22]

Not content with all this building, Morgan pressed on with a new battery between Forts Charles and Rupert. In this he was helped by the increasingly aggressive posture of the French, for as the island secretary, Rowland Powell, wrote to Coventry in July 1679, 'since the French alarmed this place[23] the inhabitants have laboured at the fortification. They have lay'd the freestone for the platformes which the King sent by His Excellency, and are now raising of a line with a batterie for 12 demi-cannon behind the old church, which will much strengthen the harbour.'[24] In fact this battery, which became known as Fort Morgan, or Morgan's Line, eventually held 16 guns,[25] which were manhandled to their place on the ramparts by sailors from H.M.S. *Hunter*. As her captain's log for 8 September 1679 records, '[I sent] 30 of our men ashore to rowle great guns upon skeeds up to ye new Fort Morgan.'[26] By September 1679 the main work of construction was finished, and Beeston writes that 'We began to cut the grass without the breastwork at Port Royal, and fell to repaving and finishing what possible of the work we could'.[27] Whereas in 1675 Port Royal had been protected by only about 60 guns,[28] by 1680 more than 100 of them guarded the approaches to the town, thanks to the efforts of Sir Henry Morgan in 1678 and 1679. There was now a complete ring of fortresses around the Point, as figure 10 shows.

This great spurt in building activity had made heavy demands on the purses of the inhabitants, and on the labour of their slaves, and had aroused a certain resentment which expressed itself in the 'Humble Address' which the Assembly offered Governor Carlisle in November 1679. There was more than a suspicion that governors or lieutenant-governors like Sir Henry Morgan declared, or extended, martial law so as to oblige the planters and others to give the services of every tenth slave, and this was felt to be a vexatious burden. All the same, the work was now finished, and more guns were steadily added to those already on the platforms, until by 1683 there were in the whole Port Royal complex 145 large cannon.[29] By then an intruder, approaching from windward, would have had to pass Forts Rupert, Morgan, and Charles before he even got into the entrance-channel. Rounding the point, he would come into range of Fort James, and then, if he attempted to attack the shipping at the wharves, might be harassed from Fort Carlisle. In the late 1680s one final link was added to this chain, when Walker's

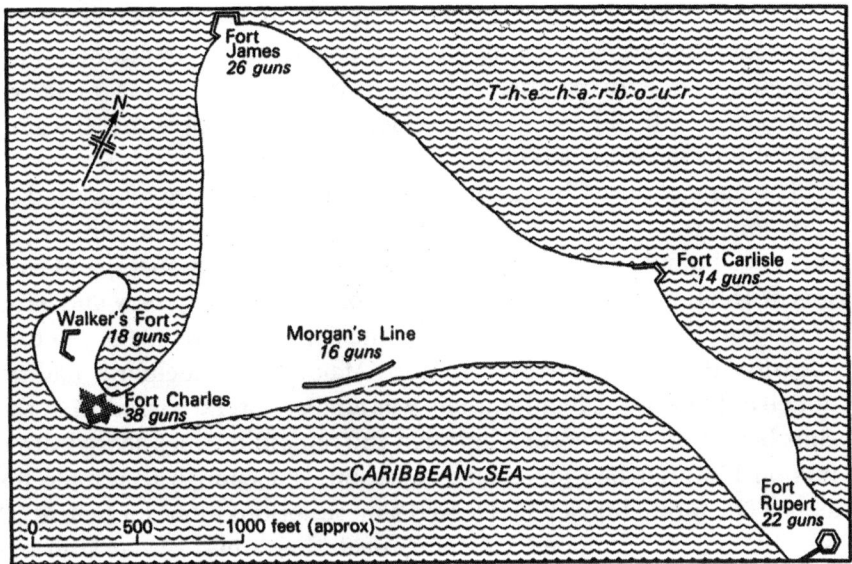

Figure 10 The fortifications of Port Royal about 1690

Fort was constructed just to the north of Fort Charles. This structure, which contained 18 guns,[30] was named after the commander of Fort Charles, and was intended to cover the area of harbour just west of Fort James. It was probably the work of a certain William Chitty, who in January 1689 received from the Assembly a medal for his 'good services and great care and industry about the new Forts at Port Royal'.[31] However, very little is known about Chitty, or indeed about the other engineers who worked at Port Royal between 1660 and 1692; it is not until after that time that a regular series of 'royal engineers' is appointed for the island.[32]

The fortifications were all under the command of the captain of Fort Charles, who in the early days was Colonel Theodore Cary. He had two matrosses, or assistant gunners, to help him, but these were the only permanent gunners at Port Royal; the guns were mostly served by volunteers from the town, with two 'files' on duty each night.[33] There was of course no local foundry capable of manufacturing cannon or shot; these, like the powder, were shipped out from England. Sometimes, too, guns and shot from sunken or captured ships were assigned to the forts.[34] Munitions of all kinds were stored in the round tower in Fort Charles, which had been converted into a magazine after the rebuilding of the fort in the mid-1660s. Carriages were sometimes sent from England, but could also be manufactured on the spot, no doubt using the excellent local hardwoods.[35] It was no easy matter to handle the great guns, some weighing as much as four tons, but seamen were accustomed to moving great weights, using a variety of ingenious arrangements with sheer-legs and tackle, and it is probable that the gunners often sought the aid of the sailors.

The guns of Fort Charles and of the other forts were often fired in ceremony, to greet a ship, for instance, or to spread an alarm. There seems to be only one example of their being fired in anger, and that was in 1684, when Captain Bannister, condemned for piracy and lying in the Port Royal gaol, seized a sloop and slipped out by night. On that occasion the commander of the fort, Major Peter Beckford, had no notice of Bannister's flight until he was almost out; he passed 14 of the guns before he was spotted, but then the remaining ones scored three hits on him; not bad for a dark night, but not enough to cripple his sloop. The pirate himself had feared a more serious blow, for he had 50 men in his hold, equipped with 'plugs of all sizes wherewith to stop any breach which could be made in him by the guns of the fort'.[36]

Fortifications, of course, can serve their strategic purpose even if they never have to fire a shot in anger, and it is arguable that no serious attempt was made on Port Royal precisely because hostile forces realized how strong the defences were. In 1694, for instance, during their major raid on Jamaica, the French sailed past Port Royal, ravaging the coast both to east and to west of Kingston harbour, but preferring not to measure their strength against the guns of Port Royal. All in all, in spite of the rather incoherent way in which they developed, these fortifications seem to have presented a formidable obstacle, and to have provided the emergent economic centre with good protection.

NOTES
[1] *C.S.P.* 1661-8, 379 of 20 October 1662 and N.L.J. MS. A1, 'The history and state of Jamaica under Lord Vaughan', fo. 54.
[2] *Interesting Tracts*, pp. 277-8.
[3] Ibid., p. 279.
[4] See figure 8, reproducing the plan mentioned in Modyford's letter of 3 September 1667, *C.S.P.* 1661-8, 1563 of 3 September 1667.
[5] N.L.J. MS. A1, fo. 54-5.
[6] B.M. Egerton 2395, fo. 163 (part of a 'state of Jamaica').
[7] In the ' Description and history of the islands by John Ogilby', part of *An Account of America* (1671) ed. W. W. Anderson (Kingston, 1851), p. 28, Gun Cay is called 'Little Island.' But this seems to have been a passing title.
[8] See figure 8.
[9] *An Account of America*, p. 28.
[10] *C.S.P.* 1669-74, 604 (i) of 20 August 1671.

11 Ibid., 827 of May 1672 and *J.H.A.*, i. 6.
12 Ibid., 933 of 26 September 1672.
13 Ibid., 1062 of 4 April 1673.
14 Ibid., 1055 of 21 March 1673.
15 N.L.J. MS. A1, fo. 55.
16 *C.S.P.* 1669-74, 1128 of August (?) 1673.
17 According to the diver Jeremiah Murphy, who found it more or less intact in 1859, and described it in a letter to the *Falmouth Post* of 7 October 1859 (see chapter 11).
18 Morgan to Secretary Coventry, Port Royal 10 April 1678, Coventry Papers, vol. 75, fo. 241.
19 Morgan to Coventry, 30 April 1678, Port Royal, Coventry Papers, 75, fo. 247.
20 *Interesting Tracts,* p. 293.
21 *C.S.P.* 1677-80, 770 of 31 July 1678 and *Acts of the Privy Council,* vol. I, 28 May 1679.
22 *Interesting Tracts,* p. 293.
23 That same month, July 1679: see *C.S.P.* 1677-80, 1107 of 30 August 1679 and also chapter 5.
24 Rowland Powell to Coventry, Port Royal 26 July 1679, Coventry Papers, vol. 75, fo. 322.
25 Carlisle to Coventry, 30 July 1679, Coventry Papers, vol. 75, fo. 324.
26 P.R.O. Adm.. 51/3870, 'A journal of a voyage . . .' under that date.
27 B.M. Add. MSS. 12430 (vol. ii), 'A journal kept by Colonel William Beeston . . .', fo. 38r.
28 According to the account found in *J.H.A.*, i, Statistical Papers, p. 41, and in Coventry Papers, vol. 74, fo. 159.
29 *J.H.A.,* i, Statistical Papers, p. 47.
30 *C.S.P.* 1689-92, 2034 of 28 January 1692.
31 Cundall, *Governors of Jamaica in the 17th century,* p. 122.
32 The careers of some of these officers are described in Buisseret, *The fortifications of Kingston 1655-1914* (Kingston, 1972).
33 See also below, chapter 8.
34 See, for instance, Carlisle's letter to Coventry of 15 September 1679 from Spanish Town (*C.S.P.* 1677-80, 1118 of 15 September 1679): '[I have recovered 20 great guns with 212 "greate shott"] . . . which come in good time for the fortifications at the Point'.
35 See, for instance, *J.H.A.*, i. 50 and *C.S.P.* 1681-5, 668 of 29 August 1682.
36 See Molesworth's letter to Blathwayt, 3 February 1685, in vol. 25 of the Blathwayt Papers.

CHAPTER FIVE

The Consolidation of English Power: The Navy 1668–1692

The years immediately following the conquest of 1655 saw a large English naval force concentrated at Jamaica, but these vessels were steadily sent back to England during the next few years, and no others came out to replace them. The result was that after about 1660 there were for a time no naval vessels in Jamaica, which had to rely on the dubious protection of privateers, and it was not until 1668 that the first regular guard-ship, H.M.S. *Oxford*, was assigned to the station. Thereafter the number of vessels sent to Jamaica tended to rise steadily with each decade, until by the early 1690s there was a squadron of half a dozen or so ships permanently stationed at Port Royal.

The fleet which had brought Penn and Venables consisted of about 30 ships, of which at least ten were fourth-rates, carrying 40 or more guns.[1] Most of these ships left in the year following the landing; in 1656 eight were left, in 1658 seven, and in 1659 six.[2] By 1660 only two were left, H.M.S. *Diamond* and H.M.S. *Hector*, and these had to be sent home by D'Oyley in that year for want of provisions.

For the next eight years there were no naval ships at Port Royal, which relied for its protection on the pirates and privateers whose activities are described in chapter 3. In October 1668 the fifth-rate frigate H.M.S. *Oxford* arrived, but was totally destroyed the following January. This accident is described by a certain Richard Browne, who was on board at the time:

> While the captains [who had assembled on the *Oxford* for a council of war] were at dinner on the quarter-deck, the *Oxford* blew up ... only six men and four boys being saved. The accident is supposed to have been caused by the negligence of the gunner. I was eating my dinner with the rest, when the main-mast blew out and fell upon captains Aylett, Bigford and others, and knocked them on the head; I saved myself by getting astride the mizzen-mast.[3]

About 250 officers and men were killed, but Henry Morgan miraculously survived. William Beeston explains his survival this way in his log of events: 'Admiral Morgan and those captains that sat on that side the table he did were saved, but those captains on the other side all killed.'[4] The sequence of vessels which followed the ill-fated *Oxford* is set out in figure 11; of the 20 ships, nine were fourth-rates, nine fifth-rates, and two 'sloops'. Many of them stayed in Jamaica for only one year, since tropical waters were, as we shall see, particularly hard on the hulls of wooden ships. In the late 1670s the number of ships increased markedly, and after that there were usually three on the station; this reflected the general increase in size of the Royal Navy, whose tonnage of ships roughly doubled between 1660 and 1690.[5]

All these ships came out as a result of directions from the Admiralty, of which the indefatigable Mr. Samuel Pepys was secretary between 1673 and 1688. Each captain received his 'instructions', usually signed by Pepys himself. A copy of the instructions for Captain Charles Talbot, of H.M.S. *Falcon*, still survives at the Pepysian Library in Cambridge.[6] Talbot is enjoined to scrupulously follow the instructions of the governor of Jamaica, and to be particularly assiduous in seizing 'shipps trading to Guiney', or 'interlopers' as they were called.[7] Captains were expected to report back to Mr. Pepys in the course of their tours of duty, sending accounts of their activity and also statistics about payments to their crews. Captain Josiah Tosier was one of the most conscientious of the commanders in this respect, perhaps because he had a certain literary turn of mind.[8] Usually these documents were sent home by some convenient merchantman; as Tosier recorded in his log for 28 October 1678:

> This day I gave master Charles Swann, commander of the *Carlisle* bound for London, four muster-books for ye Navie Board, with my letters to them and Mr Secretarie Pepies . . .[9]

Another very assiduous captain was Lawrence Wright of H.M.S. *Assistance*; he too constantly sent letters back to Pepys, during his cruise of 1687-9.[10]

It is not easy to discover what kind of men these captains were. They plainly had to be literate, but then the ability to read and write was fairly widespread in Stuart England. We cannot tell from what social background they came, any more than we can be sure what their constitutional loyalties were; as we shall see, at least one of them proved an admirable trimmer.

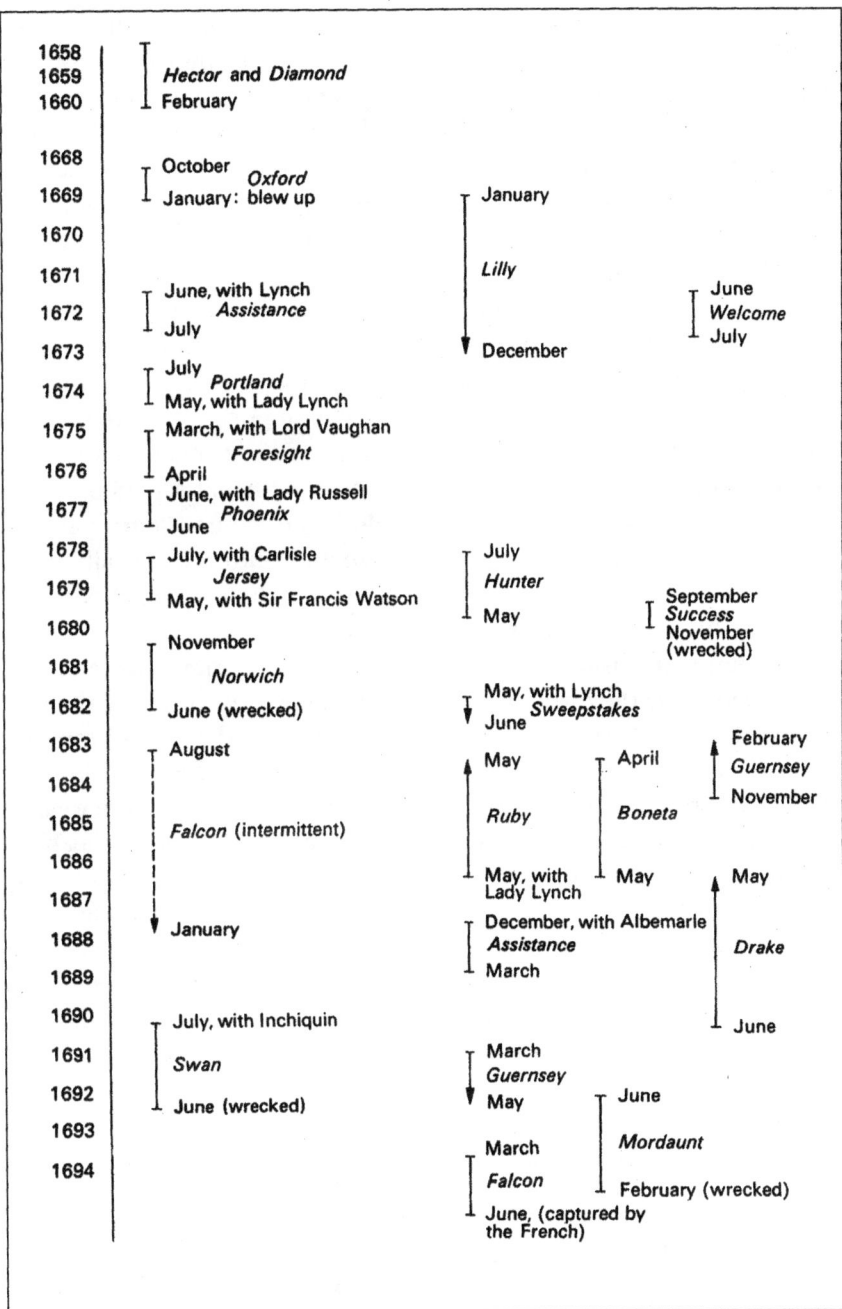

Figure 11 Sequence of naval vessels at Port Royal to 1692

The Navy 59

The captain was assisted by three or four navigating officers, and each vessel carried a ship's doctor, or 'surgeon' as he was called. The crew was made up of a motley gathering of men, many of them 'pressed' at the last moment on the quays and in the streets of towns like Deptford, Chatham, Sheerness, Woolwich, Portsmouth - and for that matter Port Royal. It was normally very hard to make up a full complement, even with the addition of these 'prestmen'. Conditions for the whole crew were bad, but at least they could usually be sure of having something to eat, which must have been more than many of them could expect ashore. When H.M.S. *Hunter* was fitting out at Deptford in February 1678, she loaded not only biscuit, peas, oatmeal, and flour, but also perishable goods like cheese, butter, beef, and pork.[11] There was rum to drink, and water in great casks; the ingredient most lacking from shipboard diet was fresh vegetables, and the virtual absence of Vitamin C led to a variety of diseases, including of course scurvy. It must have been very hard to preserve cheese and butter, especially in the tropics, and the logs are full of entries noting that 'rotten cheeze' and 'mouldie bread' had to be thrown overboard.

The ships themselves were very small by later standards, and often sailed poorly, as they were usually over-gunned. The largest of the ships at Jamaica at this time seems to have been the *Ruby*, of 540 tons; she carried about 150 men. The smallest was probably the *Boneta*, which was rated at 57 tons and carried only ten men and four guns. These weapons varied greatly both in size and in performance, but it would probably be safe to say that few were accurate at more than a quarter of a mile, though many could fire at random for more than four times that distance.

So these little ships would set out, 'rowling and labouring' as one log remarks, into the unfriendly seas of the Channel and Western approaches. Many of them made their last call at Portsmouth, which had been an important naval base since its establishment by Henry VIII, and there arranged their sailing-plans with their companions and with the merchant vessels which they sometimes escorted. When H.M.S. *Hunter* and *Jersey*, for instance, set sail in May 1678, Captain Tosier:

> received Captain Temple's order to stay for him at the Madera five days and if we misst him there to make the best of my waye for Barbados, there to stay a week for him, and then to Jamaica in case wee should be parted by foule weather or dark nights.[12]

It was hard enough to keep company with another vessel even if there was good will on both sides; sometimes too one captain would deliberately slip ahead, as happened in January 1675, when Sir Henry Morgan in the *Jamaica Merchant* was due to accompany the new governor, Lord Vaughan, in H.M.S. *Foresight*. Morgan 'wilfully lost' Vaughan somewhere in the English Channel, and was at Port Royal in time to welcome the governor, in spite of being wrecked off the Ile-à-Vache.[13]

The first part of the journey must have been extremely unpleasant, for these small, overladen ships could only wallow through the water, and must have pitched and rolled horribly in the normal rough weather. Many of them carried dignitaries, on their way to take up important posts in Jamaica, and the sufferings of these men, unaccustomed to the sea, are easy to imagine. Their purgatory would normally have lasted until the vicinity of the Madeiras, after which the waters were usually calmer. Most governors came out on naval vessels, and were often accompanied by their wives;[14] the latter were usually housed in temporary cabins. Sometimes the ladies were less than content with their treatment and accommodation, like Lady Russell, who came out on H.M.S. *Phoenix* (Captain Lawrence Wright) in June 1676 (figure 12). She complained to the Navy Board, and received a reply from Mr. Pepys, in which the secretary was at his most tactful. He was sorry, he wrote, that Lady Russell should 'miss in any degree the accomodation and content' which she expected from Captain Wright, 'not that either the perfection of courtship is to be looked for from a tarpauling,[15] or

Figure 12 The younger van de Velde, H.M.S. *Phoenix* (National Maritime Museum)

the fulness of accomodation from so small a ship as the *Phoenix*, pestered as she must be for so long a voyage'.[16] However, Pepys went on, he would let Captain Wright know that 'in this case both [courtship and accomodation] might have been bettered'.

To take advantage of the prevailing winds, the ships would pass far to the south of the great circle route, often calling in at the Madeiras. They normally made landfall in the West Indies somewhere near Barbados, after a passage which varied in length between eight and 12 weeks. From Barbados it was an easy run up to Jamaica, usually taking only two weeks. Sometimes the crews would be given gunnery practice on the way, but this is only noted in one or two logs.

The crew's first sight of Jamaica would be the splendid mountains at its eastern end. Then the coastline would slowly emerge, as they sailed along the southern edge of the island. The arrival of H.M.S. *Falcon* in August 1683 was fairly typical, as her log records:[17] 'Being Sunday att 9 we had the sea breeze fresh and att 10 we was abrest of Yallowes [Yallahs] and fired a gun for a pilott . . .' In fact they met a sloop in Cow Bay and 'took the master out to pilott us in'. He would have taken them along the Palisadoes, past Forts Rupert and Morgan, and then turned sharply north by Fort Charles, no doubt returning its thunderous salute. Then, 'att 4 we came to an anchor att Jamaica in 14 fathoms water'.

The naval vessels seem to have anchored at various points to the northwest of Fort James, anywhere from a quarter to one-and-a-half miles from the shore; this was the area in which naval moorings would eventually be provided, in the eighteenth century. It was conveniently sheltered from the main force of the sea, but had the disadvantage that a south-easterly gale could easily drive a ship which dragged its anchor onto the lee shore, under what became known as Port Henderson Hill.[18]

The captain's first act after entering harbour and dropping anchor was to call on the naval officer (or 'clerk of the Navy Office', as he was sometimes called) at Port Royal. This post was held from at least 1675 and perhaps earlier by a certain Reginald Wilson, and his responsibilities were so important to the ships at Port Royal that it is worth examining them fully.[19] To his naval office came all 'masters, merchants and others', to give 'exact accompts of their voyages, cocketts,[20] entries, dispatches, loadings, passengers etc., so that Wilson could ensure that the Navigation Acts had not been contravened.[21] It was his responsibility to collect together all these statistics, and then to forward them to the Lords of the Treasury and Commissioners of H.M. Customs in London; some of these returns signed by him are still to be found in the Public Record Office.[22] Nor was his responsibility for the enforcement of the Navigation Acts merely a passive one, as the log of H.M.S. *Hunter* for 3 November 1678 makes clear:

> This day master Reginald Wilson, Naval Officer, brought in a small vessel upon suspition. She was at anchor within the keies, and belongs to London; came from Nantes loaden with wine and brandie . . .[23]

As well as being head of the customs and immigration organization, he was also a kind of harbour-master, charged as his commission put it:

> to act as overseer of the harbour of Port Royall, and to take care that it be not endammag'd, and that none take in or throw out ballast, nor lay up ships, but where you appoint, that the port may be preserv'd, and that all that commit such offences be prosecuted and punished according to lawe and custom . . .[24]

His responsibilities towards naval vessels were still more extensive. He it was who provided them with pilots when they went cruising in the West Indies, and who paid these pilots on their return to Port Royal.[25] He ordered supplies for ships when they needed them,[26] at least until 1688, when a separate storehouse-keeper was appointed.[27] He arranged for ships to be surveyed, and in consultation with the governor made the appropriate recommendation following the survey.[28] He even, on one occasion, seems to have arranged for the construction of an 84-foot galley, with which pirates could be chased into shoal water, where the larger frigates could not follow them.[29] Finally, he sometimes made himself responsible for the reception of pirates,[30] no doubt handing them over for incarceration to the Port Royal marshal.

The naval officer was appointed by the governor, who was also responsible for naval affairs on the station. In fact, the Act of 1663 named governors as 'naval officers' for their respective territories, with the power of appointing deputies.[31] Most of our sea-captains seem to have obeyed the governors' instructions cheerfully enough, and Governor Lynch was alone in affirming that 'not one of them, out of port, heeds my instructions any more than they would a chapter in the Alcoran'.[32] If a captain were very unsatisfactory the governor could dismiss him; Lynch was reduced to this in the case of Captain John Wilgress of H.M.S. *Assistance*, who in 1671 was cashiered for his 'wicked, drunken behaviour' and replaced by Major William Beeston.[33] The latter turned out to be a skilful commander and eventually became a successful governor of the island.

The period during which the ships lay at anchor in Port Royal Harbour was one of rest and preparation for further duty. First of all, the stores loaded in England had to be ferried ashore. Many naval vessels brought arms, ammunition and powder, and these had to be taken to the storehouses on Port Royal, where they were kept for the needs of both ships and forts. The ships' own supplies were often low after the voyage, and they normally needed both to water and to lay in more food. Water for naval vessels came from the Rock, a few hundred yards to the west of what is now Rockfort.[34] There a spring came out from the Long Mountain, and from it casks were filled and then floated out to the ship's longboat. This was an arduous way of watering, but no more efficient one was devised until Admiral Vernon's work of the 1740s.

Food for naval vessels was sometimes, as we have noted, supplied by Reginald Wilson, out of the Port Royal storehouse. Often, though, merchant-ships came from England with supplies specially for the men-of-war. In November 1686, for instance, the log of H.M.S. *Falcon* records that: 'Last night arrived a pinke from London, with 6 months' provisions for us and the *Drake*.'[35] Seven years earlier it had been aboard the *Loyal*, commanded by the well-known captain, Joseph Knapman, that provisions had come for H.M.S. *Hunter*.[36]

Ships used up a considerable quantity of powder, not only in engagements, but also in exercises and in frequent salutes; much was also spoiled through getting damp. Deficiencies, not only of powder but also of shot and of match, could be made good from the magazine in Fort Charles, and captains commonly stocked up there before beginning tours of duty.[37] There was as yet no naval dockyard at Port Royal, but a little sloop like H.M.S. *Boneta* could be fairly completely refitted there,[38] no doubt using canvas and tackle provided by the naval officer.

All the ships on the station had periodically to be careened, and for this operation, in the absence of a naval dockyard, it was common to hire the merchants' careening-place.[39] The vessels were hauled down by the masts, first one side and then the other, until their hulls were clear of the water. Then the ravages of the tropical crustaceans and insects had to be repaired as best they could be; often a ship was found on careening to be so badly damaged as to need either major rebuilding (in England) or even condemnation. During the 1670s the Admiralty was experimenting with milled lead sheathing as a means of protecting wooden hulls,[40] and if the hull were much damaged then this sheathing had to be taken off. In the case of H.M.S *Hunter's* careen in February 1680, this involved the stripping of more than 2,400 pounds of lead;[41] it was three months before she could again put to sea. Two months was a more normal time for a fifth-rate,[42] and a little vessel like the *Boneta* could complete her careen in three weeks.

When a ship was found to be severely damaged, a board of survey was called - often by Reginald Wilson - and a number of experts, both from the navy and from the merchant fleet, gave their opinion. One of these reports survives among the Coventry Papers at Longleat House; it concerns H.M.S. *Phoenix*, and runs as follows:

> We, the commissioned, warrant and other officers of H.M.S *Phoenix* [have diligently but in vain searched for the leak she sprang in April 1677] . . . and having considered that our ship being sheathed in lead, this leak cannot be found outboard but by stripping it off, which will require many more carpenters than can be procured in this place, we therefore do unanimously declare that the safety and preservation of the king's ship depends upon her speedy being ordered home for England . . .[43]

This report is not typical, in that the members of the board of survey seem all to have come from the ship concerned; there is also the suspicion that their verdict may not have been uninfluenced by the desire to return to England. More typical was the board which surveyed H.M.S. *Norwich* in June 1682, after her misadventure on the East Middle Ground (see below for an account of this.) The board in this case was drawn both from the ships' carpenters and from the captains of ships - both merchant and naval - in the harbour, and headed by Captain John Temple of H.M.S. *Sweepstakes*.[44] Similar boards of survey were called when there was some question of condemning food. In April of 1679, for instance, certain merchant-captains were called to H.M.S. *Hunter* to give their opinions on her stores of food; their verdict is not recorded.[45]

Such collaboration was by no means one-sided, for the sailors helped the merchantmen and the shore authorities in many ways. In March of 1680, for instance, when H.M.S. *Hunter* was in harbour:

> At six this morning the *Golden Fleece* of 30 guns, Captain Bannister commander, overset at an anchor in the harbour, noe current nor wind, but her men going over her side to scrape her made a sallie that the guns and other weight aloft gave way at once. The captain saved himself out of the mizzen shrouds; the purser, gunner and doctor, with five others and a Negroe were drowned . . .[46]

The Navy

Hunter's men were quickly on the scene to help, and in the following days spent much time in helping what remained of the *Golden Fleece's* crew in their attempts to 'weigh' or refloat their ship. As we shall see, the naval frigates later had a less amicable relationship with Bannister.

The sailors were of course particularly skilful at handling heavy objects and at refloating sunken ones. So it was that after the 1692 earthquake the crew of H.M.S. *Mordaunt* (figure 13) were called in to 'weigh six of the guns that was sunke in Walker's Forth [Fort]';[47] 12 years earlier, it had been men from H.M.S. *Hunter* who had been called upon to 'rowl great guns upon skeeds up to the new Fort Morgan'.[48] Sailors were skilled not only at this kind of heavy moving, but also at carrying out surveys. When in September 1679 the earl of Carlisle needed an accurate account of 'all the depths of water of all the wharfes in Port Royall', it was the master of H.M.S. *Hunter* who provided this.[49] His report is reproduced in *Hunter's* logs and is a rare if rather unreliable source for our knowledge of the Port Royal waterfront at this time.[50]

Of course, relations between the sailors and the inhabitants of Port Royal were not always friendly. There seems to have been surprisingly little protest over the pressing of vessels for naval service, as the *Richard and Sarah* and a sloop were pressed in 1692.[51] It was even possible for Captain Tosier in 1680 to press a doctor, using a letter from the governor. This letter ran as follows:

> Whereas the chirugien of H.M.S. *Hunter* is deceased, and there is not a mate aboard sufficient to supply his place, these are to order you to take aboard the chirugien of Wm Chambers, master of the pinke *Saint Christopher*, he being sufficiently provided for his voyage home. Given under my hand this 10 of June 1680 to Capt. Josiah Tosier, commander of H.M.S. *Hunter*.

What made more trouble was the pressing of seamen on the wharves and in the streets of Port Royal. There were frequent complaints about this, since it hampered the commercial development of the town. However, these complaints were largely disregarded, as they were in England; the king's ships had to have men.

Back on board, life was at any rate less strenuous than at sea. Sometimes a captain would invite some local dignitaries on board for dinner,[52] though this must have been a fairly unnerving experience for some of the guests, with the crude quarters and food available, and with the constant loud noises. The crew's health was a great problem, for if they were less exposed than some landsmen to yellow fever, they were highly vulnerable to the 'griping of guts', a very descriptive term applied to various kinds of dysentery. While they were in harbour there was also the constant temptation to desert, either to seek their fortune in Jamaica, or perhaps to join a pirate crew sailing from Port Royal. The punishment for desertion was severe, to judge by that inflicted on a certain John Exill of H.M.S. *Falcon*, who on November 1686 'was duck't at the yard-arm and whipt from ship to ship, for running away and enticeing others with him'.[53] Almost as severe was the punishment for pilots unlucky or careless enough to damage the vessels which they were guiding. In January 1680, for instance, 'Captain Daniel was tried by a council of war aboard the *Hunter* (where Lieutenant-Colonel Beeston was president) for losing the *Success*, where he was ordered to receive seven lashes aboard every commissioned ship, thrice, one day after another.'[54]

Hunter does not seem to have been a lucky ship for pilots, for only the previous year Paul Abney, pilot, had been imprisoned for failing to 'find the wreck to fish up the plate'.[55] Pirates were also judged by the councils of war, often held on board naval vessels in the harbour. Sometimes too the prisoners were held aboard, as in the case of Bannister's crew, held on H.M.S. *Ruby* during his trial in 1685;[56] the prison on land at Port Royal was not remarkable for its efficiency in guarding suspected pirates. The normal composition of courts trying pirates is described in the log of H.M.S. *Assistance* for 20 March 1672:

> The governor with his officers and commanders of the ships which were in the harbour came aboard and held a council of war, in which they condemned Captain Francis Weatherbourn and Captain Du Mangles to be shot to death for their pyracys in taking Spaniards without commission.[57]

The Navy 67

Councils of war were called not only for specific problems like these, but also to decide on questions of strategy; they often met on ships when it was inconvenient or dangerous to assemble on shore, as in 1692, when after the earthquake the president and council came aboard H.M.S. *Mordaunt*[58] in order to concert the plans for resisting the French and for re-establishing a commercial centre.

The presence of naval vessels at Port Royal was tactically important, since with their broadsides they could be anchored to help the forts in time of need. However, their strategic value lay in the operations which they could carry out not only in Jamaican waters, but throughout the whole Caribbean area. Relations with the foreign powers - which meant with Spain and France - were in effect in the hands of naval captains, who were kept busy with visits to all the great centres of Spanish power in the Caribbean. They often visited the Cuban ports of Havana, Trinidad,[59] and Santiago, and sometimes put in at Porto Bello. But their most common port of call was Cartagena, the great fortress-port in what is now Colombia.[60]

Captain Tosier, whom we have already mentioned as one of the most assiduous of the commanders in his correspondence with Mr. Pepys,[61] went so far as to publish an account of his mission to Havana in 1679.[62] He sailed from Port Royal on 25 January, as he writes, 'as well in quality of Embassador, as that of my command'. By 13 February he was off the 'Moor's Castle' [the Moro] at Havana, and sent his longboat ashore with a request to the governor to release those Englishmen 'kept worse slaves than those of Algiers'. The governor was not at first willing to do this, but Tosier persisted, and described the happy outcome thus:

> the Governour caused the prisoners to be called over in a back Court near his house, and examined some of them, one after another; who before he had done said, though I have no order to deliver them to you, and that I may be blamed, yet take them all with you, and if there be any more, let them come forth immediately and they shall be discharged, at which Declaration, they all being 46 in number, gave such Cheer-ho, that they made the house ring, saying, God bless the *Blessing of England*, which they called our ship. Immediately I hoisted out the longboat, and had them all on board in less than three hours; whereupon I set sail the next day for the bay of Mestances [Matanzas] to water, and to Port-Royal, where I arrived the 20th day of March following, to the great satisfaction of all men there.

As well as requesting the return of prisoners, which was not normally so easy as in this case, the captains carried announcements of peace and of war; they were in fact diplomatic agents as well as seamen.

When war did come, the role of the naval vessels was ill defined. There was as yet no question of a blockade of hostile ports, and in any case a couple of frigates could not do much in this respect. Nor could they undertake any serious punitive expedition; when Reginald Wilson wrote in April 1691 that

> Their majesties' ships *Guernsey* and *Swann*, with the *Quaker*, ketch, and a merchant shipp of 30 gunns, hier'd and well manned ... are gone to Hispaniola to destroy by sea and land what they cann,[63]

he was showing an optimism which the events did not bear out. In fact, the captain's most useful function was that of shadowing potentially hostile fleets, as H.M.S. *Hunter* did in July 1679, when the French fleet cruised along the southern coast of Jamaica.

The naval vessels were, however, quite well able to take on most of the pirates, interlopers and other unauthorized ships. Sometimes the latter carried more men than the royal frigates, but the pirate crews could rarely sail their vessels or serve their guns well enough to put up a good fight on the high seas, though of course they could hold their own if they could reach shoal water. The best way to catch pirates was to combine a frigate with one or two smaller vessels, like the *barcoluengo* or galley constructed by Wilson in 1683 (see above); as we shall see, the pirate Bannister was taken by a combination of this kind.

Many pirates were encountered by the naval frigates between 1671 and 1692; some, like Captain Sawkins, escaped them,[64] though many others, like Captains Cornelius Essex[65] and Francis Weatherbourn[66] were captured and brought to trial. It would be tedious to examine the adventures and misadventures of all these rogues, but the story of one pirate, a certain Captain Joseph Bannister, whom we have already met above, is worth recounting at length because of its savour. We first hear of Bannister in a letter of 20 June 1684 from Sir Thomas Lynch to the lord president of the Council. 'One Banister', he writes:

> ran away [from Port Royal, about June 1st] with a ship, the *Golden Fleece*, of thirty or forty guns, picked up over a hundred men from sloops and from leeward, and has got a French commission.[67]

However, this first privateering venture was not very successful. Three naval ships, H.M.S. *Ruby*, *Boneta*, and a *barcoluengo*, were cruising off

Jamaica for pirates and interlopers, and on 27 July, while he was stocking up with turtle in the Cayman Islands, Bannister and his vessel fell into their hands.[68] Sir Thomas Lynch wrote exultantly to Sir Charles Lyttelton that:

> last night the *Ruby* brought in Bannister. He took him at Caymanos; he has about 115 men on board, most the veriest rogues in these Indies. I have ordered the ship and men to be delivered into the Admirality and commanded the judge immediately to proceed against them, because we do not know how to secure or keep such a number. We conclude they'll be found guilty of pyracy . . .[69]

However, it was one thing to capture pirates, and quite another to get them convicted at Port Royal. It turned out that Bannister had no commission from the French, for the governor of Hispaniola had refused him one.[70] He had all the same taken two Spaniards, who were found on the ship when *Ruby* captured it. But the Spaniards were induced to give Bannister a formal discharge, and the upshot was that 'the grand jury threw out the bill' of piracy.

Sir Thomas Lynch was already ill, and this vexatious experience is said to have 'much increased his disease', of which he died on 24 August. Sir Hender Molesworth, who as lieutenant-governor directed affairs after Lynch's death, did his best to persuade the jury to convict. But he found that the Spaniards would 'swear backward and forward'; the jury remained obstinate, and in the end Bannister was bound over in good security to appear at the next court for trial of pirates.[71] That was September 1684; Bannister used the following weeks to make his preparations, and then late in January:

> in a dark night a desperate resolute manner [he] past the fort, having provided himself of plugs of all sizes wherewith to stop any breach which could be made in him by the guns of the fort, for which he had (as is sayd) about 50 men in the hold that stood ready. But what by the carelessness of the centrys and the darkness of the night, being favoured also with a freshe land brieze, he was got abrest of the fort before Major Beckford that commands it had any notice given to him . . . Beckford did all that he could, but only placed three shot in him. He at once sent me word of the occurrence, which was a great surprize to me, for I thought Bannister's want of credit would prevent him from ever getting the ship to sea again . . . yet now he has obtained credit from some persons underhand, and has his ship well fitted in every respect. It was

done so artfully that no one suspected it, or I should have found some pretext for securing him.[72]

Molesworth's dismay was understandable; he sent H.M.S. *Boneta* after the *Golden Fleece*, but Captain Stanley, ' finding himself unable to do more against a ship of her size and strength', contented himself with giving Bannister a note saying that he would be treated as a pirate unless he returned.[73] To this Bannister replied that he had 'done no pyratical act as yet and intended to do none, but his design was for the bay of Honduras for logwood'.[74] He was next seen the following April, off the Ile-a-Vâche in company with the notorious French privateers Grammont, Laurens, Yankey, and Jacobs. Captain Mitchell, the commander of H.M.S. *Ruby*, asked Grammont for Bannister to be arrested for serving under a foreign commission, but Grammont and the rest insisted that Bannister had not entered the king of France's service, and as the vessels they commanded were 'all great ships', Captain Mitchell thought it best 'not to insist further'.[75] In fact, Bannister does

Figure 14 The younger van de Velde, H.M.S. *Drake* (National Maritime Museum)

not seem to have joined the French, for six months later, in November 1685, he was seen cruising alone to leeward of Jamaica.[76]

H.M.S. *Ruby* was being careened at the time, but her commander, Captain Mitchell, volunteered to hire two sloops, man them with *Ruby's* men, and go out after the pirate. This he did, but for six months saw no sign of Bannister. Meanwhile the pirate was capturing ships here and there, and May 1686 marked the beginning of the events leading to his downfall, when one of his victims reported to Lieutenant-Governor Molesworth that the *Golden Fleece* was careening off the eastern coast of Hispaniola, near the Gulf of Samana.[77] Captain Mitchell had returned to England by this time, but the news was passed on to Captain Charles Spragg, of H.M.S. *Drake* (figure 14), which had replaced *Ruby* as guardship. They at once set out in pursuit of Bannister, and duly caught him 'going to careen in Samana'.[78] However, it was one thing to find Bannister and another to lay hands on him. He had fortified his careening-place, and a regular battle now took place, described in these words by a dispatch preserved among the State Papers, Domestic Series:

> on June 24th the *Falcon* and *Drake* frigates found the chief buccaneer Bannister with two ships in a deep bay fit to go on the careen at Jamana [sic] on the north side of Hispaniola, having got his guns on shore and mounted them in two batteries. The frigates stood in, though they were warmly entertained for two hours from the batteries and with small shot from the ships, and, bringing all their guns to bear, sunk and beat almost to pieces the buccaneers' ships, but not having enough water to carry them in, the *Drake* having but eleven foot, they could not fire them. The *Drake* had thirteen killed and wounded and the *Falcon* ten . . .[79]

When the two naval captains got back to Port Royal, they were 'much censured'[80] for not destroying the *Golden Fleece*. But the critics seem to have underestimated the difficulty of attacking a beached vessel under heavy fire both from fixed batteries and from small-arms; Spragg and Talbot were obliged to break off the engagement because neither had any ammunition left.[81] After a quick refit, they sailed again in July, to 'seek out and destroy the pirate Bannister'.[82] When they reached the Gulf of Samana, they found that Bannister had been obliged to burn the *Golden Fleece*, and had sailed away in a smaller vessel.[83] They do not seem to have found any further trace of him on this cruise, but early in 1687 Captain Spragg had better luck. We do not know how or where he found Bannister, but he certainly captured him and several other pirates, and sailed with them for Port Royal. What happened after this is described in the log of H.M.S. *Falcon*, at anchor in Port Royal Harbour at the time:

> [28 January 1687] . . . this day the *Drake* arrived, with Bannister he and 3 of his partners hanged at the yards arms, and severall other prisoners . . . [84]

Molesworth was delighted; as he wrote to William Blathwayt on 9 February 1687, this was:

> a spectacle of great satisfaction to all good people and of terror to the favourers of pirates, the manner of his punishment being that which will most discourage others, which was the reason why I empowered Captain Spragge to inflict it. Bannister seemed to have no small confidence in his friends; I find from letters that he wrote some of them that he intended to plead that he had been forced into all that he had done by the French. How far this would have prevailed with a Port Royal jury I know not, but I am glad that the case did not come before one . . . [85]

So ended Captain Bannister, his confidence in the corruption of justice at Port Royal betrayed by the more direct methods of Molesworth and Captain Spragg. As well as chasing pirates, the frigates' duty was to watch for 'interlopers', or ships which brought slaves from Africa infringing the monopoly of the Royal African Company. Sir Henry Morgan, in a letter of 16 March 1681 to the Lords of Trade and Plantations, explains how these vessels operated:

> The interloping ships trading for Negroes contrary to the charter of the Royal African Company have been too successful in this island, four of them having in some 14 days (his Majesty's frigate being at sea) landed their Negroes both to windward and leeward of Port Royal. The factors here had not the least warning, whereby to make a timely seizure, before they landed them and dispersed them marked in several plantations . . . [86]

They were of course easier to intercept than pirates, both because they were more lightly armed and because they had to lie for some time off the Jamaican coast in order to unload their human cargo. H.M.S. *Boneta's* log describes the capture of an interloper in these words:

> At 7 this morning, having Port Morant harbour open and seeing a shipp at anchor, I run in and anchor'd close by her, and upon examining her

> I found her to bee an interloper, hee having landed all his Negroes, and for not giving the governor an account I put some men aboard him and ordered him to follow me to Port Royall . . .[87]

Pirates and interlopers were both outside the law; privateers were in effect licensed pirates, operating with letters of marque from some sovereign or other. Sometimes privateers might fit out quite large ships, big enough even to match the naval frigates. In 1681, for instance, Sir Thomas Lynch wrote to Lord Finch that:

> the pryvateers of Jamaica being grown numerous and desperate now prey on us as well as the Spanyard. They killed a master of the last ships, and had plundered and carried away his ship if captain Knapman had not rescued him. Two or three of them lie now before Cartagena and have the insolence to threaten H.M.S. *Norwich* . . .[88]

Often, though, quite small vessels received letters of marque, and the master's log of H.M.S. *Guernsey* describes the capture of one of these in 1691:

> this day we stood to the southward, with the *Swan* frigatt and 2 sloops with us. We se [sic] a ship at 9 of the clock this morning; we gave chase . . . at 9 of the clock this evening the sloops came up with her, and it proved to be a French privateer with 8 guns and 100 men. She fired never a gun, but struck to us. So we lay by until 2 of the clock of this morning; then we made saile, and stood in for Port Morant.[89]

When they were not running diplomatic errands, or cruising for pirates, interlopers, or privateers, the naval captains were often to be found trying to salvage wrecks. Although it is rarely mentioned by naval historians, this activity took up a good deal of the naval vessels' time, and at least one governor, the duke of Albemarle, looked for great things from the divers. Albemarle's hopes of recovering great quantities of treasure from 'the wreck', a Spanish galleon lost off Hispaniola, were in fact disappointed,[90] but in the more routine work the naval divers were often successful. When, for instance, H.M.S. *Success* was lost off the Cuban cays in 1679,[91] H.M.S. *Hunter* was sent to recover what she could from the wreck. Her crew succeeded in 'weighing' all the sunken frigate's guns, and but for bad weather might have refloated the whole wreck. That same year, too, H.M.S. *Jersey* 'brought into Port Royall twenty great guns and 212 great shott, weighed from the wreck on the Isle of As [Ile-à-Vache]'.[92] Of course, there were severe technical limitations for divers working without masks, or, as far as we know, other equipment. Forty or 50 feet seems to have been the maximum depth at which sustained work could be undertaken. [93] And it was much easier to lift small items, however heavy, than to raise a whole ship, for which flotation-devices would have been necessary.

Often, though, the vessels had run aground in relatively shallow water, by striking hidden reefs. H.M.S. *Success* (1679), *Norwich* (1682), and *Mordaunt* (1694), the three ships lost on the high seas (H.M.S. *Oxford* and *Swan* being destroyed in harbour), all sank after running aground in this way. The loss of H.M.S. *Norwich* is the best documented of the three,[94] and it makes a piquant tale. H.M.S. *Norwich*, commanded by Captain Peter Heywood, left Port Royal on 25 May 1682, bound for Cartagena on the usual diplomatic mission. She duly delivered her packets and recovered some prisoners, setting sail again for Jamaica on 13 June. Four days later, 'at 9 o'clock in the morning we saw one key to windward and one breaker to leeward'. They had made landfall in Jamaica some forty miles west of Port Royal, and consequently had to stand off and then beat up against the prevailing easterly wind. By the morning of 19 June, Norwich had reached the neighbourhood of the Port Royal cays, and was ready to enter the harbour. The wind was still blowing from the east, and the current running strongly from the same direction. Leaving the South-East Cay to port, Heywood pressed on into what he thought was the channel (see figure 15). What happened next is best described in the words of the journal of Phillip Lawson, his first lieutenant:

> we stood into the shore againe, making severall boards to weather the windermost key. About 4 o'clock in the afternoon, having weather'd the easternmost key (the wind being fresh at ESE) we stood over for the channel, but the wind shortening upon us and the current setting strong to leeward wee struck upon a ledge of rocks which lies about half a mile from the key [what is known as the east Middle Ground; see figure 15]. We kept all sails full in hopes to force her over, but finding it would not doe we furl'd sailes . . .[95]

Meanwhile Francis Wivell, waiting at Port Royal to join the crew of *Norwich*, noted that:

> about five in the afternoon [she] struck upon the rife to windward of the easternmost key. She fired guns for sloops and boates to come off. Captain Temple lent me his boate with severall men, so I went off, and by reason of the brise blowing late I could not gitt aboard until 8 when

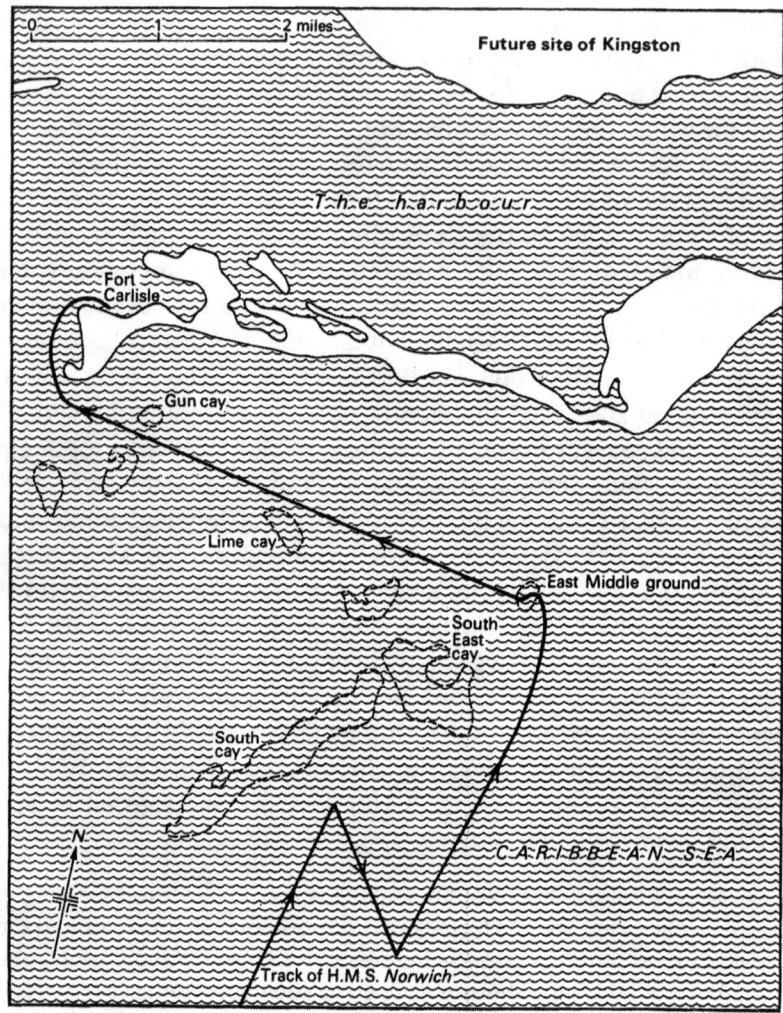

Figure 15 The loss of H.M.S. *Norwich* in 1682

I cam aboard. I found the men heaving upon the best bower which they had laid out astern. . . .

However, heaving upon the bower-cable was no more successful than had been the attempt to 'force her over', and later that evening Heywood began lightening ship, unloading certain merchants' stores which, it was later alleged, had overburdened the *Norwich*. Still she would not budge, but sprang a leak, and about 2 in the morning made about six feet of water in the hold. This meant plenty of work for the crew; as Lawson observes, 'wee went to, pumping and bayling'. Twenty guns were thrown overboard, and during the following day more stores taken off.

All these desperate measures finally took effect, when at about 4 o'clock in the afternoon of the 20th, after a whole day on the reef:

> the sea breeze pretty fresh wee sett our sailes and heaving . . . we hove her off by the helpe of the breeze and gott her into the harbour, and afftter makeing her securely fast to the wharfe fell to pumping and bayling, continuing soe all night, being supplied with fresh men from the *Sweepstakes*.

From the wharf, on the following morning, the crew warped *Norwich* up as far as Carlisle Fort, and there had to beach her. *Norwich's* men were now exhausted with the constant bailing, and so, as Francis Wivell records, on Thursday 22 June:

> the captain sent me up to Spanish Town with an express to the governor, to desire his order to beat a drum upon the Point for gentlemen to send their slaves aboard the *Norwich*, when we had cler'd the shipp of all her stores, to free her. At 12 at night I return'd with an order to Captain Wilson for to beat the drums when Captain Heywood desired it, which order I gave Captain Wilson.

On Saturday 24 June, the weather was fair and:

> This morning at 4 the drums beate in Port Royal for slaves to come aboard and free our ship. At 6 came aboard about 60 of the *Sweepstakes'* men and some men from the merchantmen and about 30 slaves from the shore. [Three gangs were formed and the ship's ballast was taken out.] At 1 the captain sent me to Captain Temple and some commanders of merchantmen, to desire them to come aboard with their carpenters . . . they all gave theire opinions that they only found a greate leake just abaft the mainmast on the starboard side, and that she might with good help be made fitt to goo for England . . .

With the ballast out, the carpenters were then able to try to patch up the leak. But this proved disastrous, for on Sunday 25 June, when they were working down by the bottom of the mainmast:

> of a suding the water flew up soo violent that a man could not come to put anything to stop it. Then the carpenters gave their opinion that the ship was bilg'd . . .

A survey was needed, and was made on Monday 20 June by Captain Temple of *Sweepstakes,* by other captains of ships in the harbour, and by their carpenters. The latter reported that 'her keel is wronged and her garboard strake abaft the mast staved in'. The captains added that:

> We the commanders . . . doe concur with them therein and doe further add that we doe verily believe that the said frigatte is wholly unfit to be repair'd and made capable of His Majestie's service.

The *Norwich* was plainly a total loss, and her stores were quickly transferred, some going to *Sweepstakes* and others to 'captain Clark's storehouse' (probably the naval store). There remained the business of assigning responsibility for the loss of the ship. On Wednesday 28 June:

> Captain Temple received a commission from the governor to call a court-martiall aboard the *Sweepstakes* to try Captain Heywood and his master about the loss of H.M.S. *Norwich*, in order to which Captain Temple hoisted a flag at his main topmast head . . .

Some of the members of the court were merchant-captains, and on 30 June at 10 o'clock in the morning 'Captain Temple spread his flagg in the mizzen shrouds and fired a gun for the captains to come aboard'. The upshot of the court-martial, which seems to have lasted for three or four days, was that 'Captain Heywood and his master [were] both cler'd about the loss of the *Norwich*', even though they had plainly made a bad error of judgement, and even though the ship was carrying a large quantity of merchants' goods, contrary to standing orders. The following day the Phillip Lawson made the final entry in his diary: 'Wee were all discharg'd from aboard His Majesty's ship *Norwich* in Jamaica.'

This verdict was not altogether to the taste of the Privy Council, and we may well imagine Mr. Pepys's fury when he read the account of a court-martial in which the partiality of the members, and the unwillingness to condemn a fellow-captain, were so manifest. Governor Lynch was ordered to send Heywood back to England in custody.[96] Whether he did so or not is not evident. But Lynch, in his usual forthright way, at any rate made his own position clear, in a letter of 12 September 1683 to the Lords of Trade and Plantations:

> I know not what the King's Evidence may prove in London, but I will perish if they prove here that Heywood or the goods he had on board

caused the loss of the *Norwich*. If Heywood was not censured and imprisoned for breach of instructions, that was due to the folly or partiality of Captain Temple, not of the Jamaica governor, for he had my orders . . .[97]

Whatever this court of enquiry revealed, it does not seem to have had much adverse effect on the career of either of our captains. Temple continued to serve in the West Indies, in command of the fourth-rate *Mary Rose*, and after some enterprising operations in the eastern Caribbean seems to have died early in 1687. Heywood's fate was more incongruous; having become a planter at Heywood Hall in Saint Mary, he joined the Council of Jamaica in 1689, became a director of the Bath of St. Thomas ten years later, was appointed chief justice in 1703, and finally became governor of the island, dying in 1725.[98] Well might the author of the *Groans of Jamaica* write in 1714:

> Our present Chief-Justice, and chief judge of the grand court, . . . was likewise bred at sea, from a boy upward, and happening to get the command of a frigat, had the good or bad luck (I can't tell which) to lose her on a rock in sight of Port Royal, without any stress of weather; so, not thinking it convenient to return home, settled here and became first a planter and then a judge . . .

And finally, as we have seen, a governor. It was very hard either for pirates or for sea-captains to receive what they deserved in a Port Royal trial.[99]

Those ships which survived their tour of duty in Jamaica - and one in four in our period did not - eventually received the coveted order to sail for England. There was no regular convoy system until the 1690s,[100] but merchantmen often took advantage of the return of the warships to form a kind of informal convoy with them. When H.M.S. *Assistance* sailed for England in July of 1672, for instance, she was accompanied by the *Friezland*, the *Thomas and Charles*, the *Huntsman*, and the *Indeavour*; they all reached the mouth of the Thames the following October, after an average run of three months.

Another duty of returning ships was to carry back governors, or more normally their widows. Of the five governors known to have come out from England on naval vessels, only two sailed back alive, a melancholy comment on the life expectancy for newly arrived Englishmen in seventeenth-century Jamaica. The most curious return journey was probably that of the duchess of Albemarle, whose husband had died in October

1688, at the age of 35. The duke of Albemarle had been very much the nominee of James II, and so when on 19 January 1689 the people of Port Royal heard of 'strange news of the Prince of Orange his landing in England an army',[101] her situation became rather precarious.[102]

However, the president and Assembly rallied round their 'disconsolate princess', and on 8 March 1689 the duke's body, preserved in pitch, was put on board his yacht. A week later the preparations for the departure of the duchess were almost complete; as Cundall puts it 'In the darkness of the night the duchess was escorted on board the frigate by Dr. Hans Sloane, who was now established as sole guardian and protector of the widowed lady. With her came her treasure, her plate, her five hundred tons of furnishings, and her numerous retinue of servants.'[103] On 16 March H.M.S. *Assistance* set sail, accompanied by the yacht and a convoy of 13 merchantmen. However, after a day's sailing Captain Wright learned that, 'the Duchess had a mind to stop at Blewfields, by reason some of her goods were left ashoare at Port Royall'.[104] She was a strong-willed and eccentric lady - she eventually had to be declared insane - and she may well have had her way.

Some days further on, a more serious problem arose. When they left Port Royal, neither the duchess nor Captain Wright knew what they would find in England. They knew that James II had fled, but they had no news of the progress of William of Orange.[105] Captain Wright, who was an adherent of the Stuarts, said that if he found the king in exile he intended to hurry to France, in order to place his frigate at the disposition of the rightful monarch. This was the last straw for the duchess, who risked being landed in a foreign country with all her chattles and her dead husband. Leavng the ungallant Captain Wright's ship in mid-ocean, she re-embarked first on the yacht and then on the *Generous Hanna*, one of the convoy of merchantmen.[106] So H.M.S. *Assistance* and the rest of the convoy parted company. What happened next is best conveyed by a felicitous passage from Cundall's book:

> They landed, on the 30th of May, at Plymouth, in a heavy rain; the Duchess, her dead Duke, her plate and jewels and treasure, her servants and all their gear. In the harbour, with astonishment, they beheld the *Assistance* riding at anchor. Captain Wright had had leisure on his voyage to consider his future prospects. He prudently sailed into Plymouth, and had sworn fealty to king William.[107]

Plymouth was almost certainly not the eventual English destination of H.M.S. *Assistance*. All the ships for which we have this information in the logs seem to have ended up at Deptford, where their crews were paid off and where the vessels themselves could be surveyed and refitted for further duty. Mr. Pepys himself often visited Deptford, to view the dockyard and to see how well his instructions were being carried out. Considering the administrative and technical problems involved, he should have been reasonably satisfied with the equipment and control of the naval vessels at Port Royal between 1668 and 1692. In size and number they were as yet too weak to play any serious offensive role, but they did act as a reasonably efficient maritime police force. They had, as we have seen, one advantage which is not usually mentioned by naval historians, in that they could always call on the help of the merchant captains. But the central administration which equipped and directed them was also sound at this time; behind the frigates in Port Royal lay the robust hand of Mr. Pepys.

NOTES

[1] It is not easy to say what constituted the different 'rates', since methods of calculation varied. But in terms of guns, ships were rated roughly like this: 96 guns upwards, first-rate: 70-96 guns, second-rate; 60-70 guns, third-rate; 40-60 guns, fourth-rate; 20-40 guns, fifth-rate; and below 20 guns, sixth-rate.
[2] These figures are derived from W. L. Clowes, *The Royal Navy* (7 vols., London, 1897-1903), A. W. Tedder, *The navy of the Restoration* (Cambridge, 1916) and A. P. Thornton, *West-India policy*.
[3] *C.S.P.* 1675-6, 1207 of 20 January 1669.
[4] *Interesting Tracts*, p. 286.
[5] According to David McPherson's *Annals of commerce* (4 vols., London, 1805), ii. 629.
[6] MS. 2867, fo. 325, 'Instructions to Captain Talbot'.
[7] See above, p. 55, for an explanation and discussion of interloping.
[8] Which, as we shall see, led to the publication of *A letter from captain John* [?] *Tosier* (London, 1679).
[9] P.R.O. Adm. 51/3870 under this date.
[10] N.L.J. 'Registered shelves': 'P.R.O. captains' journals 68'.
[11] P.R.O. Adm. 51/3870 under 7 February 1678/9.
[12] P.R.O. Adm. 51/3870 under this date.
[13] This story is well told by Cundall in *Governors of Jamaica in the 17th century*, pp. 64 and 78.
[14] See figure 11, which lists prominent passengers.
[15] A 'tarpaulin' was a captain who had come up the hard way.
[16] These extracts from Pepys's letter are quoted by J. R. Tanner (ed.) In his *Catalogue of the Pepysian manuscripts* (4 vols., Cambridge, 1903-22), iii. 271; see figure 12 for a drawing of H.M.S. *Phoenix*.
[17] The following extracts all come from P.R.O. Adm. 51/345.
[18] Modern divers are familiar with the wealth of wrecks lying in the water at the foot of these hills.
[19] Wilson's 'Commissions and instructions' are preserved in the Bodleian Library, Oxford; Rawlinson collection, A 171 fo. 199-201.
[20] An archaic term for a customs certificate.
[21] He probably acted for the governor, too, in officially receiving important news; see the Council minutes of July 1661; N.L.J. M.S.T. 60, p. 16.
[22] See P.R.O. C.O. 142/13, extensively used in chapter 6.
[23] P.R.O. Adm. 51/3870 under this date.
[24] Bodleian, Rawlinson A 171, fo. 199.

[25] P.R.O. Adm. 51/3870, 8 October 1678.
[26] Ibid., 7 January 1679.
[27] See B.M. Sloane 1599, fo. 106, 'Minutes of the Council in Jamaica 1687-9'.
[28] See for instance, the survey of H.M.S. *Phoenix* in June 1677 (Coventry Papers, vol. 75, fo. 192), and of the *Stuart*, galley, in January 1688 (B.M. Sloane 1599, fo. 5v).
[29] See his letter to Blathwayt, Blathwayt Papers, vol. 26, 15 May 1683.
[30] See the log for H.M.S. *Falcon*, P.R.O. Adm. 51/345, of 5 September 1686; the pirate Courtney was handed over on that occasion.
[31] According to C. M. Andrews, *Guide to material for American history to 1783* (2 vols., Washington, 1912 and 1914), i. 234, note 3.
[32] Quoted in *C.S.P.* 1681-5, 1563 of 28 February 1684.
[33] *C.S.P.* 1669-74, 691, 697, and 709, all of December 1671.
[34] See, for instance, the log of H.M.S. *Hunter*, P.R.O. Adm. 51/3870 for 8 April 1680.
[35] P.R.O. Adm. 51/345 for 12 November 1686.
[36] P.R.O. Adm. 51/3870 for 10 April 1679.
[37] Ibid., for 30 July 1679 and elsewhere.
[38] See the 'Journal of H.M.S. *Boneta*', Bodleian, Rawlinson A 300, under February 1686 among other places.
[39] See the 'Considerations worthy of Your Majesty's knowledge' in the Pepysian Library, Cambridge, MS. 2873, fo. 487.
[40] H.M.S. *Phoenix* was one of the earliest vessels to be equipped in this way; see Tanner, *Catalogue of the Pepysian manuscripts*, ii. 184, note 3.
[41] Described in P.R.O. Adm. 51/3870 for this date.
[42] See, for instance, the careen of H.M.S. *Mordaunt*, in the summer of 1693: P.R.O. Adm. 52/68 for April to June.
[43] Coventry Papers, vol. 75, fo. 194.
[44] See P.R.O. Adm. 51/3926.2 at this date.
[45] P.R.O. Adm. 51/3870 for 25 April 1879.
[46] Ibid. for 23 March 1680.
[47] P.R.O. Adm, 52/68 for 27 July 1692; figure 13 shows a contemporary model of H.M.S. *Mordaunt*.
[48] See above, p. 52
[49] P.R.O. Adm. 51/3870 for 5 September 1679
[50] It has been used in chapter 12.
[51] *C.S.P.* 1689-92, 2270 of 14 June 1692.
[52] See, for instance, Captain Tosier's journal for 9 June 1679 (P.R.O Adm. 51/3870): 'At noon Sir Henry Morgan and my ladie, and Collonell Byndloss with his lady did mee thee honour as to dine with mee . . .'
[53] P.R.O. Adm. 51/345 under this date.
[54] *Interesting Tracts*, p. 299.
[55] B.M. Add. MSS. 12430, fo. 38v.
[56] See below.
[57] B.M. Add. MSS. 12424. 'Journal of H.M.S. *Assistance*' under this date.
[58] P.R.O. Adm. 52/68 for 28 June 1692.
[59] Not to be confused, of course, with the island of that name.
[60] This information comes from a number of logs.
[61] See above.
[62] See *A letter from captain John* [sic; elsewhere he signs himself 'Josiah'] *Tosier, commander of H.M.S. the Hunter at Jamaica, with a narrative of his embassy and command in that frigat to the captain general and governor of Havanna* . . . (presumably London, 1679).
[63] Blathwayt Papers, vol. 26; Wilson to Blathwayt, 3 April 1691.
[64] See 'A pirate at Port Royal in 1679' by the present authors, in *The Mariner's Mirror*, lvii (1971), 303-5.
[65] *C.S.P.* 1677-80, 1188 of 23 November 1679.
[66] *C.S.P.* 1669-74, 908 of 12 August 1672.
[67] *C.S.P.* 1681-5, 1759 of 20 June 1684; this version may be amplified by Lynch's letter of 16 August 1684 to Sir Charles Lyttleton, preserved in vol. 24 of the Blathwayt Papers.
[68] See *Boneta's* log under that date; Bodleian, Rawlinson A 300.
[69] Extract from the letter cited in note 1 above.

70 *C.S.P.* 1681-5, 1852 of 30 August 1684, Colonel Molesworth to the Earl of Sunderland, 30 August 1684. The next paragraph also relies on this letter.
71 *C.S.P.* 1681-5, 1867 of 19 September 1684.
72 Molesworth to Blathwayt, 3 February 1685, Blathwayt papers, vol. 25. See also above, p. 54.
73 *C.S.P.* 1681-5, 2067 of 3 February 1685.
74 Molesworth to Blathwayt, 3 February 1685; Blathwayt Papers, vol. 25.
75 *C.S.P* 1685-8, 193 of 15 May 1685.
76 Ibid., 463 of 16 November 1685.
77 Molesworth to Blathwayt, 25 March 1686; Blathwayt papers, vol. 25. This gulf is now known as 'Sabana'.
78 Molesworth to Blathwayt, 21 June 1686; Blathwayt Papers, vol. 23; figure 14 reproduces a drawing of H.M.S. *Drake*.
79 *Calendar of State Papers, Domestic Series*; James II, vol ii, art. 961.
80 Molesworth to Blathwayt, 5 July 1686; Blathwayt Papers, vol. 25.
81 *C.S.P.* 1685-8, 1127 of 9 February 1687.
82 Ibid., 755 of 5 July 1686.
83 Ibid., 839 of 31 August 1686.
84 P.R.O. Adm. 51/345 under this date.
85 *C.S.P.* 1685-8, 1127 of 9 February 1687.
86 *C.S.P.* 1681-5, 51 of 16 March 1681.
87 Bodleian, Rawlinson A 300 under this date.
88 Historical MSS. Commission, Report on the MSS. of A. G. Finch, i, 119-20.
89 P.R.O. Adm. 52/38 under 2 April 1691.
90 This venture is described in Estelle F. Ward's *Christopher Monck, Duke of Albemarle* (London, 1915)
91 She had been chasing the pirate, Peter Harris, and followed him too far into shoal water.
92 Governor Carlisle to Coventry, St. Jago 24 October 1679; Coventry Papers, vol. 75, fo. 279.
93 See the letter from Reginald Wilson to Blathwayt of 28 April 1692, Blathwayt Papers, vol. 26; '. . . which was a great shipp, but lyes in 8 or 9 fathoms water and beleaved too laborious to worke uppon . . .'.
94 P.R.O. Adm. 51. 3926/1-2, logs of Phillip Lawson, first lieutenant, of Francis Wivell, lieutenant, and of William Lowe, navigator. See also 'The loss of H.M.S. *Norwich* off Port Royal in June 1682' by David Buisseret, *The Mariner's Mirror*, liv (1968), 403-7.
95 All the quotations used here will be found in the documents quoted in note 2 above.
96 *C.S.P.* 1681-5, 792 of 15 November 1682.
97 Ibid. 1249 of 12 September 1683.
98 These details are all taken from Cundall, *Governors of Jamaica in the first half of the 18th century* (London, 1937), pp. 66-73.
99 And, we may add, easy for pirates to escape from Port Royal jail; Sawkins got out in 1679, Bannister in 1684, and in 1686 Captain Coxen escaped with equal ease. See the Blathwayt Papers, vol. 25, Molesworth to Blathwayt, 25 March 1686.
100 Though as early as 1671 the king had ordered that such a system be instituted; see Cundall, *Governors of Jamaica in the 17th century*, p. 35.
101 From the log of Captain Laurence Wright, H.M.S. *Assistance*, P.R.O. captains' journals 68 under that date. William of Orange had landed at Torbay on 5 November 1688.
102 Most of the following account of the return of the duchess is taken from Cundall's *Governors of Jamaica in the 17th century*, pp. 115-16.
103 Cundall, op. cit., p. 116.
104 Log of H.M.S. *Assistance* under this date.
105 James had in fact fled late the previous December.
106 See Sloane, *A voyage to the island Madera, Barbados . . . and Jamaica* (2 vols., London, 1707 and 1725) ii. 344
107 Cundall, op. cit., p. 116.

CHAPTER SIX

The Economic Development of Port Royal in the Seventeenth Century

The history of Port Royal's economic development is above all the history of her traders. Merchants could also be shipowners or shopkeepers, and many eventually became planters, but the very heart of Port Royal's prosperity lay in their long-distance trading. Some English merchants had been quick to see the economic possibilities of the Western Design, which after all was only another phase in that English overseas expansion which had been going on since the reign of Elizabeth. Men like Thomas Povey, Martin Noell, and Maurice Thompson were closely connected with the expansionist group in England, whose most notable representative - both during the Commonwealth and under the Restoration - was Colonel George Monck.[1] Their contacts with the highest political figures permitted them not only to press for aggressive policies in search of new trade, but also - in the case particularly of the Western Design - to secure contracts for supplying the army and navy, as soon as these forces had been assembled in England.[2]

Until about 1660, however, the trading possibilities of the Point were not apparent. The six vessels recorded in D'Oyley's journal as arriving in the harbour between September 1657 and January 1658 all carried what might be described as 'survival stores' for the army. In the *Golden Faulcon* was a mixed assortment of building materials: 'oake boards', 'pyne plankes', barrels of tar and so forth. The *Mary, William* and *Thomas*, and *Brothers Adventure* brought food: 'biskett', 'biefe', 'pease', 'flower', and other things to keep hungry men alive. The *Francis and Mary*, it is true, brought eight hogsheads of French wine, but that was for the use of the commander-in-chief.[3]

Most of the exports were carried on naval ships, as the units of Penn's fleet were sent home. Among these shipments we find portents of Jamaica's agricultural future; nearly 40,000 pounds of tobacco, about

18,000 pounds of cacao nuts, nearly 19,000 pounds of sugar (the first shipment dating from January 1660), and an assortment of minor products like skins, fustick, ebony, and so on. The scale of operations was as yet very small, and it was not until after 1660, when political and economic conditions were alike propitious, that Port Royal began its rapid expansion as a commercial centre.

From that time onwards, we find many English merchants establishing themselves or their representatives at Port Royal. Already in April 1660, for instance, William Beeston was the Port Royal partner of Edward Pinhorne, a merchant of Southampton with a relative, William, who in 1657 was sheriff of that port.[4] The Port Royal representative of the Merchant Venturers of Bristol was Anthony Swymmer; he also had a brother, resident in Bristol, with interests in Jamaica.[5] As might be expected, it was the London merchants whose Port Royal representatives were most numerous; they included such prominent figures as John Belfield, Sir Thomas Modyford, Hender Molesworth, and Samuel Bach. Some Port Royal merchants were attorneys for more than one English-based trader, and sometimes for merchants from different centres in England. Family ties were also very important, involving groups such as the Mans, the Gordons, the Pinhornes, and the Elkins.

The Port Royal attorney necessarily enjoyed a very wide liberty of action, and could by his skill or lack of it make or break the fortune of his partner in England; hence this reliance on the traditional device of keeping the business within the family. Even so, attorneyships were generally granted through legal bonds setting out very precisely the mutual obligations of the partners. These 'letters of attorney' were 'sealed and enrolled' before the clerk of the Office of Enrolments, and many of them survive at the Island Record Office in Spanish Town, where they provide us with a general if incomplete view of the relationship between colony and metropolis. Sometimes such letters were procured for merchants already resident in Port Royal; others, as the documents themselves tell us, were in favour of some agent 'now bound for Jamaica'. That normally meant bound for Port Royal, since until the late 1680s there was no other trading centre of consequence in the island. Once the agent arrived in Port Royal, he became a statistic among the general totals recorded by Reginald Wilson, naval officer, in pursuance of the provisions of the Navigation Acts. Some of these registers survive, and provide us with precious evidence concerning arrivals of ships and their contents between 1686 and 1692.[6]

For the period before this, we have only two references. One tells us that between January 1668 and January 1670 some 208 ships of 6,727 tons 'arrived in Port Royal harbour';[7] the other claims that in the year 1676-7 there arrived from London 27 ships totalling 2,950 tons.[8] The information derived from Wilson's figures is set out below.

TONNAGE OF VESSELS ARRIVING AT PORT ROYAL, 1686-1691

Year	Vessels coming from:				
	England	Ireland	Africa	North America	Total (tons)
1686	3,605	445	1,395	1,690	7,135
1687	4,955	545	1,680	1,790	8,970
1688	5,785	750	765	2,410	9,710
1689	3,460	420	100	1,355	5,355
1690	2,590	160	250	1,165	4,165
1691	2,780	815	660	1,310	5,565
	23,175	3,135	4,850	9,720	40,880

In terms of tonnage, it looks as if the peak of arrivals for the period came in 1688, with nearly 10,000 tons. This fits well enough with the figures for 1668/60 and 1676, and suggests a steady rise from about 3,400 tons in 1670 to about 6,000 by 1676 (the London tonnage being normally a little less than half that of the total).

Within the tonnages recorded for the period 1686-91, ships coming from England enjoyed a clear predominance in their total tonnage, which in almost every case amounted to more than half the total. This did not mean, of course, that the English ships were more numerous. In fact, 240 ships came from England and Africa between 1686 and 1691, as opposed to 363 from the North American colonies. However, the latter vessels' total tonnage was only 9,720, against a total tonnage of 28,025 for the transatlantic vessels. The North American boats were quite small, averaging a little over 25 tons, whereas the others averaged about 120 tons.[9]

It will be recalled that between January 1668 and January 1670 some 208 ships of 6,727 tons 'arrived in Port Royal harbour'. The average size of these vessels was only 32 tons, and if we assume that the relative size of North American and transatlantic ships remained roughly constant at this time, then there can hardly have been within

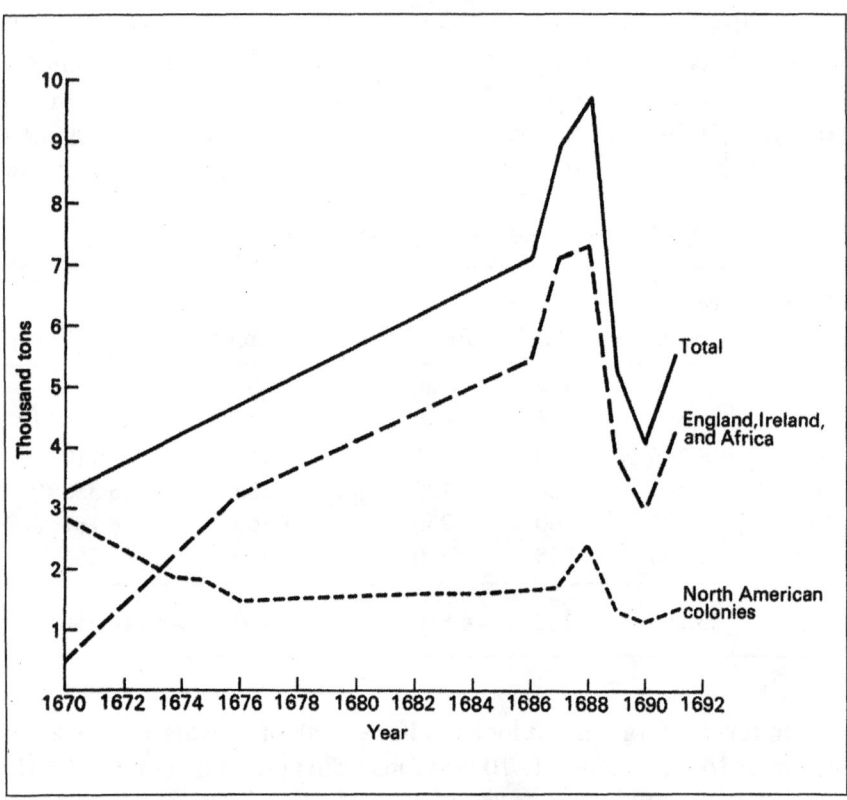

Figure 16 Tonnage of vessels arriving at Port Royal, 1670-1692

this total more than 15 or 20 ships of the transatlantic size, with a total tonnage of about 2,000. We might use this information to construct a very crude and hypothetical graph of arrivals at Port Royal down to 1692 (figure 16).

It is one thing to offer a sketch of the tonnage of shipping arriving at Port Royal, and quite another to give an account of the actual quantities of commodities landed there. Most of the goods entered the island in a bewildering variety of barrels, butts, casks, hogsheads, puncheons, and tierces, and any attempt to reduce these to statistical order would surely be misleading. About the only commodity for which a single unvarying unit of measurement was used was human beings. Between June 1671 and March 1679 there landed at Port Royal 5,396 'Christians' and 11,816 slaves.[10] This figure for 'Christians', meaning passengers and servants from the British Isles, averages 675 a year between 1671 and 1679. For the years between 1686 and 1691 the annual figures run like this:

Year	1686	1687	1688	1689	1690	1691
Passengers and servants	510	325	176	nil	nil	nil

The figure for 1686 includes 131 'convicted rebels' from the Monmouth insurrection of July 1685, so that the true number for that year would be nearer 400. Plainly, fewer and fewer persons from the British Isles were coming to seek their fortunes in Jamaica in the later 1680s; these figures form an eloquent commentary on the general trend of Jamaica's population, in which the white element declined from 12,000 in 1680 to 10,000 in 1690 and only 7,000 by 1700.[11]

In the same period, the black population rose from 15,000 to 40,000, largely because of landings at Port Royal. Between 1671 and 1679 the annual figure for Africans landed had run at about 1,500; it increased only slightly between 1686 and 1691, to about 1,700.[12] Of course, these figures do not sufficiently explain the general trend within Jamaica's slave population; not only were many of the Africans landed at Port Royal shipped out again, but many others were landed by stealth in remote parts of the island, and so escaped the attention of the naval officer in Port Royal.

The considerable tonnage of shipping from England brought a wide variety of goods, including food, drink, naval stores, arms, and dry goods. Among the foods were the usual meats: beef, pork, and bacon, and also vegetables and cereals like peas, oats, and rice. Biscuits and cheese came as well, with a good deal of butter, though the latter must surely have been often rancid by the time it reached Port Royal. Among the drink, which seems to have come in very large quantities, were cider, beer, claret, Rhenish wine, Malaga, Madeira, Canary, sherry, port, and the various brandies. Naval stores included chiefly canvas, tar, and cordage, all of which weathered quickly in the tropics; the arms were mostly muskets and pistols, for the cannon were brought on naval ships. Other goods included candles, soaps, grindstones, cart-wheels, ploughs, bricks, nails, pantiles, stills, iron pots and rollers, and even one 'coach and chariott'. There were also shipments of lead and 'coales', the latter no doubt for smithies; in short, England supplied nearly all the commodities needed not only for surviving, but also for setting up plantations. Most of these goods were loaded in London, though a few ships came from Bristol and one or two from Liverpool.

The ships which had touched at Ireland brought food. From Cork and Dublin, as well as lesser ports like Limerick, Ross, Waterford, and Wexford, came not only the foods described above, but also herrings and Irish salmon. Fish came as well from North America; not only salted codfish, but also mackerel, salmon, sturgeon, ale-wives, and oysters. Meat from this source was chiefly pork and mutton, and there was also a wide variety of vegetables and fruits, which survived the short voyage quite well: apples, cabbages, cranberries, garlic, and quinces, as well as onions and peas. Instead of the great variety of European and mid-Atlantic wines there were beer, cider, honey, and rose-water; instead of the wide range of manufactures there were chiefly wooden products like casks, chairs, shingles, staves, and tubs, with one desk as well. There were also a few manufactured products, like candles, grindstones, and small-arms, but in general the shipments from North America reflected her abundance of fresh food and wood; she could not yet match the English range of manufactures. Boston was the most frequent last port of call, though many ships came from New York and some from little ports like Burlington, Plymouth, Roanoke, and Salem.

We are not very well informed about the nature of the trade with other Caribbean islands and with the Spanish Main. From the latter came occasional shipments of hides and of tropical products like cacao-nuts. From the Campeche region came large supplies of logwood, used in Europe for providing cloth with a good base on which to apply colours.[13] Finally, from the Cayman islands came constant supplies of turtles, whose flesh had sustained Venables' army in the days when very little other food was available, and which continued to play a leading part in Jamaican cooking.

It is impossible to hazard a guess about the volume of this inter-Caribbean trade in commodities like logwood and turtles. There do seem to be certain trends, however, which are discernible in the extra-Caribbean pattern. On the whole, Jamaican imports of North American products seem to have stabilized or even declined in the 1680s, while transatlantic imports were growing. Perhaps this corresponds to an economic phase in which Jamaica was becoming increasingly self-sufficient in food and wood, and also rich enough to import European delicacies. In short, it may reflect the increasing sophistication of the Jamaican economy, in which a largish number of 'small' white settlers producing a wide range of crops was being replaced by a smaller number of considerable white landowners, producing sugar with the aid of large gangs of slaves.[14]

This trend is certainly evident enough in the figures for exports of sugar, which from very small beginnings in the later 1660s grew strongly throughout the 1680s, until in a year like 1686 or 1691 the island was sending over 7,000 tons (about 14,000 hogsheads) to England alone.[15] By then the earliest exports like hides and tobacco had fallen off almost completely, to be replaced by small quantities of exotic products like tortoise-shell, lime-juice, indigo, ginger, cotton, pimento, and cacao-nuts. All these products lay in Port Royal's fragrant warehouses, until the time came when they were loaded on to the ships and entered into the naval officer's registers.

These registers are not quite as complete for vessels leaving Port Royal as for those entering the harbour, for in the former case only those carrying enumerated goods[16] were recorded. However, the difference is only of about 20 per cent, not enough to prevent us from forming a general impression of the pattern of departures. As with the imports to Jamaica, we have few figures before 1680 of exports; we know only that in 1676-7 the Port of London received 35 ships coming from the island.[17] This number would of course represent only part of the total number of ships arriving in England, since Bristol, Liverpool, and Plymouth were also ports of entry. It is in fact only a little lower than the yearly average after 1680; the total number of ships each year carrying enumerated goods and clearing customs at Port Royal is as shown below:

NUMBER OF VESSELS CLEARING CUSTOMS AT PORT ROYAL 1680-1692

Year (March to March)	Vessels for England	Vessels for Colonies	Total
1680	42	not available	[42]
1681	14 [partial]	not available	[14]
1682	44	22	66
1683	62	24	86
1684	not available	14 [partial]	[14]
1685	10 [partial]	18 [partial]	[28]
1686	66	36	102
1687	45	24	69
1688	57	23	80
1689	45	9	54
1690	41	25	66
1691	55	13	68
...			
1704	65	30	95

Sailings for England were becoming increasingly numerous in the later 1680s, while those for North America seem only to have been holding steady; the pattern thus resembles that for the tonnage of ships arriving at Port Royal, even though, for the reasons explained above, there is no exact correlation. It is certain that the years of war following 1691 saw a greatly reduced trade, though by 1704, when figures again become available, sailings had recovered to the level of 1686.

Many of the items shipped from Port Royal formed part of a re-export trade. Logwood from Campeche and other parts of central America was shipped to England in considerable quantities; from the Spanish colonies came hides, brazil nuts, cochineal, and bullion, which were all re-shipped to England. Only occasionally were small quantities of hides, nuts, and dyewoods sent to the North American colonies, for their markets remained as yet very small, and easily swamped by trifling quantities of these exotic commodities.[18] Ships coming from Africa often brought ivory and palm oil; the latter seems to have remained in the island, but the ivory, after a longer or shorter stay in the hands of some Port Royal middleman, was nearly always shipped on to England. The most valuable 'commodity' coming from Africa was of course the slaves, many of whom were sent on to the Spanish colonies,[19] though some too went to English colonies in North America.[20]

There was also a re-export trade from Port Royal in goods which had originated in Europe or the North American colonies. Some of this trade took the form of illegal exchanges with the Spanish American colonies, but there was also a legal trade with the various English possessions. Spirits, for instance, which had passed customs into Jamaica, were commonly exported to other West Indian colonies. The *Friendship*, for example, sailed from Port Royal to Bermuda on 12 August 1687,[21] carrying eight barrels of brandy which the master had bought in Jamaica after selling his cargo of provisions. This type of exchange was very common among the captains of the little ships from North America; they were disinclined to return home empty,[22] and did not hesitate to load their vessels with cloth and other English manufactures if the local rum and molasses was in short supply or too expensive. Goods originating in North America played a much smaller part in the re-export trade; it was altogether exceptional when one Port Royal merchant shipped five bear-skins to England.[23]

The seasonal incidence of ships arriving in Port Royal from across the Atlantic was quite different from that of the small North American vessels. Curiously enough, the latter paid little attention to avoiding the dangerous summer months, as the following table shows (it covers the years 1686-91):

Quarter of year	January-March	April-June	July-September	October-December
Transatlantic arrivals	88	69	41	42
Arrivals from N. America	87	87	95	94

The large ships coming from England, whether *via* Ireland or *via* Africa, mostly arrived in the first four or five months of the year, partly to catch 'crop time' in Jamaica, and partly to avoid the hurricane months, usually designated as June to October. Ships coming straight from Europe often had to wait for very long periods in Port Royal harbour, while supplies of sugar arrived from the more distant plantations. Sometimes their masters sent their own sailors out in sloops to pick the cargo up; sometimes too, they left their agents in Port Royal to collect the cargo, and themselves sailed off to load logwood in Campeche or even to trade with the North American colonies.[24] The ships coming from Africa often stayed in harbor so as to be modified in order to carry hogsheads; they too were subject to the same delays, which lasted anywhere from one to three or four months.

Of course, there were many exceptions to the traditional route-pattern. The *Amity*, for instance, in 1686 sailed from London to New York, and thence to Barbados and Jamaica,[25] and she was no isolated example. The North American captains were particularly flexible in their choice of routes. While they usually sailed directly southwards, first to Jamaica and then to the other islands as they came, sometimes they would cruise the Caribbean very freely, searching for the best markets. Sometimes too they would venture right across the Atlantic, to arrive in Port Royal from the English ports and Madeira.[26] It looks as if the small size of their vessels made them more flexible in their operations; they were certainly fearless in venturing into the Caribbean during the summer months, as we have noticed above.

All the figures quoted so far refer to the places from which vessels came, and not necessarily to the places where they were owned. In fact, most of the ships coming from England were owned by Londoners, just as most of those from North America belonged to Yankee captains. There was a sizeable fleet belonging to Port Royal, and some of these vessels were engaged in long-distance trades. The *Loyal Ivy*, registered at Port Royal, thus departed for Newfoundland in May 1686 carrying sugar, rum, and molasses; she then went to Madeira, whence she returned in December 1686, laden with Madeira wine.[27] By 1687 at least three Jamaican-owned vessels were acting as contract ships for the Royal African Company.[28] Most of the Port Royal-owned vessels were engaged in more local trades; indeed, of 207 such ships registering their arrival in the harbour between 1680 and 1691 (with gaps in the records, of course), only 72 had come from outside the Caribbean. Most of the Port Royal fleet consisted of quite small vessels, some of which hardly left the immediate area of the island. The number of ships owned by Port Royallers appears to have grown steadily between 1670 and 1688, probably in a sequence like this:[29]

Year	1670	1675	1679	1688
Number of vessels	38	60-70	80	100

Apart from participating in the Caribbean trades in logwood and turtles, they were also very busy salvaging what they could from various wrecks. The most famous of these was simply called 'the wreck', and was in fact a Spanish galleon which had gone down in the 1640s off Hispaniola; sometimes it looks from the returns as if almost every seaworthy ship in the island must have been busy on 'the wreck.' The steady increase in the size of the fleet probably reflects not so much an increase in this salvage-work and in the Caribbean trades, as a growing need for small vessels to fetch sugar from coastal plantations and bring it to Port Royal for transhipment. In fact the fleet did not grow at the same pace as the general population of the town (see chapter 8); no doubt its economic importance was relatively greater in 1670 than in 1690, though it would be impossible to adduce figures to prove this.

The great problem during the 1660s and 1670s often seems to have been a shortage of ships to take produce back to England. As Governor Carlisle wrote in March 1679, 'our present trouble here is for the great plenty of sugar and scarcity of shipping to carry it off'.[30] Some Port Royal merchants did their best to hedge against such a shortage by buying either vessels or shares in them; it is of course impossible to say how significant such participation was, in terms of the total investment in shipping.

After giving this general view of the scale and nature of maritime operations, it may be helpful if we take three categories of ship - those owned in England, those owned in North American colonies, and those owned in Port Royal - and describe the actual operations of two or three of them. In the first category, we have particularly full records for eight ships: the *America Merchant* (captain, Thomas Masters),[31] the *Arthur and Mary* (George Winter), the *Cadiz Merchant*[32] (Charles Johnson, figure 17), the *Jamaica Merchant* (Richard Browning), the *Lambe* (George Colwell), the *Loyall Merchant* (Joseph Knapman, a

Figure 17 Edward Barlow, *The Cadiz Merchant* (National Maritime Museum)

famous captain), the *Richard and Sarah* (Thomas Stubbs), and the *William and Mary* (Francis Mingham). Of these, the *Richard and Sarah* and the *Lambe* will serve well as examples, for the first was a London ship of about 200 tons, and the second was based in Bristol and was rated at only 80 tons.

The *Richard and Sarah*, which carried about 30 English sailors and mounted 20 (or sometimes 22) guns, first came to Port Royal some time in 1683 - our records are deficient here - and sailed for London in September of that year.[33] Her captain, Thomas Stubbs, had taken on a very characteristic cargo, consisting of 429 hogsheads of sugar, 28 hogsheads of cocoa, 28 bags of cotton, 24 barrels of indigo, 20 tons of logwood, 20 hogsheads of pimento, and 86 hides. Presumably Stubbs returned safely to England, and then perhaps traded for a year or two elsewhere in the world, for he did not return to Port Royal until 21 June 1686.[34] This time he brought 46 'passengers and servants', 25 tons of beer, 12 casks of mum (a type of beer), 4 hogsheads of cider, 40 whole and 20 half cases of spirits, 3 tons of flour, 60 firkins of butter, 2,500 pounds of cheese, and '90 tons of dry goods as per cocketts'.

Having unloaded this cargo in the latter part of June, he seems to have been rather late for the bulk of the sugar crop. It was not until 28 August that he was able to sail again, and he then carried only 43 hogsheads of sugar.[35] However, there was a wide variety of tropical produce: 63 bags of cotton, 32 barrels of indigo, 15 tons of ginger, 30 tons of logwood, two tons of fustick, 23 hogsheads of pimento, and 41 puncheons of lime-juice. The *Richard and Sarah* would almost certainly have taken the (normal) Windward Passage route between Cuba and Santo Domingo, and probably arrived in London towards the middle or end of November. By 29 June 1687 she was back in Port Royal,[36] with the usual kind of cargo: no passengers this time, but plenty of food, drink, and dry goods including beer, mum, Rhenish wine, Canary wine, butter, cheese, candles, flour, and soap.

Captain Stubbs was now later than ever from the point of view of the sugar trade, and the *Richard and Sarah* seems to have lain in Port Royal harbour for six months, until on 4 January 1688 she was able to sail with a good cargo of sugar and other staples.[37] In addition to these, she carried 231 'elephant teeth' and ten tons of ebony, part of the re-export trade in African commodities. During 1688 Captain Stubbs seems to have followed more closely the conventional pattern of sailings, for he arrived back at Port Royal on 21 November 1688.[38] In addition to the usual food and drink, he had '45 tuns provisions and 50 tuns ammunition, the King's stores'. By the beginning of April he had assembled a new cargo, which consisted of 574 hogsheads of sugar - the largest consignment which he ever collected - 53 hogsheads of pimento, 7 hogsheads of indigo, 37 bags of cotton, and 50 tons of logwood. He sailed for London on 4 April 1688, and that is the last we hear of Thomas Stubbs.[39]

The operations of the *Richard and Sarah* offer a characteristic image of those of the larger English vessels. Captain Stubbs does not seem to have been very skilful at timing his arrivals at Port Royal, but he usually shipped a fair-sized cargo in the end, carrying the predictable goods. We have, alas, no means of knowing what kind of financial success (or failure) Stubbs made, since our documents offer no hints in that direction. When we come on to consider the voyages of George Colwell,[40] in command of the 80-ton *Lambe* of Bristol, we can at once see that the Lambe operated more nimbly than the *Richard and Sarah*. For the years before 1686, we have figures only for sailings from Port Royal of June 1682 and April 1683, and for an arrival of January 1684. On his sailings - which fell in the most favourable part of the year - Colwell took the conventional commodities, in smaller quantities than Stubbs, of course, but in much the same proportions. When he arrived at Port Royal in 1684, too, his cargo was what one would expect in a ship coming from Bristol and Cork: food and drink and a variety of dry goods including 20 grindstones and 10 sheets of lead.

From 1686 to 1691, with a gap for 1690, we have full records of Colwell's yearly visits to Port Royal. They ran as follows:

Year	Date of arrival	Date of departure	Time in port
1686	17 March	5 May	7 weeks
1687	28 April	30 June	8 weeks
1688	2 March	28 April	8 weeks
1689	17 January	19 April	13 weeks
1691	6 August	10 November	13 weeks

Colwell's ability to follow a regular schedule between 1686 and 1688 - and for all we know before that as well - is surely very remarkable, as is the consistency with which in those years he found a cargo and sailed again within two months. By 1689, of course, he may have been put out by the need to avoid French privateers; later on the whole routine of shipping would change, with the adoption of the convoy system.[41] It may be of some interest to tabulate the quantities of various goods carried by Colwell in his seven recorded trips out from Port Royal:

Year	Sugar (hogsheads)	Cotton (bags)	Indigo (bars)	Fustick (tons)
1682	226	222	20	20
1683	194	58	-	25
1686	251	52	-	8 [logwood]
1687	203	75	3	-
1688	239	20	2 chests	15
1689	215	80	-	10
1691	222	13	11	8

For a little ship of 80 tons, this is surely a remarkable record; the consistency of the cargo seems to indicate also that captains who arrived at the right time could take on what commodities suited them best.

None of the ships from North America for which we have abundant records was even as big as the *Lambe*. The *James* (Job Prince) was 70 tons, the *Katheryne* (Thomas Berry and then John Pullin) 45 tons, the *Mary and Elizabeth* (Nathaniel Car) 45 tons, and the *Sara and Abigail* a barque of only 25 tons; they all came from Boston. The *James* visited Port Royal five times in the period for which we have records:[42]

Date of arrival	Date of departure	Time in port
25 November 1687	30 December 1687	5 weeks
5 May 1688	30 May 1688	4 weeks
24 September 1688	12 October 1688	3 weeks
3 April 1689	22 April 1689	3 weeks
10 September 1689	28 October 1689	7 weeks

Clearly, Job Prince obeyed no very strict seasonal pattern, and he was able to turn round more quickly even than George Colwell. From New England he brought the predictable lumber, fish, food, and on one occasion five horses. His return cargo normally consisted of about a dozen or a score of hogsheads of sugar and a bag or two of cotton, and on one occasion of 2,260 pounds of tanned leather. For the sailing of

28 October 1689, however, he appears to have departed radically from this pattern, and took on 209 hogsheads of sugar, 11 barrels of indigo, and eight bags of cotton, and sailed for London. Unless the records have made a blunder, this was a very unusual tactic for a North American captain; it is a pity that we can follow him no further.

The *Katheryne*, a pink of 45 tons, was an exceptionally frequent visitor to Port Royal; we know that she came in 1682, 1683, and 1685, and we have singularly complete records of her operations after that date:[43]

Date of arrival	Date of departure	Time in port
24 January 1684	8 March 1684	2 weeks
19 April 1686	15 June 1686	8 weeks
24 November 1686	25 December 1686	4 weeks
11 June 1687	4 July 1687	3 weeks
12 January 1688	9 February 1688	4 weeks
23 July 1688	11 August 1688	3 weeks
29 December 1688	8 February 1689	5 weeks

It looks as if captains Berry and Pullin simply operated a kind of shuttle between Boston and Port Royal, arriving when they could and loading what was available. They usually brought the normal timber, food, and fish, and took off sugar and cotton, both the latter in small quantities. Indeed, to judge by her possible capacity - on 8 March 1684 she sailed with 78 hogsheads of sugar - the *Katheryne* must normally have been at least half empty on the return voyage.

The smallest of the vessels which we have mentioned from Boston was the *Sara and Abigail*, a barque of 25 tons mounting between two and six guns according to the voyage. We have records for four of this little ship's visits to Port Royal:[44]

Date of arrival	Date of departure	Time in port
6 March 1686	3 April 1686	4 weeks
6 September 1686	16 October 1686	5 weeks
18 January 1687	18 March 1687	8 weeks
31 December 1688	5 April 1689	14 weeks

Of course, her capacity was not very great, and once she had a dozen hogsheads of sugar and a dozen of molasses on board, as she had in March 1687 and April 1689, there cannot have been room for very much else. However, she seems to have been very enterprising in her cruising. When she arrived in 1686 Captain Edwards had come merely from Boston with the usual commodities, but in January 1687 the *Sara and Abigail* was 'laden with Braziletta wood' from 'Providence', and in December 1688 she had come from Cork in Ireland, laden *inter alia* with two barrels of neats' tongues and five firkins of salmon. Not bad going for a ship of 25 tons.

Even the *Sara and Abigail* would have counted as a sizeable vessel among the craft operating out of Port Royal, many of whose ships were rated at ten tons or less. By far the largest seems to have been the *Loyal Factor* of 130 tons, commanded by Samuel Kempthorne.[45] We are short of information about this vessel because, as in the case of many of the Port Royal ships, she often did not carry enumerated goods when she left, and so escaped Wilson's registers. However, we do know that on 7 March 1689 Kempthorne arrived from 'Angolah' with '286 Negroes'. After that he completed the next leg of the conventional triangle, by sailing on 19 April for London with 142 hogsheads of sugar as well as other tropical products.

The *Loyal Factor* was however quite exceptional among Port Royal vessels because of her size. Much more typical was the *Bonadventure* of 25 tons, captained by John Taylor.[46] This little ship too went to Africa in 1691. Arriving at Port Royal on 17 January 1691, with a cargo of food, drink, and dry goods from Bristol, she must have unloaded hastily and sailed for the West African coast, for on 20 October 1691 she came into the harbour carrying '59 Negroes' from 'Gambo'. This may well have been an altogether exceptional voyage; certainly we should not expect a ship of this size to make a habit of transatlantic crossings.

The pattern of operations of the *John and Joseph*, while taking her out of the Caribbean, was altogether more modest.[47] In March 1687, she arrived from Curaçao with 30 tons of salt and one passenger; this probably rated a full cargo for a sloop of 30 tons and six guns. She then sailed for Boston, whence she returned in November 1687 with a load of fish, tobacco, wood, and candles. Her captain, Richard Baker, then took her to work on 'the wreck' for a while, and the following June she returned from it with a good haul of 'whole and broken pieces of eight'. Much of the silver having by then been recovered, Baker set off for the

Bay of Campeche, whence he returned in October 1688 with 30 tons of logwood. After that he seems to have resigned as captain, but on 23 September 1690 we find the *John and Joseph* returning from New York with a cargo of flour, beef, pork, and staves. All in all, this little sloop's operations were very characteristic of those of the larger ships in the Port Royal fleet.

The *Sarah*, captain William Lord, 20 tons and unarmed, will provide us with a final example from Port Royal.[48] In April 1688 and July 1689 she came into the harbour carrying Madeira wine, having gone to that island via Salem, presumably with some small quantity of tropical produce. In the summer of 1687 she sailed directly to New England, whence she returned in September with a cargo of fish and staves. Varying this Atlantic pattern, in the summer of 1688 Captain Lord took her after logwood in the Bay of Campeche; she loaded 25 tons of it and sailed back into Port Royal Harbour on 10 August. Her very flexible style of operating is of course characteristic of the smaller vessels whether from Port Royal or from the North American colonies. These captains chased round the Caribbean and its borders, picking up cargoes where they could and adhering to no particular patterns. Their operations contrast sharply with those of the much larger English vessels, which were in general tied to a seasonal routine connected both with the sugar crop and with the condition of the weather.

The pattern of sailings both known and predicted was of course a crucial element in the calculations of the merchants at Port Royal, as well as of their counterparts in North America and England. A letter from Henry Gleed, merchant of Port Royal, to Richard Wooley, citizen and baker of London and Gleed's partner, describes market conditions in 1672:

> my last to you of 9th April, wherein I gave account of the goodness of the market I came to, but since then two ships have arrived here with wines, so that our wines stick on hand . . . the large credit given by the merchants, and my resolution to sell no wine without ready money hath done some prejudice for the partnership . . . your beer proved all very good and well conditioned, excepting [that] which proved very sour, the which when beer was scarce worth 40 [?]. Mr Forthe's beer far surpasseth yours in both freshness and goodness, but sold both at one rate at £12 per tunn . . . the brandy generally sold for 6s. 6d. and 7s. per gallon. Your mum proves all very naught and good for little. There

is no sale for it, [for] little of that liquor drunk in this island. Your butter disposed of at 30s. per firkin, flour at 22s. 6d. p.c. [per hundred pounds?] and candles at 8d. per pound. I have sent you by captain Stubbs two hogsheads of sugar and one cask of cocoa and I shall send you more as fast as money comes to my hand.[49]

Later that year, 1671, Gleed again wrote to Wooley, commenting on the general trading situation:

Freight very high and scarce to be obtained. Logwood at £8 per ton and coffee £10 per ton freight, so that indeed have no encouragement to send home my goods, for that they are dear here and will not answer friends' expectations in England.[50]

Obviously, the Port Royal market was already quite highly developed, and a quick turnover depended on the right goods arriving at the opportune moment, since several ships arriving simultaneously with similar cargoes could result in stock remaining unsold and capital tied up, with the possible consequence that favourable opportunities for local purchases would be lost. Since communications were so slow and uncertain between Port Royal and the other commercial centres, the partners at each end must often have had to act more or less by instinct; a man with flair might prosper, but the opportunities for losing money were equally obvious.

There are, of course, no general statistics covering commercial operations at Port Royal, but we do have a good many of the papers of Thomas Brailsford, merchant of Coleman Street, London, and these permit us in some degree to reconstruct the activities of one large house towards the end of Port Royal's most prosperous period.[51] It was on 20 July 1687 that William Hall, Brailsford's associate, sailed for Jamaica with his brother Francis, in order to set up a business establishment in Port Royal. The Halls were to operate with Brailsford much as Gleed worked with with Wooley.

The most lucrative of the commodities sold by the Halls were wines, 'stuffs', and silks; the gross turnover for the 29 months came to £4,031. 14s. 10d., with a net return after all local expenses of £3,089. 4s. 5 1/2 d. This represents 76.6 per cent, but the invoices and accounts do not reveal either the original cost in England, or the loading charges levied in London, or the cost of freight to Jamaica.

When money could not be satisfactorily laid out in Port Royal, because of high prices or a shortage of appropriate goods, hard cash was sometimes shipped to London. Surviving invoices give us the following shipments:

Date	Vessel	Quantity	Shipping premium
23 August 1688	*Joseph*	400 pieces of eight	none
?	*Diamond*	571 pieces of eight	none
7 September 1688	'Per Brooks'	800 pieces of eight	?
?	*Thomas and Elizabeth*	600 pieces of eight	4. 10s. 0d.

The shipment of September 1688 is in fact referred to not in an invoice but in the routine correspondence between the Halls and Brailsford; they decided to send home specie on this occasion 'sugars being dear, 15 to 20 per cent rising occasioned per the Bristolman'. Whoever the Bristolman was, he was forcing prices up beyond what the Halls were prepared to pay; in the same letter they mention that the price of indigo was expected to fall, and that they had no intention of buying until it had done so. The Halls had of course to pay not only freight from Jamaica to London, but also insurance.

The Halls had a part not only in this conventional trade, but also in unconventional and even illegal ventures in other areas. Their correspondence hints at the Spanish trade as well as bartering with 'pyrates'. In the latter case, when some sherry and hock were slow to sell, they sent several dozens 'in a sloop and thought would have sold it to the pyrates but did not meet with them'. It was no doubt such illicit ventures that prompted William Hall to say in one of his letters to Brailsford 'as padlocks upon people's mouths are convenient at this time, so do put it upon my pen'. Even when more documents like those concerning the Brailsford-Hall operation have been discovered, it is likely that these 'padlocks upon the pen' will prevent us from ever fully reconstructing the flow of trade into and out of Port Royal. Nevertheless, we can already build up a composite image of its rough scale and type: the big ships bringing increasing quantities of certain goods from Europe, the smaller North American vessels fetching staples from the northern plantations, and the little local boats bustling about the Caribbean, sniffing out any opportunities for trade, whether legal or illegal. At the centre, come the Port Royal merchants, concerned not only to supply the local market, but also to re-export certain commodities and increasingly as time went by to draw on Jamaica's own sugar crop. All this activity seems to have reached its height about 1688, but even then the system was beginning to reveal certain inherent contradictions and hostilities which, even without the earthquake, would have led to a slowing down in the process of growth at Port Royal.

The basic contradiction lay in the inescapable hostility of merchant to planter.[52] As the latter became more and more powerful, it was inevitable that the plantations would begin trying to bypass those middlemen in Port Royal who, it was rightly felt, made their profit from exploiting the rather vulnerable position of the primary producers. As the plantations developed in the hinterland, so towns emerged as rivals to Port Royal in the business of shipping sugar, and planters increasingly relied on English factors both to sell their crops and to supply them with the necessities of plantation life.[53] Many merchants of Port Royal, foreseeing this trend, began even in the 1680s to shift their operations to the metropolis; the deeds of that period are replete with sales of property, mortgages, and letters of attorney for merchants 'formerly of Port Royal, now of London'.[54] Other prominent Port Royal merchants themselves bought plantations and moved out to live on them. In chapter 2 we noted the case of Lieutenant-Colonel William Ivy, who moved to Clarendon from Port Royal in 1665; he was among the first of a long line of Port Royallers turned planter. At first these ventures were often unsuccessful; Sir Martin Noell's plantation was a spectacular failure,[55] and so was Cary Helyar's.[56] As time went by, however, successful merchants invested more and more in plantations, so that 'between 1680 and 1689 the merchant community [of Port Royal] accounted for approximately one-fifth to one-quarter of all the recorded agricultural transactions on the island'.[57]

Port Royal, thus in a sense, committed suicide, for some of the merchants moved out of the island altogether, and others left it for plantations and for an economic mode of life ultimately hostile to the role of the resident merchant. By the late 1680s, even though all the signs of apparent prosperity were present, the craftsmen of the town - whose activities we shall examine in the next chapter - were already feeling the pinch, as the market for their services began to diminish. The coming of the French wars in 1689 and of the earthquake in 1692, fully described in chapter 9, was thus a series of blows which consummated a decline which was already in train.

CONCLUSION

It was Port Royal's advantages as a trading centre which enabled it to grow in 25 years from a barren sandy spit to the largest and most opulent town in the English Americas. At first the plantations of the hinterland played little part in this development, and then in the end they contributed to the precipitate decline of the little town. However dazzling its rise, we should not forget that it was a little town, and its merchants relatively insignificant figures, by the side of their European contemporaries. Of the wealthiest inhabitants, only Daniel Hicks succeeded in amassing wealth comparable with that of the richer London merchants, and Hicks seems to have made his money through the manufacture in Liguanea of the clay pots used in the refining of sugar. The other substantial Port Royal merchants were worth less than £10,000, whereas the greater London merchants might have accumulated nearly £20,000.[58] Moreover, the prosperity of Port Royal was both fragile and short lived; the economic advantage in a system of this kind always lay with their metropolis.

NOTES
[1] On this group see Ramsay Muir, *A short history of the British Commonwealth* (2 vols., London, 1920) and James A. Williamson, *A short history of British expansion* (2 vols., London, 1965).
[2] On these contracts see Maurice Ashley, *Financial and commercial policy under the Cromwellian Protectorate* (London, 1934) and also Claypole, 'The merchants of Port Royal', pp. 57-65.
[3] On these imports see B.M. Add. MSS. 12423, fo. 37r, 47v, 52r, and 60v. In February 1656 the English Council of State had issued a warrant to James de Senne, master of the *Bonaventure* of Dieppe, to trade with Jamaica, but this seems to be an isolated example of French enterprise (*C.S.P.* 1574-1660: p. 436 of 8 February 1656).
[4] This information comes from Malcolm Pinhorn of Shalfleet Manor, Isle of Wight. Readers who need a full account of grants of attorney between 1664 and 1674 will find it in appendix 4 of the first edition of this work.
[5] See P. McGrath (ed.), *Records relating to the Society of Merchant Adventurers of the city of Bristol in the 17th century* (Bristol, 1952), concerning the Swymmers and other merchants.
[6] For a discussion and analysis of these registers, see W. A. Claypole and D. J. Buisseret, 'Trade-patterns in early English Jamaica', *J.C.H.*, v (1972), 1-19.
[7] *J.H.A.*, i. 27 of 'Statistical Papers'.
[8] P.R.O. C.O. 324/4, 58-9, quoted by A.P. Thornton in 'Some statistics of West Indian produce, shipping and revenue 1660-1685', in *Caribbean Historical Review*, iii-iv (1954), 251-80.
[9] Our figures concur neatly with those of Ralph Davis in *The rise of the English shipping industry* (London, 1962), p. 280. Davis (op. cit., p. 15) gives the total tonnage of English merchant shipping as 340,000 in 1686, so that the Jamaican trade as yet concerned only a very small part of it.
[10] *C.S.P.* 1677-80, 945 of 25 March 1679.
[11] These approximations come from Richard S. Dunn's *Sugar and slaves* (Chapel Hill, N.C., 1972), p. 312.
[12] The figures given in P.R.O. C.O. 142/13 agree well with those provided by K. G. Davis in *The Royal African Company* (London, 1957), p. 363.
[13] For a brief summary of this trade see Carl and Roberta Bridenbaugh, *No peace beyond the line* (New York, 1972), pp. 338-42.

[14] In *The development of the plantations to 1750* (Barbados, 1970) Richard Sheridan gives a concise general view of this development.
[15] According to Dunn, *Sugar and slaves*, p. 203; his figures tally well enough with those given in P.R.O. C.O. 142/13.
[16] 'Enumerated goods' were those mentioned in the Navigation Acts as being exportable only to the possessions of the English Crown.
[17] C.O. 324/4, 58-9, quoted by Thornton, 'Some statistics of West Indian produce', p. 253.
[18] Richard Pares, *Yankees and Creoles* (London, 1956), p. 94.
[19] It seems to be impossible even to hazard a guess as to the importance of this traffic, though its directors have been recently described by F. J. Osborne, S.J. In 'James Castillo-Asiento agent', *J.H.R.*, viii (1971), 9-18.
[20] See, for instance, P.R.O. C.O. 142/13, p. 197.
[21] Ibid., p. 130.
[22] On this point see Pares, *Yankee, and Creoles*, pp. 95-101.
[23] P.R.O. C.O. 142/13, p. 131.
[24] See, for instance, the *Mary*, P.R.O. C.O. 142/13, pp. 91 and 92.
[25] P.R.O. C.O. 142/13, pp. 7 and 13.
[26] Some of these vessels were as small as the brigantine *Dolphin*, 15 tons, which arrived from Madeira on October 1688; P.R.O. C.O. 142/13, p. 211.
[27] P.R.O. C.O. 142/13, pp. 18 and 125.
[28] Claypole, 'The merchants of Port Royal', p. 141.
[29] These four references come from *J.H.A.*, i., Statistical Papers, p. 20, from the Coventry Papers, vol. 75, fo. 305, from P.R.O. C.O. 1/143, fo. 51, and from the Taylor MS., p. 499. Sloane (*A voyage to the islands*, i. xvii) gives a figure of 180 for 1688, but this is surely exaggerated.
[30] Coventry Papers, vol. 75, fo. 161.
[31] Sometimes the captains changed, of course, but in general they seem to have survived a good many voyages.
[32] The operations of the *Cadiz Merchant* between 1675 and 1684 have been described by Ralph Davis in *The rise of the English shipping industry*, pp. 346-57. Plate 7 reproduces Barlow's drawing of her.
[33] P.R.O. C.O. 142/13, p. 184; for the remaining ships taken as examples, we shall give all the appropriate references under the first note.
[34] P.R.O. C.O. 142/13, p. 4.
[35] Ibid., p. 113.
[36] Ibid., p. 30.
[37] Ibid., p. 119.
[38] Ibid., p. 6.
[39] Ibid., p. 220. It would probably be possible to trace his fortunes in greater detail, using the London entry-books, but that would be an immense task before which we have recoiled.
[40] In chronological order, P.R.O. C.O. 142/13, pp. 179, 184, 189, 8, 112, 25, 117, 45, 120, 211, 220, 93, and 145.
[41] P.R.O. C.O. 142/13 first reveals the application of the convoy system in the first quarter of 1691, when ten ships arrived together from England. There had occasionally been convoys before that; see William Beeston's journal in H.M.S. *Assistance*, B.M. Add. MSS. 12424, 10 July 1672.
[42] In chronological order, P.R.O. C.O. 142/13, pp. 36, 192, 51, 194, 63, 198, 222, 219, 234, and 131.
[43] In chronological order, P.R.O. C.O. 142/13, pp. 180, 183, 188, 186, 191, 10, 125, 17, 127, 28, 130, 43, 192, 57, 193, 210, 233, 199, and 88.
[44] In chronological order, P.R.O. C.O. 142/13, pp. 7, 125, 14, 127, 20, 128, 210, and 217.
[45] P.R.O. C.O. 145/13, pp. 217 and 220.
[46] Ibid., pp. 217 and 220.
[47] Ibid., pp. 21, 36, 52, 201, and 78.
[48] Ibid., pp. 17, 30, 50, 61, and 229.
[49] I.R.O. Deeds, liber I, pp. 215-16. It is just possible that the 'captain Stubbs' mentioned was Thomas Stubbs of the *Richard and Sarah*.
[50] I.R.O. Deeds, liber I, fo. 215v.
[51] See P.R.O. C. 110/152, correspondence and accounts of Thomas Brailsford.
[52] Well explained in P.R.O. C.O. 1/54, 139, concerning an Act of 1683 to prevent 'forestalling and regrating' by Port Royal merchants.

[53] On the economic forces generally favouring the factor at the expense of the resident merchant see Richard Pares, *Merchants and planters* (Cambridge, 1960), pp. 47-8.
[54] Claypole, 'The merchants of Port Royal', p. 225.
[55] Recorded by Pares, *Merchants and planters*, p. 6, note 29.
[56] See J. Harry Bennett, 'Cary Helyar, merchant and planter of seventeenth-century Jamaica', in *The William and Mary Quarterly*, xxi (1964), 53-76.
[57] On 'merchants as planters', see Claypole, 'The merchants of Port Royal', pp. 168-94.
[58] Figures quoted by Richard Grassby in 'English merchant capitalism in the late seventeenth century', *Past and present*, xlvi (1970), 92. However, the merchants of Port Royal did at least as well as their counterparts in New England; see Dunn, *Sugar and slaves*, p. 182.

CHAPTER SEVEN

The Topography of Port Royal 1660–1692

In chapter 2 we described the genesis of the town upon the Point. Chapter 4 sketched out the boundaries of Port Royal, behind its fortified line, and chapter 6 described its economic growth. Now it is time to examine in more detail the physical growth of the town, describing as far as possible who lived where and in what kind of structure. As we have seen, many of the early inhabitants of the Point were soldiers, sailors, or officials; the sites of greatest potential lay along the northern harbourside and these were quickly taken up. Almost as quickly, land on the shore between Fort Cromwell and the northernmost point of the cay, bordering on the shoal water called Chocolata Hole, was also claimed; thereafter the less influential had to accept plots on the southern coast and in more central locations.

At no time in the seventeenth century was the area of the town greater than 60 acres, and this lack of space conditioned every aspect of life there. In particular, it meant that there was continuous division and sub-division of property, so that houses, shops, taverns, and storehouses came to be cramped together on every square foot of land.[1] Figure 18 gives a good idea of the way in which houses were crowded together, particularly in the central area. This crowding also meant that from the 1670s onwards those merchants who had come to control the greater part of the land bordering on the harbour began requesting (and receiving) grants of 'shoal water', to be reclaimed 'out of the sea'. This reclaimed land then provided them with both private wharves alongside which large ships could berth, and also additional space for warehouses. Landowners on Fishers' Row, the street which ran parallel to Chocolata Hole (see figure 19) followed suit and eventually provided berthing facilities for the local fleet, based on Chocolata Hole.

The map, taken from one of a number of roughly reliable street-plans of Port Royal before the earthquake, sets out the major streets of

Figure 18 John Fletcher's land, New Street, 1692

the town. They were surprisingly wide; Thames Street for instance averaged at least 20 feet in breadth. From as early as 1664 the width of Church Street and Tower Street had been fixed at 30 feet and it is probable that all the other principal streets were of this breadth.[2] On the other hand, small lanes and alleys which gave access at irregular intervals from one major street to another varied in breadth, and were dependent on arrangements made between adjacent landowners. In general, the plan of Port Royal, established it would seem by Firemaster Nicholas Keene,[3] was reasonably logical if not particularly elegant. It consisted essentially of a rough triangle, with right-angled 'blocks' running from its base up to each of the roughly equal sides; along each of these sides then ran two or three major streets, Fishers' Row and Lime Street to the west and Thames Street, Queen Street, and High Street to the east. Outside this general schema lay Fort Charles to the west and the section of High Street leading to Fort Rupert in the east.

The streets were poorly surfaced with unconsolidated sand, and remained in this condition from the start until 1692. Their disgraceful condition was a constant source of embarrassment and, no doubt, the bane of housewives. A grand jury in November 1662 complained to the governor and council of the need for 'hardening and making even the streets', and there ensued a proclamation, issued more in hope than expectation:

> The Governor and Council, presuming upon the inclinations and readiness of all the inhabitants fit so to work, are not forward to impose upon them by order, but had rather recommend the same to masters of families and other owners of houses, to make choice among themselves of well-qualified, discreet and deserving persons to carry on so good a work by the assistance of Mr John Man, Esq., Surveyor-General.[4]

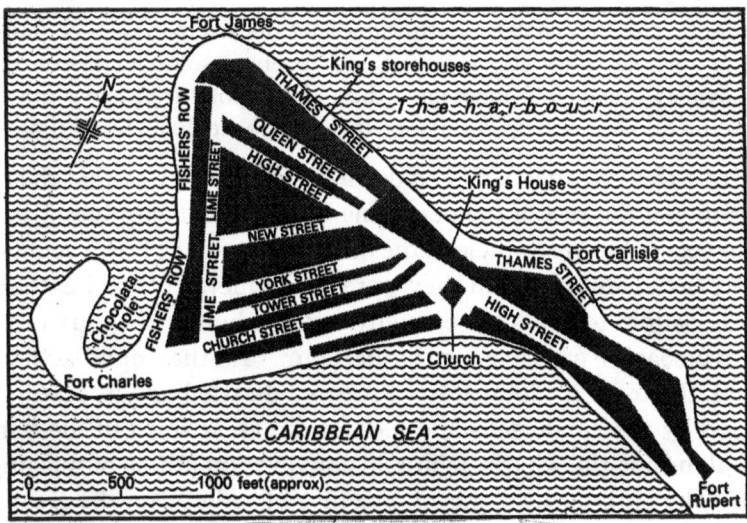

Figure 19   Street plan of Port Royal before 1692

Topography   111

Few if any volunteers seem to have come forward, and the streets remained in the same deplorable condition. It would in fact have been very remarkable if the inhabitants of Port Royal had troubled to pave their streets, particularly with stone in relatively short supply, for scarcely any of the towns of 'English' America had done so at this time.[5] The only area so treated was the general parade ground 'nigh the Palisado gate', where the town's infantry regiment went through its paces; this was paved with brick.[6]

The physical topography of the town remained much the same until the earthquake, though the years 1683 and 1684 did see temporary modifications. In 1683, fierce northerly winds caused havoc in the harbour,[7] so that:

> most of the shipps and others vessels ... broke loose from their moorings and fell foule with one another, and beat their sides on the wharfes; nay, such was the force of the blustering and turbulent seas that Port Royal was in danger to be sunk, for the sea broak in upon the Point and overflowed it to Morgan's Line, and seeing the point lies very low, and that the surface above the rock is only a loose sand, the sea by its breaking in made several channels quite through it to the harbour, and much damnified the edifices and buildings towards the sea by washing and spoyling their foundations ....

The following year the weather left a more ominous mark still upon the little town,[8] for:

> there came such violent south winds that the sea rose and overflowed the port, such was its violence that it oversett some houses on Port Royal and made a channel quite through the point from the south sea to the harbour, soe deep and long that ferry-boats [could sail] therein.

By 1688 this channel had been drained and bridged, so that the burial ground and the rest of the peninsula beyond the Palisadoes gate were again accessible; nevertheless, the inhabitants of Port Royal could never forget the extent of which they were at the mercy of the weather.

All visitors to the town came by water, whether they arrived from far overseas or from across the harbour.[9] As they approached Port Royal, the town itself must have seemed dwarfed and its features obscured by the spars, sails and flags of the great ships in the harbour and alongside the wharfs; figure 20 conveys something of this impression. The harbour itself was often a hive of activity, for the great ships lay alongside the wharves during as short a time as possible before hauling off to anchor in the harbour, and there was a constant traffic

Figure 20 Edward Barlow, View of Port Royal (National Maritime Museum)

between them and the shore, mixed in with residents' sloops, shallops, and rowing boats. These small vessels anchored or were moored in the relatively shallow water of the Chocolata Hole, leaving the northern side of the harbour to the big ships. Picking their way through the mass of shipping, these would slowly warp up to one of the wharves which stretched in an almost unbroken line from Fort James to Fort Carlisle; only before the King's House was there no wharf.

Often visitors came ashore at the Wherry Bridge, where was perhaps the main landing-stage.[10] This gave directly on to Thames Street,

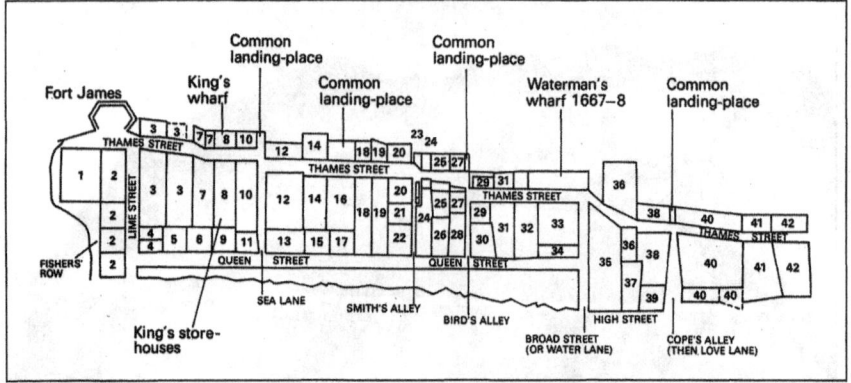

Figure 21 Detailed plan of part of Port Royal before 1692

the broad sandy roadway which stretched the whole length of the harbourside. This waterfront scene was one of continual movement between the berthed ships and the warehouses on the south side of the street; imported goods of all kinds moving southwards into the storehouses and sugar, indigo, rum, and other tropical goods moving northwards on to the wharf and into the ships' holds.

Across Thames Street and slightly to the west of the Wherry Bridge was the fish market; directly opposite the bridge was the entrance to a private alley surmounted by a brick archway.[11] On the land to the west of this alley stood 'The Feathers', a tavern leased in July 1681 by Thomas and Ann Mills from Edward Moulder, who owned the whole site (marked '49' on figure 21).[12] This building, though referred to as a tavern, seems in fact to have been designed for the sale of wines and to have occupied the site of an earlier 'Feathers' tavern; it was 'newly-built with brick' and comprised 'a large shop with a large entry with a large balcony room over them and another room over that, behind which said premises there is a large room or bed-chamber and a cellar, all of very old buildings'. The tavern yard included 'an arbour and house of office, a cookroom of brick next to it, a large lower room with a partition, and a billiard-room over that, with a large pair of stairs going upp to it'. On the eastern side of the alley was another inn, 'The Three Tunns'. This tavern was already operating in December 1665, when it was bought by Thomas Freeman from Charles Whitfield, merchant.[13]

From the Wherry Bridge, a visitor could reach the High Street either by going westwards, through the fish market and so through an eight-foot passage, or else by turning eastwards and taking Honey Lane. The latter route would take him past Captain Penhallow's tavern 'The Three

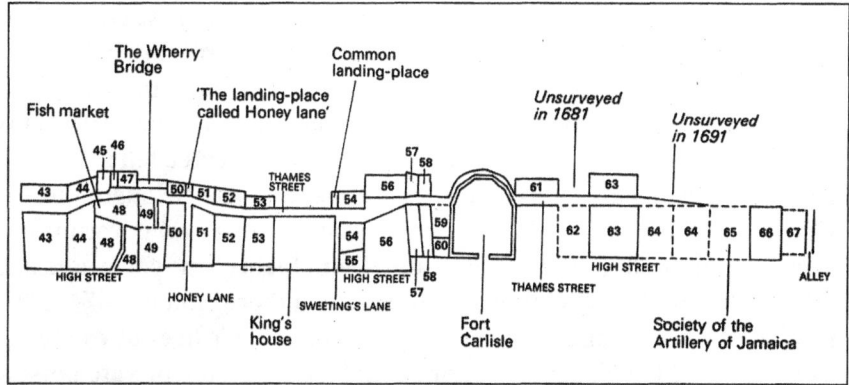

Figure 21 (continued)

Mariners' (50). Honey Lane derived its name from the original patentee, Lieutenant Thomas Honeyman, and was about 150 feet long.[14] 'The Three Mariners' was originally owned, and probably built, by a Frenchman, Peter Bartaboa, who operated it for many years in partnership with a fellow-countryman, John Grandmaison.[15] Bartaboa was a carpenter of some repute; he built the town gallows in 1666 for £3[16] and probably the ducking-stool as well, for which the fee was £10.[17] South of 'The Three Mariners' on Honey Lane was a complex of houses and yards, in which the principal building was the house and shop of Thomas and Alice Lockyer, a well stocked drapery (50).[18]

The plot on the eastern side of Honey Lane was patented to Mr. Peter Coveney in 1663, but it was soon sub-divided. Next to this plot was the land and wharf (52) owned in 1682 by Henry Watson, goldsmith. On the northern part of the site, fronting on to Thames Street, stood 'The Salutacon', a tavern leased for many years to Randolph Bolton. To the east again of this property lay the land and wharf of Peter Beckford, described in 1681 as a merchant of Saint Jago de la Vega (53). This plot had originally belonged to Captain Cornelius Burrough, steward-general of the army, and was granted to him by D'Oyley in September 1659. When it came into Peter Beckford's hands it probably still retained Burrough's original buildings - the timber dwelling-house and the storehouse built between September 1659 and April 1660.[19] It was not until four years after he had purchased the land that Beckford applied for and received 'a parcel of land being shoalwater to be recovered for wharf-ground'.[20]

Next to Beckford's property to the east was the most important official site in the town - the King's House and grounds. We do not know its

Topography 115

exact dimensions, but it is likely to have been the largest site in Port Royal. As we have noticed in chapter 2, the whole structure was at first surrounded by a stockade, but by 1683 this had been replaced by a brick wall.[21] King's House does not seem to have found favour with many of the governors or their lieutenants, and being neglected fell into disrepair. Lord Vaughan referred to it as 'a mean house belonging to the King',[22] but in spite of its dilapidation the arrival of a new governor was always celebrated there with a great dinner. Lieutenant-governors and other high-ranking officials sometimes stayed there, and in 1674 it was resolved by the Council 'that when no public officer lives at the King's House in Port Royal, the governor should let it to some private person, that the rent might value the reparation'.[23] In short, the old house was kept up with a minimum of expenditure,[24] to survive until 1692.

The King's House and its yard fronted north on to Thames Street, south on to High Street, and east on to Sweeting's Lane. The latter was named after Mr. Henry Sweeting, merchant of London, who early received the northern section of the next block (54). On the southern section, allocated to Surveyor-General John Man (55) there were in 1682 several messuages, including a shop 'whereof containeth 25 feet in length and 19 feet in breadth, together with the dining-room and other rooms over the same, being of the like dimensions, and the storehouse thereto adjoining containing 19 feet square and also a kitchen'.[25] John Man, by his will of 9 November 1664, appointed William Beeston his executor, and Beeston sold the plot on 22 June 1668 to John Belfield, who in turn left it to his son John. Belfield the elder, a notable Port Royal merchant, had rented the house on the site to Mr. John Maxwell, who was still in possession at Belfield's death.[26] Maxwell, 'a Scotchman', was minister at the Port Royal Anglican Church, but had to find his own lodging. As Sir Thomas Lynch reported in 1671:

> in all the parishes on the south side there is not a foot of land to be had for a church, king or public; all is appropriated after so disorderly a fashion that the town of Port Royal is rendered unhealthy for want of streets and public commodities, nor is there hardly left landing-places, and there is neither house, land, nor other conveniency for the king or his ministers.[27]

Lynch was surely exaggerating, but it is true that public buildings occupied a relatively subsidiary place in the general plan of Port Royal.

The next plot to the east (56) was that patented on 20 February 1661 to Richard Brock. He was a carpenter who almost certainly came with the expeditionary forces of 1655, and helped to build many of the early public buildings: the King's House itself, the first (oak) church or 'market house', and the wooden court-house. He died leaving 'two only daughters being then orphans', and his land was sold by the justices of the peace and churchwardens of the port to Hender Molesworth to defray the cost of maintaining the children.[28] Still moving east on High Street, we come to the plots originally owned by the merchant John Loving (57) and Edward Tunstall (58). Neither of these has been identified with buildings of any commercial or social significance, but there is little doubt that they too were heavily built up with dwelling-houses and stores.

Between Tunstall's plot and the western wall of Fort Carlisle was a waterside plot (59) granted in Brayne's time to Captain Marke Harrison of the naval ship *Gift*. Other than a brief reference to the holding by D'Oyley in his journal,[29] we have no documentation to throw light on later owners; neither can we trace any grant of the shoal-water. This absence of references suggests that the land escheated at an early date to the Crown, and it may well be that on this undeveloped site either the Marshallsea prison for men or the Bridewell prison 'for lazie strumpets' was subsequently built. In his manuscript, Taylor makes contradictory statements on the subject, for after affirming that 'the Marshallsea is the prison house standing nigh the Palisadoes gate', he adds that 'now we pass along by the wharf-side untill we come up to the Marshallsea, where we find another strong breastwork called Carlisle Fort'.[30] Since Fort Carlisle and the Palisadoes gate were separated by a considerable length of High Street, the Marshallsea could not be close to both of them; no doubt Taylor was confusing the two prisons.

Passing the forecourt of Fort Carlisle, and continuing eastwards along High Street, the land began to narrow towards the Palisadoes gate. On the left soon appeared the land bordering directly on the harbour (65) which had been purchased by Simon Musgrave as treasurer of the Society of the Artillery of Jamaica in January 1677;[31] this served both as headquarters and as practice ground. The Society, which had some 50 members resident in Port Royal,[32] does not seem to have been directly connected with the Honourable Artillery Company in London, though some of the members of the Jamaica Society may well have been former members of the company. To the east of the society's grounds was a plot (66) patented to Mr. John Mayne in August 1668,[33] when it was sold to a planter from Vere, it had been for a while in the occupation of Captain John Coxen, the notorious buccaneer.[34]

Figure 22 William Hack, Plan of Port Royal (British Library)

High Street ended in the parade ground, and beyond this was the gate and bridge giving access to the burial ground, which lay well outside the town. Here too was the site of Barre's tavern, a popular rendezvous in the cool of the evening.[35] Figures 20, 22 and 23 all show some kind of structure beyond the gate, and in his map of 1683 (figure 22) William Hack goes so far as to call these buildings 'Islington'. Taylor does not mention Islington, but he does claim that on Pelican Point there was 'a fine house and garden built by one Mr. Swettman'.[36] Otherwise the Palisadoes spit was probably neglected, and partially covered with the same kind of scrub and cactus as grows on much of it today.

Retracing our steps along High Street, we should eventually come back to Honey Lane and the Lockyers' shop (50). The plot to the west of them (49) had originally been granted to Captain Epsley Englefield,[37] and in May 1670, after several other changes of owner, was sold to

David Gomez, merchant of Port Royal. On the plot was an old house called 'Corker's house', and in the north-east corner of the land was an area five feet square 'whereon an oven is now erected'.[38] As this oven is mentioned in several transactions concerning the property, it was probably of some commercial significance.

To the west of this plot was a site which eventually came into the possession of Mr. John Loving (48 east), followed across the alley by one which had been bought in 1664 by Ceasar Carter, churchwarden of Port Royal, from the victualler Mary Dayton (48 west). When Carter sold the land in April 1689, it contained several dwelling-houses and other messuages, one of them occupied by Mr. Fox the shoemaker.[39] Westwards again was a plot originally owned by Captain John Wilgress, who in October 1658 was building a wooden house there.[40] Wilgress subsequently left Jamaica, returning to Lower Shadwell 'in the parish of Stepney, Middlesex', and the land was eventually sold to Dr. Anthony Cartwright in 1670.[41] Further transactions concerning this plot have not survived, but if its ownership followed the trend of that of other plots on the northern side of High Street, it would not long have remained in Dr. Cartwright's hands but would have passed into those of some wealthy merchant.

A similar absence of information prevents us from writing much about the next plot westwards, owned in the early days by Mr. Arthur Towne (43; see also chapter 2). On the plot to the west of this (42) we are better informed; it was first patented by Mr. John Man, surveyor-general, and remained in his family until September 1670, at which date it contained 'a dwelling-house, a storehouse and other buildings'.[42] It was then bought by the merchant Samuel Lewis, who four years later sold it to another merchant, Thomas Hudson. The latter proceeded 'to pull down a greate part thereof and has erected thereon since one large messuage or mansion house and other tenements which are now, or late were, in the possession of Captain Samuel Bach and the said Thomas Hudson'.[43]

Westwards again lay the plot owned first by Captain John Shaw, and then by Richard Pepys (41). This site is a good example of the rising value of harbourside properties, for while Pepys sold it for £22 in August 1667 to Hender Molesworth, the latter sold it in May 1672 for £55 to Benjamin Whitcombe, after whose death it was sold by his creditors in August 1680 for £250 to Edward Yeomans, and even this figure did not include the 'Shoal water for a wharf', which Yeomans bought the following year for £15.[44] Incidentally, the lowness of this price surely attests that the land had not been reclaimed.

The same Edward Yeomans also acquired the northern part of the plot immediately to the west of here, part of which he subsequently let to Robert Snead (or Sneed) 'late of the city of London, architect', for a term of 13 years from 14 August 1684.[45] The deed referring to this transaction contains one of the most illuminating references to the style of building in Port Royal at this time. Snead, 'at his own proper cost', was required to 'build three or four substantial houses, fronting to the harbour, each to have a cookroom and a house of office, with a balcony to each house fronting to the sea northward, of eight feet long and three and a half feet in the cheare'.[46] There follows a detailed description:

> The foundations of all the buildings to bee of stone, two and a half feet thick, and one foot above the surface and superfices of the ground, and 22 feet southward, and from the stone building thence to be built upp to the water-table two and half bricks, and from there to the first floor two bricks thick, which to be ten feet in the cheare and carried with a brick and one half cleare upp to ye gable ends, and that the carpentry work and scantlings of timber and other necessaryes bee as followeth; viz.,
>
> The door-cases in the front to be seven and an half and six inches, the lower door cases to be five feet wide in the cheare and nine feet high with a proporconable light in each door, and that the gerders of the first floor shall be twelve inches and thirteen, and the joists shall be six inches and three and framed at fifteen inches distance, and that the principal rafters shall be of no less than nine inches and six at the bottom and six inches square at the top. The purloines to be six and eight inches, wall-plates the same, and that the beams of the upper floor shall be ten and nine inches, the joists four and three inches at fourteen inches distance, and for the roof that it bee framed and the rafters and joists all well tenanted and primed with substantial and lasting prime.
>
> The gerders and beams planed and moulded, the joists also planed on both sides, and that the . . . bee framed and painted in all lengths of the front, with good large cornishes, and the shingles bored, primed and laid, and a sufficient pent-house even with the balcony the whole length of the house, and that all and every of the necessary timber for the building be of some or of one of the following: mahogany, cedar, bullett tree, yellow saunders, black-hearted fiddle-wood, base terre, lignum vitae, fustick, manchioniel or logwood and no other, the roof only excepted, in which it may be lawful to use Spanish elm, the timber and windows shall be suitable and proportionable to the buildings, with Lutherian lights in the garretts, and the windows shall be painted, the garretts sealed, and the balconyes well leaded.

From about 1679 onwards, it seems to have become the general practice when new buildings were planned to specify the following foundations for outer load-bearing walls:

> *Single-storey buildings:* two bricks thick to the water-table and then one-and-a-half bricks to the wall plates *Two- or more storey buildings:* two and a half bricks thick to the water-table (or sometimes stone in place of brick), and then two bricks thick to the first floor.

These specifications seem to have applied not only to buildings by the harbourside, but also to those in the rest of the town; they might help future archaeological investigators to determine with considerable accuracy the pre-earthquake water-table level.

To the west of Snead's four houses was an alley originally known as Cope's Alley, after Major John Cope, an early patentee.[47] Some time

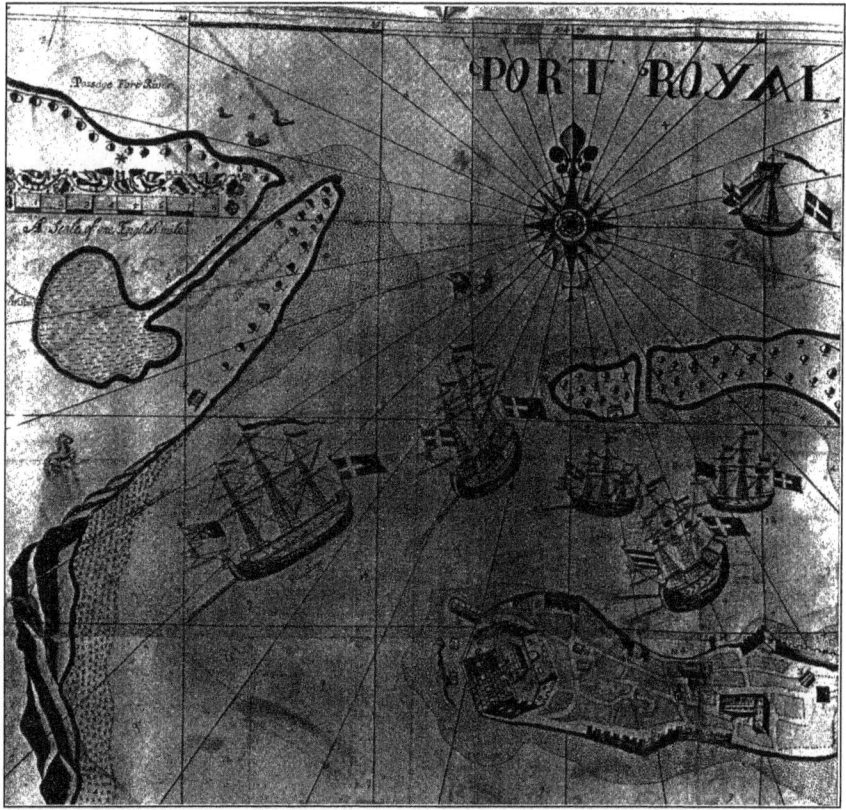

Figure 23 John Taylor, Plan of Port Royal (National Library of Jamaica)

between January 1663 and August 1664 its name was changed to Love Lane; at its northern end, across Thames Street, was a common landing-place. The land bordering on the west of Love Lane was originally granted in two sections. The northern part (38) belonged to Major John Cope, and by 1686 had passed to Mr. Thomas Sutton,[48] while the southern half had a succession of owners.[49] In 1663 it was owned by a cordwainer who left it to his son; a moiety of it was then split again to be acquired by two coopers. The two halves were then combined again and sold to a merchant, who in turn sold the plot to a vintner, and by January 1689 it was again in the hands of a merchant - Charles Knight.

Simon Musgrave, treasurer of the Society of the Artillery of Jamaica, owned the southern part of the next plot to the west (39). He did not retain it for long, for having received his patent in October 1681, he sold the land six months later to Sir Thomas Lynch.[50] Lynch's major Port Royal holding was the plot he acquired to the west of Musgrave (35), patented to him on 3 March 1664,[51] though he probably occupied it long before the patent was granted. He built on the site a large timber house described in 1664 as the 'New Prison';[52] indeed, it served for many years in this capacity. It was not until 1685 that the Council of Jamaica ordered that the work on another prison should begin, following a recommendation to them which remarked *inter alia* that 'there having been hitherto none in this island . . . [save]. . . that belonging to the late patentee for the Marshall's place, which would now be converted to other uses, whereby the island would be wholly destitute of a place of security to keep prisoners in'.[53] Lynch, then, had been provost marshal from 1661 until his death in August 1684, using his house as a prison. Even before his death he had been selling off some of the land around his prison-house; in February 1683, for instance, he sold a section to Lieutenant-Colonel William Parker for £300,[54] and almost a year later bought from Parker at the same price the latter's land and wharf to the east of Fort Carlisle (63).[55]

Lynch's plot, one of the largest private ones in Port Royal, provided the western end of the landholdings bounding north on Thames Street and south to High Street. From this point westwards, marked by what was originally called Broad Street and later became Water Lane, High Street continued westwards until it joined Lime Street at the western end of the town, and a further highway called Queen Street now paralleled High Street some hundred feet to the north. This had the desirable effect of splitting into a reasonable size what would otherwise have been plots of excessively large north-south dimensions.

We have sited the Watermen's Wharf at the head of Water Lane (the change of name may well be significant), because only here was there sufficient room to allocate the watermen a space 150 feet long by 42 feet deep, and only here were there no grants of shoal water for private construction. Here the watermen had an area set aside 'for the use of their boats and wherryes to make wharfs or bridges', patented on 10 February 1668 to 'Joel Clements and the rest of the watermen of Port Royal'.[56] Clements was the negotiator for the patent and no doubt the watermen's representative; from here they must have distributed huge quantities of water each day, for there were virtually no local supplies of drinkable water (see chapter 8).

As we have seen, Queen Street struck off westwards about 100 feet up Water Lane, and it is this route that we must follow in order to examine the rest of the harbourside properties, stretching westwards to Fort James. The first of these belonged to Marke Harrison, at any rate in its northern section (33), but we know little about it.[57] The same is true of the next plot to the west, in the possession of Edward Tunstall (32). The one to the west of this (31) originally belonged to Richard Povey, and was leased for many years to the merchant William Crane;[58] unfortunately the boundary measurements are never mentioned in any deed relating to the property.

The next site to the west was originally allotted in two parts, the northern (29) to Abraham Langford in July 1659,[59] and the southern (30) to Richard Richardson in January 1669.[60] Both plots eventually came into the hands of the merchant Anthony Swymmer. The most unusual architectural feature of the site was the size of the main warehouse, which 'fronted the said harbour and extended to Queen Street', making it close on 130 feet in length; it was called 'the long storehouse'.[61] There were at least four other buildings on the northern boundary of the land fronting to Thames Street. One was at the intersection with Bird's Alley; Swymmer let this to Henry Ward, merchant. To the east of this was the house and shop occupied by Swymmer himself, then a shop in the tenure of the merchant George Cole, whose wife was a Negress, and then a shop rented by Swymmer to John Tull the cooper. Tull also rented the whole of the wharf from Swymmer, but permitted him the use of it 'to shipp, load or unload all manner of goods and merchandizes which shall be the produce of Swymmer's plantacion in Saint Thomas, and also the use of the weights'.[62] The weights were part of the standard equipment of a Port Royal wharf; in view of the high berthing charges, Swymmer's goods were 'not to remain on the wharf above the space of two full working days together'.

The harbourside from this point and stretching as far west as Humphrey Freeman's wharf was known colloquially as 'the little seaside' (the name recurs in several deeds). This part of the harbour was of course fully taken up with wharves, and certainly had no beach; clearly the name 'seaside' had a connotation rather different from its present one. On the western side of Bird's Alley was the plot owned by another of the port's early merchants - Richard Bird. It was at first two separate plots, the northern one (27) owned by Arthur Towne, but this was early purchased from him by Bird, who already owned the southern one (28) and so now the whole site.[63] The most notable building here was the one known as 'the white storehouse', rented by a certain Elizabeth Howatt (or Hewitt), who by profession was a 'femme sole, dealer'.[64] The next plots to the west were first granted to William King (25) and Arthur Towne (26); by 1672 Towne's land had become the property of John Ellis and by 1679 Bird's was in the hands of the merchants Bach and Hudson.[65] Both these plots, like the others in this vicinity, contained a wide variety of buildings.

The most westerly plot between Bird's Alley and Smith's Alley was that owned by William King (24) and patented to him in November 1662.[66] Smith's Alley (the western boundary of the original King's Land) derived its name from the house and forge situated in its own small plot at the exit to Thames Street. The forge was built during D'Oyley's administration, in 1658, and it was here that the 'iron worke, as lockes, keys, hinges, bolts, staples etc.' were made for the commander-in-chief's house, later called the King's House. Whether or not the house and forge eventually passed into private hands is not specifically revealed by the surviving documents, but in 1668 a storehouse measuring 20 feet by 40 feet and bounding 'north on the smith's shop' was sold by John Lewis to George Hume (or Home).[67] Eventually the site came into the hands of Robert Phillips, sailmaker, and no doubt contained a sail loft.

The owner of the next plot (20) was Humphrey Freeman, who in June 1659 received land 'between the state's storehouse and the state's forge'.[68] He still owned the site in March 1683, when he let to Thomas Watson and John Wells, merchants, 'all that messuage or tenement front to the little seaside commonly called or known as the King's Arms, adjoining to a messuage or tenement now in the occupation of Josua [sic] Feake, merchant, on the one side and Smith's Alley on the other side, with all storehouses etc. and the use of the yard'.[69]

Immediately south of Freeman was land patented in 1662 to Colonel Samuel Barry (21),[70] and south again from Barry's land was a plot belonging to Henry Sweeting. This latter plot came into the hands of Jacob Haynes and with it the tavern called 'The Green Dragon'. This inn was let in September 1679 to William Hanson, blacksmith of Port Royal, with the proviso that Hanson:

> at his own proper cost and charge shall within twelve months next ensuing well and sufficiently repair, rebuild and make upp all the old houses which now are or were late standing upon the demised premises, and build one room more upon some part of the premises, at least 18 feet long and 16 feet broad, which said room shall be built of brick, the wall thereof to be at least two bricks thick to the water-table, and to the wall plates 1, and likewise so to make up and set up a new cook-roome in place of the old one, to be at least of the same dimensions, which cook-roome shall be built with brick, the wall thereof to be at least two bricks thick to the water-table, and to the wall plates 1. The chimney also to be well and substantially brought up with brick, and also that he, the said William Hanson, shall from time to time during the lease maintain and keep the said messuage and premises in good condition.[71]

The next two plots to the west (18 and 19) were originally a single holding granted by D'Oyley to Captain Collyer and Lieutenant Edgoose on 13 December 1660.[72] It seems that each took a moiety, Collyer the western half and Edgoose the eastern. By January 1676 Thomas Martyne, merchant, had acquired almost the whole of Edgoose's plot, while Sir Thomas Lynch and Nicholas Hicks (another merchant) had acquired Collyer's land.[73]

On the western boundary of Collyer's plot was the land granted to Henry Archbould by General Brayne and patented to him in November 1664.[74] Although the specific deeds are missing, we know that he sold it to William Shute, who owned it in April 1682.[75] Three years earlier a certain Captain Shotter was noted by H.M.S. *Hunter*'s captain as owning a wharf here, as well as others on the harbourside; our Shute may well be none other than this Shotter.[76] Between Shute's plot and Sea Lane to the west, were the lands of Joseph Deakins, Colonel Thomas Freeman, and Colonel John Colebeck (12, 13, and 14). No doubt these too were heavily built up with storehouses and dwellings, but nothing of architectural significance is mentioned in the deeds concerning them.[77] Across Thames Street and opposite the entrance to Sea Lane was the site of the most westerly 'common landing-place' on the harbourside.

Immediately to the west of Sea Lane was Sir James Modyford's land (10), which had been leased to William Moire (or More) in March 1679, at which date it contained 'all that messuage or tenement and three warehouses commonly called and known as Sir James Modyford's house and storehouse'.[78] This was part of Moire's lease; he also had 'the free use of the wharf lying before the same'. South of Modyford's land was a small plot (11) which had originally belonged to Captain Thomas Fuller. It escheated to the Crown at an unknown date and was eventually patented to the astute merchant, Anthony Swymmer, who sold it in January 1677 to the sailmaker Robert Phillips.[79] Also included in Swymmer's plot was part of the next plot to the west (9b), which in 1665 belonged to Lieutenant Edward Willis.

From the northern boundary of this last-named plot, stretching up to the harbourside (8), was the land on which the original state's storehouse had been built before the Restoration. Evidence suggests that the land set aside for this purpose encompassed all that area from Sea Lane in the east to the land later acquired by Roger Hill in the west, a plot 165 feet wide and 150 feet deep (7, 8, and 10).[80] However, the grants made to Modyford and Hill eroded a considerable amount of this area, so that the Crown never enjoyed an unbroken stretch of warehouse land 234 feet wide.[81]

When Roger Hill was granted a patent on 7 May 1669 for land directly to the west of the king's storehouses (7) he also received one of these storehouses.[82] Two weeks after the date of the patent, Hill sold a portion of the land to Sir Thomas Modyford, who five years later sold out to the merchant Nicholas Hicks. On the land he retained for himself, Hill built 'a certain messuage or tenement one storey high containing four rooms',[83] which, together with the land, he left to his wife Ann. She remarried after Hill's death, and with her second husband, Richard Holman, then sold the building (and probably others erected at a later date) to the merchant John Moone. By July 1680 the property had come into the hands of a gunsmith, John Phillpot.[84]

West of Roger Hill was an extensive plot (3), surveyed in July 1669 and patented the following September to John Hay, who was first victualler and then merchant. Here Hay built the tavern 'The Catt and Fiddle' and ran it with his wife Susannah. This tavern was on the western part of the plot, which Hay eventually sold to James Lyttleton, merchant of London. It is highly improbable that Lyttleton ever ran the place himself, or even visited Port Royal for that matter; after his death the property descended to his son James, gentleman of the parish of Saint Thomas and planter there, who no doubt continued the lease to William Nash. On 25 March 1689 James Lyttleton sold the land and 'The Catt and Fiddle' to Moses Watkins, carpenter of Port Royal, for £800;[85] it is from this tavern that some of the artefacts recovered by the Link-Smithsonian-National Geographic expedition are believe to have come.[86]

The intersection of Lime Street and Thames Street marked the end of the major harbourside properties and wharves. Lime Street continued almost due south and ended in the open parade area in front of Fort Charles, whose development has been described in chapter 4. Thames Street terminated in the large block held by John Man, and eventually in Fort James, also described in chapter 4. The latter fort was built on 'Bonham's Point', but the only thing we know about this person is that the adjacent grant to John Man (1), of either 28 November 1664 or 18 March 1665,[87] described his plot as being '100 feet east on land now or late of . . . Bonhor's (a copyist's error for 'Bonham'). Bonham's land (2) became the forecourt of Fort James, providing room to assemble and muster troops in the event of an alarm; it must have escheated to the Crown quite early on. However, not all of Bonham's land remained in the possession of the Crown, for two plots to the south (2), granted to Anne Thorne and James Galloway, are described as land formerly 'King's ground for a forte'.[88]

The stretch of harbourside which we have been describing no doubt contained the majority of the largest warehouses and finest dwellings, but it would be a mistake to imagine that even here there were nothing but merchant mansions, for among the large houses were plenty of humble artisans' dwellings; rich and poor were similarly mixed together in the rest of the town,[89] which became just as heavily built up as the harbourside. None of the houses at Port Royal had chimneys, for heating was unnecessary and cooking was done in the cook-room, a separate building in the yard. Some of these yards are described as having a 'well', but this could not of course have been a well in the accepted sense of the term, since brackish, salty water lies everywhere just a few feet (or even sometimes inches) below the surface. What were called 'wells' were probably in fact cisterns, built of brick in the traditional round shape, and sunk a little way into the ground (figure 24).

Port Royal, like most towns of seventeenth-century England, had its own parish land or common. This consisted of 1,100 acres 'which appurtences, situate, lying and being in the parish of Port Royal, com-

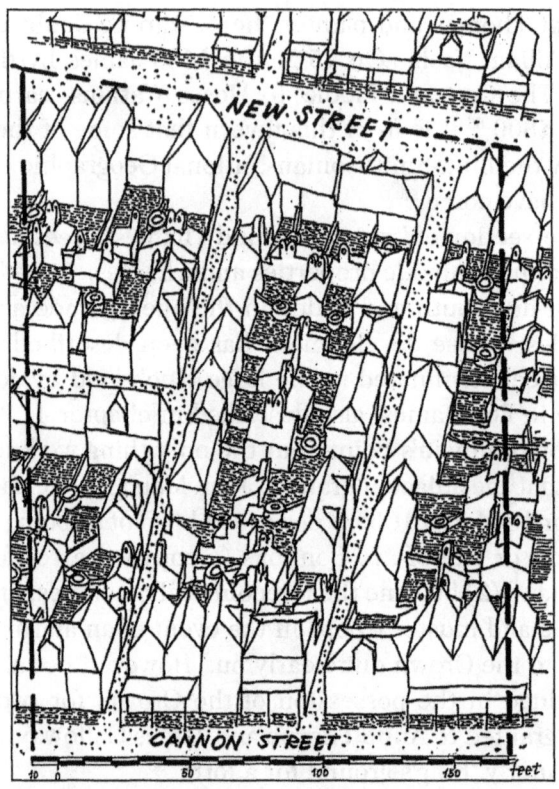

Figure 24 Houses and backyards between Cannon and New Streets, c. 1690. The outlined area represents one acre.

monly called or known by the name of the Pallisadoes', and was granted by letters patent dated 23 March 1667.[90] Such an acreage must have comprised most of the long chain of cays which spread eastwards from Port Royal itself to the mainland. Its western extremity was only a short distance to the east of the Palisadoes gate, and the topography of this area is neatly revealed by a deed of 29 January 1689 between Mary Barre and Elias Norero (or Norarrau), a merchant of Port Royal.[91] In June 1684, it seems, Reginald Wilson and John White, churchwardens of the parish:

> did let unto Edith Cottman of the Parish aforesaid a certain parcel of land lying and being without the Pallisadoes towards the harbourside, containing 80 feet in breadth and 140 feet in depth with all edifices, houses, buildings, etc. thereon erected, and also two acres of pasturage beyond the bite not far from the said parcel of land, being part and parcel of the said 100 acres [i.e., the common] from the 14th June for a

full term of eleven years at a yearly rent of one pound current money of Jamaica payable to the said Churchwardens by quarterly payments.

On 30 July 1685 the new churchwardens, Henry Ward and Joseph Jennings, reaffirmed Cottman's lease, and in the following November Cottman sold to Charles Barre 'all her right, title and interest in both parcels, together with 90 goats, 6 cows, 1 bull and 7 calves' for an unknown sum. Barre ran a tavern there with his wife Mary, and after his death she on 20 January 1689 sold to the merchant Norero the lease of the land with the tavern and pasturage for £450. Included in the goods were one bull, eight milch cows, two heifers, six calves, two steers, 90 goats (still), one canoe, one white maid servant called Elizabeth Fuller, and all the household appurtenances.

At the eastward end the Port Royal common did not quite reach the intersection with the mainland, for in September 1683 John Bendfield of 'Yallah' and Eleazer Wignall of Morant, gentlemen, 'as guardians to the children of Jacob Stokes deceased', rented to Samuel Richardson, bricklayer of Port Royal, 'all the parcel of land commonly called or known by the name of the Goate Pens, lying in the parish of Port Royal and containing by estimation 300 acres bounding north upon the sea within the harbour, south upon the great sea and west upon the parish land of Port Royal'.[92] The town limits, then, ended at the Palisadoes gate, at which point there was a bridge across the channel formed by the hurricane of 1684. Immediately beyond this on the northern side, quite close to the harbour, was the Barres' tavern, and a little further to the east lay the burial-ground, of unknown dimensions. After that came the pasturage, which terminated in the 300 acres called the Goat Pens.

Of the public buildings, we have described the fortifications in chapter 4 and have said something about prisons and the governors' residence in the course of our description of the town. As we shall see in chapter 8, there were several varieties of religious belief represented at Port Royal, but the places of worship of their adherents are singularly hard to identify, except for the Jewish synagogue. The site of this is precisely given by a deed of 29 January 1677,[93] in which John Peeke sold for £57 a plot of land 63 feet in length and 36 feet in breadth to the Jewish community of Port Royal represented by Abraham David Gabay, Moses Jesurum Cordosa, Arpenasus, and a further Gabay. The plot bounded south on Cannon Street, north on New Street, east on George Pattinson, and west on Michael Marriott, and the synagogue was constructed some time between January 1677 and March 1686.

The Presbyterians or Nonconformists certainly had a meeting-house, but it does not appear to be identifiable; perhaps they met on the premises of Colonel Samuel Bach, one of the leading members of their community. Certainly the Catholics had a room set aside for them in the house of James Castillo, agent for the asiento; this was a chapel 'capable of holding 300 persons',[94] but all trace of it has vanished. The leading Quakers were altogether less prominent men, and the site of their meeting-house is completely unknown. Even the site of the successive Anglican churches is the subject of much speculation; we have attempted to set out their sequence in appendix 3.

In the earliest days at the Point, as we have seen, each naval vessel had a special berth assigned to it on the waterfront, with an adjacent storehouse. This system rapidly faded out, as the naval ships went back to England and more and more merchants became eager to buy plots of land on the harbourside. By 1685 it was being drawn to the attention of the king.[95]

> that the Governors of Jamaica hitherto have minded soe little Your Majesty's service and interest doth appear by want of care to preserve a place in Port Royal for Your Majesty's ships to careene, and several sums of money have been paid for a storehouse. It appears a strange neglect, not to have reserved a place for His Majesty's service, the Governors themselves being they that disposed of all the land at Port Royal, not above 15 years ago. They have not been soe negligent in their own concerns . . .

Following this criticism, it appears that a careening-place was assigned to the navy at a certain unpatented wharf. But even this semi-official facility was subject to mercantile encroachment; in 1687, for instance, a 'bridge lately built upon the wharfe where His Majesty's shipps usually careene'[96] had to be removed. One way and another, the position of naval captains with vessels needing repair must have been very unsatisfactory.

This inadequacy of arrangements for careening reflects the way in which Port Royal had developed primarily under the impetus of private economic pressures, and only very secondarily in response to the requirements of the Crown. In this respect, as in many others, Port Royal offers a striking contrast with the Spanish town at Saint Jago de la Vega. There, the Spaniards had laid out a chequer-board city in which, as usual with them, pride of place went to the public buildings, lay and ecclesiastical. There is no problem in discovering where the main church or the governor's palace or the main courthouse is in a Spanish-designed city. In comparison with this orderly and public-minded plan Port Royal presented a less coherent layout in which public buildings were inserted at random; even when the Crown had secured plots like those of Fort James and the king's storehouses, for instance, they were liable to encroachment, and King's House itself seems to have fallen into a pretty squalid state.

Of course, the Spaniards had the advantage of much more space than was available at Port Royal, when they laid their city out at Saint Jago on the broad plain beside the Rio Cobre. They also had the advantage of a longer experience of building in the tropics; though the main buildings might be noble edifices of stone, the private houses were for the most part unpretentious structures, described by Taylor as 'low timber-work houses, thatched with palm-leaves, being but one storey high, paved with tiles, having lattice windows and great doors . . .'.[97] The English, on the other hand, built at the Point just as if they had never left some shire-town in the Old Country, putting up - especially after the 1670s - splendid brick houses of several stories,[98] and building a church which with its battlemented tower and splendid aisles might have come straight from East Anglia. It is a great pity that we have no really reliable views of the town before 1692. Figures 20 and 22 seem to be sketching in high-gabled houses like those in contemporary Bridgetown, Barbados, and this has led one authority to write of the 'Dutch influence' at Port Royal.[99] It may be that we should visualize the town as looking rather like one of those shire towns of eastern England which were growing fast in the seventeenth century, but we can probably never be certain about this. What we do know is that the English, in contrast to the Spaniards, made very little allowance at first for local conditions.

CONCLUSION

The chief impression of Port Royal's appearance that we should retain is probably its concentration of buildings and of vessels, all huddled together at the end of the otherwise bare peninsula. Within the town, the general trend of ownership was for properties at first owned by officers and others to pass into the hands of merchants, who came to form by far the most prominent group in the community. The town was laid out in the rather incoherent fashion characteristic of English towns of the period, and the individual houses also reflected very strongly the northern European origins of the settlers. In short, Port Royal looked very like an English shire town, perched on the end of a tropical spit.

NOTES

[1] The liveliness of the market naturally prevents any precisely accurate account being given of the whole town at any one time; our effort at a description must be considered as an attempt to show what was there for much of the two decades in question.
[2] See, for instance, Jamaica Archives, Patents, liber I. fo. 141. According to Oliver Cox in his report, the revised London Building Code of 1667 (after the Great Fire) seems to have been adopted in Port Royal around 1678.
[3] See above, p. 13
[4] Minutes of the Council of Jamaica, 9 November 1661, N.L.J. M.S.T. 60, p. 61.
[5] See Carl Bridenbaugh, *Cities in the wilderness* (New York, 1960), pp. 155-8.
[6] Taylor MS., p. 493.
[7] Ibid., p. 308.
[8] Ibid., p. 498.
[9] The fare from Passage Fort was 2s. 6d. by day, and 3s. by night, 'or of every person 6d.'. See *The Acts of Assembly and laws of Jamaica*, p. 141.
[10] The word 'bridge' is here used in its seventeenth-century sense meaning a landing-stage.
[11] I.R.O. Deeds, liber XXI, p. 100.
[12] This map has been compiled from individual plot-measurements, and is thus accurate in detail, even though its general shape is stylized and does not take into account the gentle curve of the harbourside.
[13] I.R.O. Deeds, liber I, p. 16.
[14] N.G. card 482.
[15] N.G. card 67.
[16] P.R.O. C.O. 138/1, p. 158.
[17] Ibid., p. 142.
[18] I.R.O. Deeds, liber I, p. 154 and N.G. card 579.
[19] B.M. Add. MSS. 12423, fo. 76 and 87.
[20] N.G. card 84.
[21] N.G. card 85.
[22] N.L.J. MS. Al, fo. 51.
[23] *C.S.P.* 1674, 1352 of 16 September 1674.
[24] See, for instance, B.M. Sloane 1599, fo. 42, 106-7, and 118.
[25] I.R.O. Deeds, liber XIV, p. 183.
[26] See the article by G. S. Yates in the *Bulletin of the Jamaican Historical Society*, iii (1961), 243-5.
[27] *C.S.P.* 1671, 640 of 14 October 1671 and 704 of December (?) 1671.
[28] I.R.O. Deeds, liber VI, p. 74.
[29] B.M. Add. MSS. 12423, fo. 99.
[30] Taylor MS., p. 493.
[31] I.R.O. Deeds, liber VIII, p. 103.
[32] Ibid., where there is a list of these members.
[33] N.G. card 649.
[34] I.R.O. Deeds, liber XVII, p. 75.
[35] Taylor MS., p. 503.
[36] Taylor MS., p. 498.
[37] N.G. card 346.
[38] I.R.O. Deeds, liber III, p. 77.
[39] I.R.O. Deeds, liber XXI, p. 91.
[40] B.M. Add. MSS. 12423, fo. 58^v.
[41] I.R.O. Deeds, liber XII, p. 174.
[42] I.R.O. Deeds, liber XVII, p. 165.
[43] I.R.O. Deeds, liber VI, p. 86.
[44] I.R.O. Deeds, respectively liber IV, p. 280, liber IV, p. 278, and liber XI, p. 141.
[45] I.R.O. Deeds, liber XV, p. 159.
[46] 'In the cheare' appears to mean 'broad'; 'purloines' (or better 'purlins') are roof-beams and 'cornishes' are cornices.
[47] N.G. cards 183 and 184.
[48] I.R.O. Deeds, liber XVII, p. 144.

[49] I.R.O. Deeds, liber XV, pp. 10 and 60; liber XVII, p. 162.
[50] I.R.O. Deeds, liber XIII, p. 223.
[51] N.G. card 599.
[52] I.R.O. Deeds, liber XV, p. 7.
[53] Quoted by F.G. Spurdle in his early *Early West Indian government* (Palmerston North, New Zealand [1962]), pp. 138-9.
[54] I.R.O. Deeds, liber XV, p. 39.
[55] Ibid., p. 24.
[56] N.G. cards 243, 235, and 892.
[57] N.G. card 452: this patent covers only a part of the whole area between Queen and Thames Streets.
[58] I.R.O. Deeds, liber VI, p. 17 and liber VIII, p. 246.
[59] B.M. Add. MSS. 12423, fo. 101.
[60] N.G. card 741 and 743.
[61] I.R.O. Deeds, liber VII, p. 117.
[62] I.R.O. Deeds, liber XIII, p. 132.
[63] N.G. card 107.
[64] I.R.O. Deeds, liber XV, p. 57.
[65] I.R.O. Deeds, liber VI, p. 156.
[66] I.R.O. Deeds, liber X, p. 112.
[67] I.R.O. Deeds, liber V, p. 123.
[68] B.M. Add. MSS. 12423, fo. 80.
[69] I.R.O. Deeds, liber XIII, p. 187.
[70] N.G. cards 60 and 62.
[71] I.R.O. Deeds, liber X, p. 224.
[72] B.M. Add. MSS. 12423, fo. 99.
[73] I.R.O. Deeds, liber VI, p. 139.
[74] B.M. Add. MSS. 12423, fo. 99.
[75] I.R.O. Deeds, liber XIV, p. 10.
[76] Captain Josiah Tosier (see chapter 5) had sent his sailing-master to chart all the wharves, but the result is an incomplete and unsystematic compilation, P.R.O. Adm. 51/3870 of 5 September 1679.
[77] N.G. card 311, I.R.O. Deeds, liber III, p. 53, and N.G. card 242.
[78] I.R.O. Deeds, liber X, p. 100.
[79] I.R.O. Deeds, liber VIII, p. 186.
[80] See, for instance, I.R.O. Deeds, liber VIII, p. 44.
[81] N.G. card 552 appears to be incorrect in this respect; neither does it show Modyford's land and wharf.
[82] I.R.O. Deeds, liber VIII, p. 36.
[83] I.R.O. Deeds, liber VIII, p. 36.
[84] I.R.O. Deeds, liber XI, p. 106.
[85] I.R.O. Deeds, liber XXI, p. 84.
[86] *The National Geographic*, cxvii (1960), 172-4.
[87] N.G. card 611 and I.R.O. Deeds, liber XVII, p. 165.
[88] N.G. card 382.
[89] We do not know what can have led Richard Dunn in *Sugar and slaves* (pp. 249 and 270) to assert that 'domestics lived segregated in huts behind their masters' houses'.
[90] I.R.O. Deeds, liber XXI, p. 31.
[91] Ibid.
[92] I.R.O. Deeds, liber XVII, p. 70.
[93] I.R.O. Deeds, liber VIII, p. 87. This John Peeke may in fact have been a Quaker.
[94] See F. J. Osborne, S.J., 'James Castillo-asiento agent', *J.H.R.*, viii (1971), 11.
[95] Pepysian Library, Cambridge, MS. 2873, fo. 487.
[96] B.M. Sloane 1599, fo. 2.
[97] Taylor MS., p. 508.
[98] Taylor MS., p. 492.
[99] Bridenbaugh, *No peace beyond the line*, p. 316. 'Curvilinear Flemish pediment roofs' are shown in the reconstruction suggested by R. W. Nicholson and Worth Bailey in *The National Geographic*, cxvii (1960), 153.

CHAPTER EIGHT

Everyday Life at Port Royal before the Earthquake

It is not easy to say how many people lived on the Point at any given time. As we have seen in chapters 2 and 6, economic activity began there almost as soon as the spit had been militarily occupied; by 1660 there were already 200 houses,[1] and four years later there were 400.[2] For one of the intervening years, 1662, we have the following population-figures for Port Royal:

Free men 400   *Free women* 200   *Free children* 90   *Slaves* 50.[3]

This makes a total of 740 persons in all, which seems a little low for a town of about 300 houses. However, this was the start of the occupation, and these early houses may well have been very small. About ten years later another survey was carried out, by Sir Thomas Lynch, and this gave the following results:

Free men 714   *Free women* 529   *Free children* 90   *Slaves* 50.[4]

This total of 2,181 persons apparently lived in about 800 houses,[5] a figure which again seems to imply rather small structures. As Port Royal prospered, however, the houses probably grew in size as well as in number. By 1688 there seem to have been 1,200-1,500 of them,[6] and by 1691 some authors claim as many as 2,000.[7]

The only serious figures for the population of Port Royal, between 1673 and the earthquake, appear to be those of the census of 1680.[8] According to this, Port Royal at that time had a little over 2,000 'whites' and about 850 'blacks'. This population, to judge by the figures for houses given above, would have lived in about 1,000 dwellings of various kinds. By the time of the earthquake, to judge again by the figures for houses, this number may well have more than doubled, for the proportion of slaves was constantly rising, and the latter did not normally occupy their own houses.[9] In 1692, then, we should probably visualize Port Royal as a town of about 6,500 inhabitants, of whom perhaps 2,500 were slaves.[10]

Within the free population the pattern of sex and age seems to have differed markedly from that in other parts of the 'English Caribbean', where adult males greatly predominated.[11] Even by 1673, as we have seen, the number of women (529) was approaching parity with the number of men (714), and there was a truly remarkable number of children (426). By 1692, then, we may suppose that the continuation of this trend had led to a more or less balanced pattern, with perhaps 1,600 men, 1,400 women, and about 1,000 children.[12] Of the composition of the slave population ('Negro and Indian slaves', Taylor calls them) we know less, save that it surely contained fewer children. The only figures bearing on this question are those of the 1680 census, in which the number of male and female 'blacks' was about equal; respectively 414 and 431.

Many members of the nominally free population were in fact indentured servants, bonded to their masters (or mistresses) for a period normally of ten years. Some of these indentured servants had been shipped to Jamaica as a punishment for various criminal misdemeanours;[13] there was also at least one occasion on which political prisoners were transported to the island. That was in 1685-6, years in which 355 'convicted rebels' from Monmouth's rebellion, 'as well Scotch as English',[14] were landed at Port Royal with instructions to the governor to see that they duly served their ten-year indenture, '... and that they bee not permitted in any manner whatsoever to redeem themselves by money or otherwise until that term by fully expired'.[15] Some no doubt escaped, and others went to the interior, but many surely stayed at Port Royal, where a living could be scuffled better than anywhere else.

The arrival and sale of one batch of these servants was described by John Taylor, whose manuscript has been so precious a source to us. Taylor arrived in the *Saint George* at Port Royal Harbour on the morning of 3 January 1688. He had lunch with the master of the ship, Captain James, at 'The George', and then went across to Spanish Town to pay his respects to the governor, Hender Molesworth.[16] To the latter he showed his letters of recommendation from 'the Worshipful Sir Thomas Ducke, Kt., and Mr. Jeremiah Arnold, both members of the Merchants' Royall Company trading hither from London'. No doubt Taylor also enquired of Molesworth where he might best dispose of his 'servants';[17] Molesworth advised him *inter alia* 'to go to Port Royal, it being the most commanding place for proffit and advantages on this island'. Taking their leave, Taylor and Captain James returned to Port Royal that night.

The next day, the *Saint George* was brought to the wharf 'over against *La Vera Cruz* [a hoy]', and began to unload her cargo. Meanwhile, Taylor went ashore and found lodgings with Mr. Thomas Tilley, a merchant; he took off his books and all his goods except his 'servants'. These remained aboard the *Saint George* 'with the other convicts until the day of the sale, which according to an Act of the island is not to be until the end of the day after their arrival there, soe the planters may have notice thereof and soe to supply themselves with such servants as they want'. In fact, the sale did not take place until the following Wednesday; meanwhile Taylor, complaining of the 'very hott drie weather with much thunder and lightening', remained about the port watching the shipping.

On the day of the sale for 'the convicts and servants', Captain James about ten in the morning hoisted his ensign and fired a gun 'according to the custom to give notice there of sale'. Taylor immediately went on board, no doubt along with a number of prospective purchasers, and soon 'had the opportunity to dispose of his three servants'. He sold the manservant, Charles Gold, for 60 dollars to William Ross, the marshal at Port Royal; Ann Sharp went to Mr. Moss, a merchant, for 45 dollars, and the other servant, Susanah —, went to the Withywood vintner Colson for 40 dollars. After paying Captain James 72 dollars passage-money for the servants, Taylor was left with 73 dollars, 'a proffit not soe considerable' as he expected. Captain James sold all his convicts, though some were not at once removed from the ship, since we know that the following night one fell overboard and was drowned. In the absence of any area in the town of Port Royal designated as a slave market, we must assume that slaves too were sold upon arrival in the same way as these servants and convicts.[18] Those destined for the inland plantations were passed over the side of the boat to waiting wherries, which could take them to Passage Fort or other disembarkation-points in the harbour; slaves and others destined for more distant plantations probably went on local sloops.

We have, alas, no account by an African of his or her arrival, but we do have *A memorandum of the wonderful providences of God* . . . (printed London, 1849), which is an autobiographical account of the arrival and adventures of an indentured servant, a certain John Coad. He was a Somerset carpenter and dissenting preacher, who had got caught up in Monmouth's rebellion of 1685. Captured and taken to London, on 17 October 1685, he 'went a ship-board and lay at anchor till the next day evening; then I pretty comfortably and contentedly left my native country, wife, children, relations and estates, committing them and myself to the protection and good providence of our God . . .' The master of the ship, a certain Edward Brooke,[19] took on 100 convicts, and shut them 'under deck in a very small room where we could not lay ourselves down without lying one upon another'. Partly as a result of this treatment, 22 of the convicts died, but the rest kept up their spirits by praying and 'singing praises to our God'. It is the most extraordinary image, the little ship of 190 tons ploughing her way out into the Atlantic, with guards armed with blunderbusses at the hatches, and this godly chorus going on below. The survivors berthed at Port Royal in November, and found the townspeople friendly:

> As soon as we came into the town the people took pity on us when they saw us almost starved, and ran and provided what they could get ready soonest; bisket and butter, a fresh fish fried, and fresh water, which was rich provision for such poor miscreants . . .

John Coad himself was soon in contact with Robert Speere, a dissenting preacher. Then came the sale: 'at the fire of a gun out of the ship the market begins'; Coad was sent 'to serve one Colonel Bach [Samuel Bach, a leading merchant], which was the best place [Speere] could think of on the island'. Coad's adventure in fact ended happily, for after only four years of servitude he was freed, and arrived back at Plymouth five years to the day after he had left England.

Coad was lucky. Many of his companions must have died, for newcomers were particularly vulnerable to various forms of lethal dysenteric infection. As George Ellwood put it, writing in 1672:

> The diseases generally are here, at first coming, the flux, which turns to the bloody flux and a violent fever, which seldom keepes any one above 4 days, for in that space of time they either recover or dye, and the gripes, which in a very short time takes away the use of their limbs.[20]

The 'flux' (bacillary dysentery) often seems to have been aggravated by excessive consumption of liquor; as Francis Hanson put it, while Jamaica in general was reasonably healthy for sober people, 'I think it as pernicious a place to debauch in as any in the world.'[21] The fate of John Coventry offers us a good example of this. Nephew of Sir William Coventry, John set out for America in 1671, probably in order to establish himself on one of the northern plantations. His ship was however obliged to put in at Jamaica, where she no doubt required considerable repairs, since he had to unload his possessions. What happened next is best told in the words of a letter from Sir Thomas Lynch to Sir Charles Lyttelton, dated 'Jamaica, 27 September 1671':

> It seems Monday he could not get from the Point, but at night with a mate and passenger fell into a debauch that made him sicke. The next daye he fell desperately ill; he lay at Captain Edgoose's a very good house, and Mr Thornton took care that he had the best doctors . . . [but still he died].[22]

Coventry's melancholy fate was shared by many other intemperate newcomers, as we know from a variety of sources.[23] The newly arrived slaves were vulnerable not only to these physical infections, but also, it seems, to ailments brought on by despair and disorientation. As usual, though, we have no accounts or statistics by which to gauge their sufferings.

While various fluxes attacked chiefly newcomers, those established in the island tended to suffer more from Ellwood's 'gripes', often known as 'the dry gripes'. This in fact seems to have been due to a kind of lead-poisoning, brought on by drinking (considerable quantities of) rum distilled in leaden pipes.[24] Hans Sloane describes several such cases, though he did not know what caused them. His 'case-book'[25] in fact provides a most curious record of illness in early Jamaica. Apart from flux and gripe, tuberculosis seems to have been common; Colonel Walker, for instance, was tubercular and eventually died of the disease in England.

Those who died at Port Royal were interred at the burial-ground outside the Palisadoes gate; it was this cemetery which, as we shall see, was disturbed by the earthquake of 1692. Others too were sometimes buried on the spit; this was the case with Sir Henry Morgan. As the journal of H.M.S. *Assistance* puts it:[26]

> this day [25 August 1688] Sir Henry Morgan died, and the 26th was brought over from Passage Fort to the King's House at Port Royall, from thence [sic] to the church, and after a sermon was carried to the Pallisadoes and there buried.

Mortality, then, must have been high in seventeenth-century Port Royal. However, it would be a mistake to conclude from this that the town was an unhealthy spot, judged by the standard of the West Indies (or indeed of many large European towns) of the time. On the contrary, the air there was generally accounted very healthy,[27] and children particularly seemed to thrive. The present climate of the town makes this easy to understand, for there is often a breeze either from the land or (more often) from the sea, and rain is relatively rare. The great squalls which periodically sweep down the spit rarely last for long, and the water which they leave quickly drains away into the sand.

In fact, this scarcity of natural water catchments posed grave problems to the early inhabitants. Such drinking water as could be tapped in the ground was always brackish, and even suspected of carrying the flux.[28] Relatively good water was fetched by wherry and canoe in great casks from the mouth of the Rio Cobre, but this too was suspect at least to Dr. Trapham, who suggested that it would be better to draw it from the spring at the Rock, where the vessels of the Royal Navy later watered. Many of the inhabitants of Port Royal in fact never touched the stuff, preferring to quench their thirst among the wide variety of stronger drinks available in the town. Wines were abundant and relatively cheap, especially those from Madeira; there was also a wide range of beers. George Ellwood wrote that 'our drink is chiefly Madeira wine, lemmonadoes, punch and brandy; for cool drinks, mobby wee have made of potatoes, cacao-drink, sugar-drinke and rap made of molassis'.

Food was both varied and expensive. As Francis Crow wrote in 1687, 'this is one of the most expensive, dear places in the known world for all manner of provisions'.[29] Much of this food came from overseas, though some was already produced locally. Three separate markets dealt in different categories of food, and each was supervised by a special town official. At the central market on High Street were sold herbs, fruits and fowls.[30] We do not know precisely what herbs and fruits were available, though cassava, potatoes, yams, and plantains surely were,[31] and so too must have been the apples, cabbages, onions, peas, and pears which came from England and North America.[32] Taylor is more specific on 'fowls', for he assures us that 'turkies, ducks, cappons, widgeon, teel, pidgeen, doves and parratts' were daily available.[33]

The market for 'flesh and turtle' was at the west end of the High Street, near the turtle-crawls. Here, 'in the cold of the mornings and evenings', could be bought 'beef, mutton, veal, lamb, kid and hog's flesh', as well of course as local turtle. Much of the beef, veal, and pork was reared locally, shipped to Port Royal by sea or across the harbour, and then slaughtered 'in the morning just before day'.[34] The fresh meat bought at the market must have been cooked almost at once, for there is no mention of ice coming down from North America, and no other means of refrigeration was available.

The third market was for fish, and was held 'on the wharf nigh the wherry bridge';[35] we may guess that this was chiefly stocked with locally-caught fish, though there would also have been codfish from North America, herrings from England, and salmon from Ireland. Just about the only European food not available at Port Royal was good fresh bread, for although there was at least one baker, William Wingar, the flour which he used tended to be too stale for a good loaf; Ellwood tells us that it was 'not well rellish't',[36] and Taylor confirms this view.

William Wingar was one of those craftsmen whose names are set out in appendix 4. His residence, shop, and bakery were situated at the western end of Queen Street, roughly opposite site 11 on figure 21. An inventory of his goods and chattels, taken on 9 May 1684, reveals that he had a substantial house and premises.[37] The buildings included a lodging chamber 'in the back house', another chamber used by Wingar himself, a bake-house, a store-house, several garrets in 'the great house', a 'great room' under the garrets, two 'little rooms', a 'great room up one of the stairs' and so on. There was also the usual yard with its cookroom, the baker's shop itself and a 'brickt room on the left hand'; in short, Wingar owned an extensive establishment. Like many other townsmen, he had horses, mares, colts, calves, sheep, and lambs 'in the savanna', which no doubt meant the Common of Port Royal.[38] All this was built out of the 'sutable quelque choses for regalles as cheesecacks, custards, tarts etc.', which Taylor assures us were on sale in the town.[39]

It is clear from appendix 4 that there were many other lesser enterprises catering for the mercantile community. Some were directly connected with the sea; we are not surprised to find carpenters, a chandler, fishermen, mariners, sailmakers, shipwrights, watermen, and wherrymen. Many of these men would in fact have had some particular specialization; among the mariners, for instance, are no doubt to be found those divers who worked in Port Royal harbour and also on wrecks further afield. Others were connected with commerce, and among these the art of the cooper was one of the most essential. Almost all Jamaica's exports depended on the durability of the casks, hogsheads, and barrels which they built, some working on the plantations, but many others plying their trade on the wharves of Port Royal, where in addition the 'staves and hoops for casks' were unloaded on their arrival from the New England colonies.

Appendix 4 lists a remarkable number of 'chryrugeons' or surgeons. Can there really have been as many as a dozen doctors at Port Royal? Or were they chiefly barbers? It seems a large number for so small a community, but then the merchants probably prized their health, and could afford to pay those who claimed to preserve it. They certainly had their other needs well catered for, from guns to clothes, hats, and shoes. We have the inventory of John Waller, a cordwainer (i.e., shoemaker), and curious reading it makes.[40] His house, of modest proportions, had an entrance porch and a hall which gave access to an 'inward chamber', a bed-chamber and a cellar. There was also a passageway leading to the shop, which when the inventory was taken contained only 'foure and twenty pair of French fall shoes and two pair of slippers', valued at seven pounds. In the yard was the 'currier's roome' (curing-room) in which were stored '7 calve-skins, 3 yearling-skins and one olive leather hide, 9 green (uncured) sole leather hides and 3 sides of mangrove upper leather'. There was also a tanning-house in which were '35 mangrove hides, 4 olive leather hides and 70 goate- and sheep-skins'; standing in a corner of the yard were '4 old tan vatts and severall old lyme tubbs'.

Most of the work of artisans like John Waller has perished, but a few of them worked in materials which have survived. It was at Port Royal that Governor Inchiquin had his 'good plate' worked up,[41] and as all gold- and silver-ware made on the island had to be appropriately marked,[42] it must surely be possible one day to identify some of it. The same ought to be true of the work of Abraham Coxshott, cabinet-maker; among those possessions listed in his inventory[43] was 'one Spanish elm scretore inlaid with ivory and tortoiseshell', valued at £25. The heavier work of the blacksmiths and carpenters has also survived, and much has been recovered by recent archaeological investigations. Particularly remarkable among this work is the carved roof-boss from the Anglican church.

Then there are the smaller, more delicate objects made by the tortoiseshell-workers, the ivory-turners, the pewterers, and the pipe-makers. The comb-makers worked in tortoiseshell (or rather turtle-shell, to be strictly accurate), and several of their combs with cases are now to be seen at the National Gallery of Jamaica (see figure 25); the earliest is dated 1671, and bears the arms of Sir Henry Morgan. When Sir Henry wanted in 1676 to send a present to Sir William Coventry, he chose 'two large turtle-shell combes in a case of the same', explaining that though it was 'of no value', it might be of some interest.[44] As well

Figure 25 Comb case from Port Royal, dated 1673 (National Library of Jamaica)

as combs, little boxes and caskets were also made, some of which had silver mounts, also no doubt provided by town craftsmen.[45] In 1672 Lady Lynch sent one of these boxes to Secretary Lord Arlington's wife, 'with combs and vanillas'.[46] The National Gallery of Jamaica has a similar box; it is a magnificent example of the craftsmen's art, with richly embellished silver work and handle-terminals in the form of turtles. Some of this work has undoubtedly produced by Paul Bennett, who in July 1673 purchased from 'Denis Macragh, gent, and Margery his wife, all those two little houses or tenements where the said Paul and one Mathew Comberford inhabited, fronting northwards on High Street, abutting east and south on the other lands of the said Denis Macragh, and west on the great house belonging to Benjamin Bryan'.[47] As Paul Bennett had been, prior to the sale, a tenant of one or both of the two little houses, he may very well have been working there for some years already.

Large quantities of ivory arrived at Port Royal from Africa, and by no means all of it was re-exported.[48] Some was worked up locally, by men like William Clifton, 'ivory turner'; the Link expedition of 1959 (see chapter 11) recovered a number of ivory rings which may very well have been made in the town.[49] Pewter has survived in much greater quantity, 47 pieces having been recovered merely from the underwater excavations carried out between January 1967 and March 1968.[50] However, pewterers were relatively common at Port Royal ; we know of Simon Benning in 1667, John Childermas in 1670, and John Luke in 1679 - and as we shall see in chapter 11, the work at least of Benning has been recognized and studied.

A deed dated 1 June 1680 identifies the name of a pipe-maker, John Pope the younger. No similar craftsman has been found earlier than this, nor is there any recorded in later surviving deeds. Pope seems to have been the man behind the local industry of making pipes from the 'red claie' found in the Liguanea plain and around Spanish Town. According to Taylor, 'the Negroes make tobacco pipes [from this clay]',[51] and many of these red clay pipes have survived. Unlike their English counterparts,[52] these pipes nearly always bore a mark of geometric design on top of the stem where it meets the bowl; they were very popular with the 'common women' of Port Royal, who 'in their smockes ore linnen peticotes, bare-footed without shoes or stockins, with a straw hatt and a red tobacco pipe in their mouths, [would] trampouse about their streets in this their warlike posture, and thus arrayed will booze a cupp of punch cumly with anyone'.[53]

There was, then, a considerable range of craftsmen at Port Royal in its first few decades, some of them producing work which competed with the best which could be imported. With such a variety of craftsmen at work in the town, it is not surprising that the houses were increasingly elaborate and fully furnished. The private dwellings might comprise anything from one room to perhaps four or as many as seven.[54] A house might be entirely occupied by a single family, or partially or wholly rented out, often room by room. Under the standard conditions of rental agreements, the use of the yard, cook-room, and (if it applied) the 'well' was always included, together with the 'shade' (an outside lean-to offering protection from the sun) if this existed. The shade was a regular feature of Port Royal yards in deeds of the 1660s and early 1670s and early 1680s, but as lands (and even yards) came to be extensively sub-divided in the late 1670s and early 1680s, this feature gradually disappeared.

The main function of the yard was to provide an area away from the main buildings, where meals could be prepared without risk of fire to the principal dwelling. This 'dressing of dyett' was performed in the 'cook-room', usually a rather small brick-built structure incorporating a hearth, perhaps an oven, and a chimney.[55] It was furnished with an assortment of cooking utensils such as copper pans, iron pots, a skillet, a spit, a frying-pan, a grid-iron, a pair of bellows for the fire, a brass kettle, a pestle and mortar, a 'pull-up jack' (for raising and lowering pots on the fire), one or two trivets, several pot-hooks, iron racks for holding pots and cooking utensils, trenchers of differing sizes, and occasionally a 'qualdron' and washing tubs, all of which were of course provided by the person renting the property. It is curious that surviving documents make no mention of the kind of fuel used in cooking. No doubt wood or charcoal was generally used, but it must have been imported from the mainland.

Another essential feature of the yard was the 'house of office' or latrine. In the seventeenth century, this usually consisted of a small wooden structure mounted on sills which totally covered the pit - a hole measuring some three feet by four feet and about four feet deep. Sometimes, if it was feared that the wind might blow the whole structure down, the supporting wooden sill might be strengthened or replaced by four short corner posts, sunk into shallow holes in the ground. This apparent lack of permanence is explained by the fact that at a certain stage the whole house would have to be moved to a fresh site, and a new hole dug.[56]

Furnishings of private dwellings depended on the wealth of the individual concerned, but were not in general very ostentatious. The main difference between one house and another seems to have been in size - in the number of the rooms and the quantity of furniture - rather than in quality. One of the more modest houses in Queen Street (see figure 21, site 5) was that of Arthur and Alice Lloyd. It was furnished as follows:[57]

> *In the first roome comeing in*
> 1 old table and bench
> 3 jointe stooles
> 2 low chaires
> 2 old chests   1 single hamacher [hammock]
> 1 parcel of old pewter, qt. 48 lbs. at 8*d*.
> 1 old carpett
> 1 paire of stilliards and payle
> Weights and scales
>
> *In the outwarde chamber uppstaires*
> A sute of curtains and vallances, one old feather bed, one bolster, one blankett and three small feather pillowes
>
> *In the outward chamber*
> One bed, three feather pillowes, curtains, vallances and blankett and bedstead
> 1 small table
> 2 small trunckes
> £30 ready money in the chest at his death
> Two paires of sheets, one pillowcase and other old linen
> 1 old chest and box
> A pl. of plate, qt. 34 ounces at 5*s*. per ounce
> 1 old chest
> 1 lookinge-glasse
>
> *In the shedd*
> 3 doz. bottles at 6*s*. per doz., 1 stone jugg, 1 pestle and mortar, 1 old caske.

The majority of the larger private houses occupied sites on the northern side of High Street and Queen Street, and were invariably owned or occupied by merchants, factors for overseas merchants, or prosperous artisans like sailmakers and coopers, all of whom needed to be close to the wharves. Here, for example, was the house of Sir Thomas Lynch, large enough to serve for many years both as a residence and as the only prison in Port Royal.[58]

The combination of shop and dwelling-house was more common than the single lock-up type of retail establishment. We have, for instance, the inventory of Captain Thomas Mathews, a merchant of considerable estate who lived on the southern side of High Street at the eastern end of the town. This inventory lists not only the furnishings, contents, and stock of the combined shop and dwelling-house, but also the contents of the smithy and the stock at Dr. Rose's pen. Mathews enjoyed a substantial property, for the site had a frontage on High Street of 27 feet and stretched south to the sea some 74 feet. The ground floor rooms comprised a shop, a counting-house, a warehouse, a buttery, and a cellar; above these were the dining room and two chambers 'next the street and next the sea', and above them a garret. The yard must have been of fair proportions, for apart from the usual cookroom there was at least one and probably two storehouses, as well as the smith's shop with its own storehouse. Curiously, there is no mention of the 'house of office'; perhaps this was too insubstantial to count.

Taverns, ordinaries, and punch-houses, listed in appendix 5, are rarely distinguished as such in deeds covering property transactions in the town. Such establishments are invariably introduced by the wording 'commonly called or known by the name of . . .', which in itself gives no proper identification. Often a single tavern had a special name for each of its rooms. 'The Salutacon', for instance, had a special room reserved for the lessors; this was 'known and called by the name of the Mary Gold'.[59] An even better example is provided by a tavern of unknown name, kept by Mr. Thomas Taylor who died shortly before 1 November 1674.[60] The building had five rooms and a cellar, and contained at Taylor's death the following effects:

In a roome called the Vinroome
A great wooden chest, a signe, a stripe carpet and an old saddle

In the Queen's Head
An old planeen [sic] bed, a cedar bedstead and three old leather truncks, a green rugg, a pillow and bolster
Two diaper table-clothes and seaven napkins

In the bar room
Two punch bowles, two earthen potts and a silver dram cup

In the Nag's Head
A tobacco knife, a copper pott, two spitts, a table and two formes, a wooden pestle and morer, two old gunns.

In the seller
About 20 gallons of Madera at 3s. per gallon
About 18 gallons of brandy at five shillings and sixpence per gallon
About a hogshead of sower clarett
A payr of carriers and eight pounds of candles

In the Rose
An old truncke with severall old clothes with a set of green curtins; a table and two formes

In the King's Head
Six joynt stooles, elleavon red leather chaires
A fuzends [sic] and old chest, fower hamockers
A man servant, about elleavon months to serve
A brasse kettle and skellet, a small brasse pan, a frying-pan and a paire of andirons, a lattin dripping-pan and an ax
Seaventy-five pounds of pewter, being five dishes, sixteen plates, two salt-sellers, three basons, one porringer, one sawcer
Two old chamber-potts, a pottle pott, two pint potts, two gill potts, a quart pott and a half-pint pott.

It looks from this inventory as if patrons could get a drink in a number of different places under Taylor's roof, and the quantity of pewter suggests that he provided meals as well. Attached to the inventory was a list of 'sundry people, debtors to Thomas Taylor deceased', which contained the names of 52 persons, including four doctors and 'Samuel the barber'. These debtors owed £302. 2s. 8d., out of a total estate of £396. 17s. 1d.; he surely allowed very generous credit.

Sir Thomas Lynch, governor of Jamaica, died on 24 August 1684. His inventory[61] shows that his possessions were divided between his own house, King's House in Spanish Town, and King's House at Port Royal. However, the poor quality of the furnishings in the latter house suggests that he did not live there much:

Att the King's House att Port Royal
1 set of old yellow curtains and vallances with one bolster, two old quiltes and one lookinge-glass with gilded frame . . . . £4. 0s. 0d.
1 close stool . . . . 5s. 0d.
3 small pillowes and one old night-gown, capp and slippers, and one course blankett . . . . £1. 5s. 0d.
2 diaper table-cloathes and three doz. napkins, very old . . . £2. 1s. 6d.
3 pillowes, 2 silke cushions and one table, one broken gunn barrell, one pewter dish . . . . £1. 1s. 6d.
1 embroydered holster and a case of pistolls . . . .£10. 0s. 0d.

It is an entertaining thought, to imagine Lynch peering out from between his yellow curtains, dressed in his night-gown, cap, and slippers. No doubt during the day he was more fashionably clad, for at Port Royal the latest English clothes were soon on sale. One of the more fashionable merchants seems to have been Mr. James Downes, who lived on High Street, and died intestate in 1674.[62] He had appeared wearing 'a Turkish garment of black watered chambles lined with crimson taffety, a black cloathe coat lined with blew sarconet, breeches, crimson velvet, a silke crimson Turkish shash [sic], a pair of Turkish shoes, gloves and a periwig'. His personal jewellery included a 'sealed gold ring, a silver ring with a blew stone in itt and a pair of silver buckles'. In short, it sounds as if Mr. Downes must have closely resembled the fashionable man about London town, who in the late 1660s was learning to wear what was called 'the Turkish fashion', patterned on the dress of Charles II.

The way in which Port Royal fashion closely followed that of London is neatly illustrated by a letter of September 1688 from William and Francis Hall, Port Royal merchants, to their London associate, Thomas Brailsford. They advise him 'to be searching out for new pretty things cheap and good for men's and women's apparell, yet newest gymps[63] in fashion and silver foots, or what is in fashion with you'.[64] Their instructions were often more specific; send, they write,

> a few curious silks cheap, some silver and gold twist, 3 silver and 1 gold is enough, silver and gold butons, women's laced shoes may do well, your narrow sletia [Silesia] launes will not go off, the broad very well, however, in blew papers. 100 will be enough, and if you have in Stubbs[65] send no more of them until [we] advice you . . . the silk hose account is drawn out; if you send any more here they must be long to roll up, about 12 paire of blew, 6 of purple and 12 of scarlett, not carnation.

In 1687, Taylor observed that the merchants at Port Royal were living 'to the hight of splendor, in full ease and plenty, being sumptuously arrayed, and attended on and served by their Negroa slaves, which always waits on them in livereys, or otherwise as they please to cloath them'.[66] Most of the male slaves were in fact arrayed not in livery but in the cheapest and coarsest of clothing, cut from 'brown Ozenbrigge', a coarse linen originally made at Osnabrück in Germany, which in 1674 sold in the town for 12$d.$ per ell from the roll and 10$d.$ per ell if bought as remnants. The white indentured servants were clad little better than the slaves. Clothing for the males consisted of 'plane canvas drawers' which cost 2$s.$ a pair, a shirt costing 4$s.$, a canvas jacket at 1$s.$ 6$d.$, cheap stockings and perhaps shoes, and a neck-cloth.

The merchants' wives were dressed much as their counterparts in England, with long pointed waists, tucked-up skirts, and very large lace collars. All the materials necessary for making these clothes could be bought in the haberdashery shops and merchant houses of the town. Among the records we have mention of Ghentish Holland,[67] dimity,[68] platillas,[69] plain silk, flowered silk, Persian silk, plain and coloured calico, 'Lincey Woolsey',[70] parragon,[71] fine serge, coloured serge, 'French falls',[72] fine women's hose, ribbons, cotton gloves, 'country blew thred', 'whited brown thred', and hooks and eyes. One merchant was even offering a 'Pertian goune £1. 1s. 0d.' The female slaves who worked around the houses of Port Royal were probably clad in less ostentatious versions of their mistresses' clothes - often, no doubt, in their cast-offs.

The children too were well catered for. The Lockyer's shop on High Street (see figure 21, site 50) sold children's shoe, hose and cotton gloves, 'frockes for children at 2s. 6d. each' and capps for boys at 1s. each', as well as children's coats at 15s. 6d. They even stocked what would today be called fitted sheets: 'one sute of child's bed linnen at £1. 10s. 0d.' To complete our image of the various kinds of dress found on the streets of Port Royal, we should include the militia, rather dashingly clothed in 'scarlet coats lined with blew'.[73]

No doubt the citizens reserved their finest clothes for public occasions, which were much more numerous and socially significant in early modern European towns - like Port Royal - than they are in any industrialized country today. Perhaps the grandest of them involved the reception of a new governor. Sir Henry Morgan, for instance, gave the following account of Lord John Vaughan's reception in March 1675:

> The 14th of March in this roade arrived His Excellency my Lord Vaughan in the *Foresight* frigat, which as soon as she came to an anchor, his lordship immediately came ashore in the barge, attended by severall gentlemen, where he was received by the seaside by myself and severall of the chiefest persons of Port Royall with all the civility and respect imaginable, the forts having fired many guns, and from thence conducted to the King's House, before which were drawn up in arms severall companies of the inhabitants, and afterwards entertained at a splendid supper.
>
> The 15th about 2 in the afternoon His Lordship's commission was read by Peter Beckford [Deputy Secretary of the island] . . . this ceremony being ended, His Excellency went to visit the forts upon this place, where he was likewise nobly entertained by the commander, who ordered the severall guns to be fired . . .[74]

Like his predecessors and many of his successors, Vaughan then crossed to Passage Fort in order to go to Spanish Town. One of the most elaborate of these receptions must have been the one accorded to Christopher, second duke of Albemarle. In 1687 Port Royal was near the peak of her prosperity, and as the occasion was carefully recorded by John Taylor,[75] it seems worth reproducing his account *in extenso:*

> [there was an exchange of artillery salutes off Port Morant] and by this shooting at sea the windward part of the island of Jamaica was allarmed, and soe the curious of Morant with all expedition gave the alarm to Yallows [Yallahs], and Yallows to the Port, and sett all their beakons on fire in sight of all men, soe that by fower aclock on Monday morning, being the nineteenth of December 1687, the port was all in arms at their respective posts, and they fired two shotts from Charles Fort over the Salt Pond hills to give notice to warn.
>
> After which the forts hung out their Flages of Union, and also hung out four very large chevrons, or pendants, on the fower points of the tower of the church. Then one hundred men (of the militia of the port) were drawn upp in armes at each fort with gunns sufficient to play the artillery and two hundred men were drawn upp in the court of King's House in order for a guard for His Grace's progress. The rest of the redgiment which was about 1300 men were drawn up in armes on the Parade . . .
>
> The Duke then approaching, some of the chiefe gentry of the port and the chief ministers of state went out in wherrys to meet His Grace, namely Sir Francis Watson, Sir Richard Dereham, Sir Charles Modiford the Chief Justice, Major Reeves secretary of state, Captain Musgrave the King's Attorney General, Smith Kelly esq. the Provost Marshall, Coll. Beckford president of the port and others, who were received on board the *Assistance* by His Grace with all the kindness and respect imaginable.
>
> Meanwhile the gentry from all parts of the island went from Passage Fort and Liguonea into the Port, soe that the harbour seemed to be covered with wherrymen plying to and froe, and all the shore round the port was lined with spectators joyfully to congratulate His Grace's happy arrival, the which they had so long weight[ed] for,[76] soe that there were here seen such a concourse of people as was this day gathered on the port since the island hath been inhabited by the English nation.
>
> Now comes the joyfull triumph of His Grace's reception, for about one aclock this afternoon His Grace safely came to anchor in Port Royall harbour with his illustrious Duchess aboard this *Assistance*, which had then three Union flaggs flying, the one at her foretopmast head, with her Jack and Ensign and twenty-one pendants or shevrons flieing at her yard-arms and other usual places.

Now as His Grace passed by each fort in towards the harbour, he was received thus: first the fort salutes him gradually with three several shouts of huzas for joy, and then all with a peall of their great artillery; after that the infantry all round the port (beginning at Charles Fort) gradually salutes him with five volley with their musquetts. Then the yacht, captain . . . and Captain Saunders gradually salutes the fort with thirty-nine guns; then His Grace, being now come to anchor, answers all by way of a generall thanks with thirteen gunns, then all the shipping, by way of gratulation, fires againe gradually, some with twenty others with five guns.

And then the forts, port and shipping gave His Grace three shouts, and the drums and trumpets joyfully sounded their marshall blasts, and then the Right Honourable Hender Molesworth, esq., Deputy Governor of the said island, with the rest of the ministers of state, went on board the *Assistance* to perform the ceremony of delivery to His Grace, presenting to him the mace and seale of the island, which with them were formally received by him. And soe the port and whole island remained in arms all night, making boon fires and other signals of joy.

On the morrow, being Tuesday the 20th of December 1687, about ten aclock in the morning His Grace's flagg was taken down and placed in the stern of his barge, in which his Grace, attended with the chiefe gentry of the island, were then rowed ashore by ten watermen, arrayed in whight, as His Grace's body of honour, and was attended with the *Faulcon's* barge and other shipp's pinnaces to the Wherry bridge.

As soon as His Grace had put off from the shipp's side, the *Assistance* fired twenty-one gunns, then all the other shipping in the harbour discharged all their artillery, gradually speaking forth that joy which was now received by the happy presence of His Grace; then the forts also fired and soe continued firing for about one half hour, that the loud echos of the mountains loudly thundered with the noise thereof; then the infantry gave all a volley [and] a loud shout gradually at His Grace's approaching.

His Grace being landed at the Wherry bridge on the port was waited on by the ministers of state [and] gentry of the island all in their respective orders, and all the street from the Bridge to the King's House was covered with green cloath, and two hundred soldiers drawn upp from the Bridge to the door and at each side to make a passage for His Grace's steps. Without the court, the soldiers gave a volley at his entrance into the court of King's House; within the courtyard a volley as soon as he was entered the King's House, and three shouts.

Hender Molesworth esq. standing on his right hand, and the Provost

Marshall carrying the sword before him, and the Secretary Major Ryves esq. carrying the mace and seale before him, and Mr. William Peat the deputy marshall going before all with the Marshall's staff, in this order His Grace entered King's House, when after some small stay and some compliments passed as is expected on such occasions, His Grace in the same manner went from the King's House to the church, all the way being covered with green cloath, and gunned as before.

In this order they entered the cloysters or Exchange on the north side of Saint Paul's church, at the east end of which cloyster was placed a chair of state, covered with azure velvet, richly prest, fringed and embroidered with gold in curious work, with nine steps of assent, with gold lions, like Solomon's throne, all covered with rich embroideries; over this chair of state hung a canopy of blew sattin, fringed and embroidered with silk, gold and curious work with a cushion of the like for his feet, in which was said to be 2,000 pistolls of gold, which with the chair of state was presented to His Grace by the Spanish factor seignior San Jago and senior Alverious a Jew, merchant on Port Royal; over this chair of state was curiously paterned the king's arms of England and the arms of this island.[77]

This chair of state His Grace seemed to slight, neither would he sit therein. As soon as prayers was ended in church, then there in public he audienced the Secretary of the island about His Grace's commition from His Majesty of Great Britain, in which he was honourably instituted Christopher, duke of Albemarle, the Supreme Governour of His Majesty's island of Jamaica and Lt. General of all His Majesty's dominions in America.

Which being read, and the ceremony of reception finished with, His Grace returned from the church to the King's House, having the right honourable Hender Molesworth esq. on his left hand and the other ministers of state marching in the same order as before, where His Grace was entertained with whatever amenities the island could afford, the drums and trumpetts joyfully sounding forth their marshall blast, the Marshall tending on him at dinner, and the chiefe ministers of state and gentry of the island were admitted to sit at the table with him. His Grace now had a guard of 200 men with their arms [and] swords to attend him.

His Grace then being sett down to dinner, the forts fired their ordnance gradually, beginning at Carlisle Fort, then the infantry which guarded the forts and were drawn up on the Parade gave each gradually a volley with their musquetts. Then the *Assistance* fired twenty-one pieces of ordnance, the *Faulcon* twenty-one, the *Elizabeth* yacht eleven, then all the other shipping in the harbour fired all round gradually, one after another.

Now His Grace having dined, about two aclock all the regiment of the infantry in the port were drawn upp in batalions in the court of the King's House before His Grace, the drums beating several points of turn and the infantry discharged severall volleys before him, and then marched off each to his respective post, only [except] those of His Grace's guard which still remained in their orders at the King's House.

About fower aclock in the afternoon, His Grace with his attendance in his barge went off from the port, and soe went aboard the *Assistance*, and as soon as His Grace was quit of the shore, the forts discharged all their artillery gradually beginning with Charles Fort. Then the *Assistance* fired twenty-one gunns, the *Faulcon* twenty-one, the *Elizabeth* yacht elevon, and then the other shipping continued firing gradually all round, giving three shouts or huzzas; soe the militia of the port were discharged from their arms and those of the dayly guards.

All this night the drums continued beating and the trumpetts joyfully sounding on shore, with other musick, with boon fires and all other possible signals of joy, which was fully demonstrated by the great concourse of gentry and others from all parts of the island gathered together now in the port; yet the like was never seen since this island was inhabited by the English. Also, about eight aclock at night Captain Thomas Smith, commander of His Majesty's ship the *Faulcon*, lighted about one thousand candles which were placed at the yard-arms, trunks, topmast heads, in the shrouds, rigging, all along the gunwell, bulkheads and other convenient places aboard the shipp, soe that it gave a shining and mighty light, and continued burning for about three parts of one hour, in order to congratulate His Grace's happy reception.

The receptions of governors were only one of the occasions on which Port Royal enjoyed spectacular sights and sounds. The king's birthday, in particular, was another opportunity for loyal manifestations with flags and cannon. In 1678 this celebration turned inauspiciously:

> Being the king's birthday [29 May] and all the flaggs abroad upon all the fortes, the great flagg on Fort Charles blew down, which we doubted was ominous, being so noted a day and on the most noted fort . . .[78]

Not only the king's birthday, but also the day of Charles I's death, were marked by some persons, especially when this was politically advantageous. On 30 January 1688, for instance, Lieutenant Thomas Smith of H.M.S. *Faulcon* recorded that 'this day being the death of King Charles the 1st we fired 20 guns, and all the ships in the harbour fired . . .'.[79] Captain Lawrence Wright of H.M.S. *Assistance*, who later turned his coat so decisively (see pages 80-81), recorded the same day with greater feeling: 'In remembrance of that horrid murder of our blessed sovereign Charles the First, we wore our colours half mast.'[80] Life at Port Royal, then, was much more ceremonial than we can easily imagine it; the middle ages were not so far away, with their hierarchic and symbolic conception of society.[81] The elements of symbolism and public display were conspicuously present in the way Port Royal was governed. Everybody knew and instantly recognized the resident judges of the Court of Common Pleas, which regulated minor civil cases. These judges were always men who were prominent in other respects; in 1671, for instance, they were Colonel Robert Freeman, Reginald Wilson the naval officer, and Samuel Bach, a leading merchant.[82] Four years later Reginald Wilson was still serving, but now his companions in office were William Beeston and Anthony Swymmer, both prominent merchants.[83]

The Court of Common Pleas had several minor officials. There was the clerk, who kept its records, the marshal, who looked after prisoners, and the crier, who made public announcements. When the latter had a proclamation or other document to publish, he was preceded in his rounds by a drummer, to catch the ear of the public. All important directives were published in this way, 'by beat of drum' as the phrase went. Law enforcement was the task of the provost marshal, whose office was described by Vaughan as 'a mixed employment like those of sheriffs, bailiffs, gaolers etc.'. In May 1688 the holder of this post was a certain Mr. Holly (or perhaps 'Kelly'), whose functions emerge clearly from the following petition, sent to the governor by some French settlers:[84]

> the said petitioners arrived here on Friday last, being the 27 April 1688, and were entertained at the house of one Charles Barree, a vintner on Port Royall.
>
> Where being drunck some of them with unparralleled impudence affronted some Spaniards that were peaceably here about their lawfull occasions, saying 'Dammee, you cowardly doggs, are you here while wee have been looking for you in the south seas?' and other scurrilous language . . . [so they were imprisoned].
>
> Then His Grace [Albemarle] demanded of Mr Holly the Provost Marshall if he could not secure the said prisoners without putting them in irons, to which he answer'd that the prison was very full, having at least four score prisoners in itt att present, and the building very slight . . .

Taylor, writing in 1688, describes not only the Marshallsea, for male prisoners, but also 'Bridwell . . . a house of correction for lazie strumpets'.[85] Not all offenders went to jail, of course; there was a stocks 'in the heart of the High Street', and down by the turtle market a 'cage for common strumpets'. As we have seen, Peter Bartaboa had built a ducking-stool and gallows; there was also a pillory.[86] One way and another there was a considerable variety of punishments available in old Port Royal, some of them disagreeably public.

Almost every free and able-bodied citizen played a part in the maintenance of public order, for the regiment of infantry numbered something over 1,500 men in 1688,[87] divided into ten companies. Sir Henry Morgan had his own company, and the commanders of the nine others are mostly well known to us: Lieutenant-Colonel William Beeston, Major Hender Molesworth, Captain Samuel Bach, Captain Charles Morgan, Captain Anthony Swymmer, Captain Richard Herne, Captain Charles Penhallow, Captain Thomas Hudson, and Captain Thomas Hodgkins. One of these companies watched each night and day (beginning at 6 p.m.) both for internal disorder and for seaborne assault. If they saw five or more unidentified ships approaching, their duty was to 'fire off two cannons laden with hollow balls, from Charles Fort over Salt Pond Hill [Port Henderson Hill], which by their great report and the thundering echos of the mountains, all the whole island both horse and foot are forthwith in arms . . .'. [88]

Captain Josiah Tosier was riding at anchor in H.M.S. *Hunter* among the cays off Port Royal in July 1679 when one such alarm occurred. He describes it in these words:[89]

> [At] night we heard Fort Charles fire 4 gunns with shott and a great many musketts fired att Port Royall and at Liguinie and beating of drums. [This] put us in a maze what the uproar should bee, thinking that the Negroes be risen,[90] but in an hour after, the lieutenant came on board and brought a letter from Sir Henry Morgan to acquaint mee that hee having then received advice from Port Morant that eight saile of French men-of-war was seen off that place, which caused the allarme, and that hee advised mee not to wait till daie lest I should find myself amongst them . . .

In fact, the French squadron had merely come for wood and water, and it was a false alarm. Normally there was a strict rule forbidding the firing of guns after sunset, for obvious reasons.[91] Just who manned the forts and their guns is not entirely clear, but it looks as if this must have been the task of certain members of the militia, under the supervision of a few permanent officers.[92] As we have seen in chapter 7, there was a practice ground in the premises of the Honourable Artillery Company by the Palisadoes gate, and each fort no doubt carried out its own practice shoots. From Fort Charles the gunners often aimed at a cask set up on the adjacent cay; that is how Gun Cay, *cayo blanco* to the Spaniards,[93] got its name.[94]

Naval affairs were largely the responsibility of the naval officer, whose activities have been described in chapter 5. Reginald Wilson was a very prominent figure in Port Royal, and the customs dues on wines, which he assessed, were the most considerable source of public revenue. Another public income was derived from quit rent, collected after 1675 by Receiver John Crompton from all those who had received grants of land. Crompton was supposed to work out a general rent roll, 'so that in future the king's books may be exactly made, that His Majesty can be informed what he ought to receive', but that was surely too ambitious an undertaking, given the confusion which had arisen over grants of land since the English conquest.

The establishment of a post office was another praiseworthy and desirable venture which in the end proved unpracticable. It seems to have been in 1687 that James Wale became postmaster for the island,[95] but there were soon complaints that he was over-charging. In January 1688, for instance, we read in the minutes of the Council that 'it is a general complaint of the merchants living on Port Royal that the petitioner hath by colour of his office . . . imposed upon His Majesty's good subjects here, and exacted and taken from them 7 1/2*d.* currant mony of Jamaica for every single letter . . .'.[96] In the end, Wale's service seems to have broken down, and letters continued to be delivered at Port Royal in the time-honoured way by simply entrusting them to homeward-bound merchants, who in turn freely delivered letters from abroad.[97]

It is hard to say how many of the inhabitants of Port Royal could read these letters. Presumably the unfree section of the population was generally illiterate, and most of the merchants were probably more at home in the counting-house than in the library. There does not seem to have been any formal schooling at Port Royal until 1689, when Mr. Peter Bird came to live there, and probably gave classes in the house which he rented from Jonathan Pym the gunsmith.[98] The children of the very wealthiest citizens no doubt went back to England for their schooling, and the others would have been instructed at home by their parents. As early as 1670 John Belfield, merchant of High Street, was selling books for schoolchildren - primers, psalters, testaments, and horn books - and there may as well have been informal dames' schools; after all, there were a great many children to cater for.

Religion was much better served than education, for Port Royal comprehended a complete range of creeds, from papists to atheists. There must have been many Catholics among the early French buccaneers, just as there were many among the various visitors from the Spanish territories. When, in 1684, James Castillo came to Port Royal as agent for the *asien*to, he established a chapel in his house, big enough to hold 300 persons, where his chaplain said Mass.[99] We do not know how many attended this chapel, but we may suspect that the number was not very large; 50 at most.[100] When Albemarle came to Jamaica in December 1687 he brought with him Father Thomas Churchill, nominated by James II to be chief chaplain to His Majesty's Catholic subjects. An unseemly quarrel ensued between Castillo and Churchill; Albemarle naturally took the latter's side, and Castillo was forced to leave Jamaica until 1692, when the new regime in England made it possible for him to return.[101]

The Anglican church has left fewer evidences of its activity at Port Royal, if only because no such spectacular quarrel arose to trouble its calm. Appendix 6 sets out the sequence of ministers and churchwardens of the established church; it will be noticed that Reginald Wilson is prominent, in yet another capacity. We should probably visualize the Anglican congregation as comprehending the greater part of the free populace as well as the most powerful merchants; at Port Royal as in England, its great strength - and eventual weakness - lay in its power of accommodation to the *status quo*, in the breadth of opinions which it could contain.

One of the greater merchants who did not adhere to the established church was Samuel Bach. He had carried on 'his public exercise at Port Royal for many years with good success',[102] probably preaching in what Taylor calls the 'Presbeterian meeting house'. After 1686 his efforts were supplemented (and he may have been supplanted) by those of Francis Crow, whose interesting letter of 7 March 1687 from Port Royal has often been reprinted.[103] Crow claims that 'the better sort of merchants and mechanics adhere to us', but he offers no figures to substantiate this claim. He also mentions the abundance of Quakers, 'both here and in the country parts'. Several members of this sect had reached the island as early as 1658, driven out of Barbados; Governor

D'Oyley welcomed them and they reciprocated by giving out godly books among the soldiery.[104] No doubt what Taylor calls the 'Quacker's meeting house' was established in the 1660s, and it probably had a following of between 50 and 100 persons. Certainly the community corresponded yearly with the Friends in London between 1686 and 1708,[105] but its members do not seem to have been very prominent in public or economic life; indeed, of the 60 or so Friends known by name to us, only two can be positively identified among the notarial records, and these are Thomas Hillyard the shopkeeper and John Pike the joiner.[106]

The Quakers shared with the Jews certain disabilities though the latter at least were able and permitted to bear arms, which the Quakers could not. The Jews at Port Royal were said by Francis Crow to be 'a multitude',[107] and there were complaints from various Gentiles that they 'eat us and all our children out of all our trade'.[108] However, these assertions seem to be the normal exaggerations. Although groups of Jews reached Jamaica in 1661 (from Brazil), in 1663 (from London), in 1664 (from Cayenne), and in 1667 (from Surinam), and although many of them surely remained in Port Royal, they do not seem to have played a very prominent part in the economic life of the town. The historian of Jamaica's Jews could find only seven land-patents to them at Port Royal between 1664 and 1681,[109] and of the 125 or so merchants listed in appendix 4, only about 15 have Jewish names. The synagogue, which in 1686 had as its overseers Jacob Rodriguez de Leon and Jacob Lopes Torres,[110] probably had a congregation of about the same size as the Quaker meeting house, between 50 and 100 persons.

We have no means, of course, of knowing how many of the population of Port Royal never attended any of the established religious houses. Presumably very few of the slaves did, and there were probably many laggards, agnostics, and atheists among the free population. Indeed, it would have been very hard to ensure any kind of religious discipline, such as was common in Europe at that time, in a community offering so many varieties of worship. Jamaica was exceptional in this respect among all the overseas European plantations, whether controlled by Catholic Spaniards or by puritan Englishmen. The instructions and proclamations of governors from Lord Windsor (1662) onwards insist that liberty of conscience must be observed,[111] and this policy seems to have been implemented; as Taylor remarked in 1687, 'they allow of a free toleration of all sects',[112] so that Roger Elletson in 1683 had to answer to the Council for having advocated the enforcement of penal laws against dissenters.¹¹³ This forebearing attitude changed only with the arrival of William, second earl of Inchiquin, in May 1690. Inchiquin was a supporter and friend of the prince of Orange, and naturally could not stomach Catholics. We therefore find this passage among his 'instructions':¹¹⁴ You are to permit a liberty of conscience to all persons except papists, so [provided that] they be contented with a peaceable and quiet enjoyment . . .'. No doubt Inchiquin put this unfortunate instruction into effect, with the result that Catholicism in Jamaica was almost wiped out during the eighteenth century.

Going to church was of course not only a source of spiritual solace, but also a social diversion. Other forms of recreation were necessarily limited by the site; there could be no hunting, of course, nor even any riding, as the Port Royal spit was still heavily covered with unsuitable vegetation like cactus-plants. When evening came, and the shops were closed, some inhabitants liked to go for a stroll out of the Palisadoes gate, to the spot where Barre's tavern stood, noted for its light refreshments.¹¹⁵ Others remained within the town, frequenting a wide variety of inns, which offered a wide range of entertainment. Cockfighting was common, and so was 'shotting at the targett'.¹¹⁶ There were a bull and a bear, 'for sport at the Bear garden',¹¹⁷ which may have been in the yard of one of the larger taverns, like the 'Three Crowns'. Several taverns had billiards-rooms, which always seem to have been situated in the yard, away from the main bars. One such hostelry was 'The George', which 'fronted to the old Market Place' and had a special room for the game; another was 'The Feathers', whose billiards-room was sited over another room in the yard. Among the effects of Mr. James Downes, the fashion-conscious merchant mentioned above, were '3 ivory billiard-balls' valued at 6*d*.¹¹⁸

Some of the merchants and others may have been reading men, though this seems rather improbable. Most merchants' inventories include a few books on general topics and occasionally some school books, but the only evidence of a sizeable library is that provided by the inventory of Mr. Thomas Craddock, who died in 1685. His library was kept in the garret of his house and comprised six folio books and 39 unbound volumes, together with 30 'play or pamphlet songs'. Though this was not a large library, its range was quite wide, from Hooker's *Ecclesiastical Polity* to *The contempt of clergy*, and from Spenser's *Faree Queen* to the *Anatomy of vegetables*, interspersed with several history books, poetry books, an English dictionary, and Paul Hesteman's French grammar.¹¹⁹

The taverns ranged, of course, from those in which a sober and godly man might enjoy a quiet read, to those low-class drinking establishments called punch-houses, many of which, Taylor observed, 'may be fittly called brothel houses'.[120] These were haunts of 'such a crew of vile strumpets, and common prostratures, that 'tis almost impossible to civilize [the town], since they are only its walking plague, against which the cage, whip nor ducking-stool would prevail'.[121] It was hoped by the more sober citizens that Bridewell prison would do something 'to allay the furie of those hot Amazons', but it may be doubted if this worked out so. The most celebrated of them was Mary Carleton, the 'German princess,' who was hanged at Tyburn in 1673, and whose supposed capacities gave rise to a great deal of fanciful literature.[122] They have given Port Royal a very lurid reputation, but we may doubt if in fact it was any more vice-filled than any other sea-port with an abundance of suddenly rich and temporarily idle seamen. The census of 1680, it is true, mentions a certain John Starr, whose establishment contained 21 'white women' and 2 'black women'; as Professor Dunn puts it, 'Starr appears to have operated the largest whorehouse in town'.[123] However, what is really significant is not the existence of Starr's establishment, but the fact that it is the only one we can identify.

CONCLUSION

In fact, everyday life at Port Royal seems to have been very similar to what might have been observed in any English seaport of similar size. There was very little evidence of 'creolization' amomg the richer inhabitants during the four decades after 1655; food, clothes, buildings, and recreation all obstinately followed English norms, however unsuitable these might be. Modification to suit the climate was found mainly among the poorer inhabitants. Because of the restricted area of the site, and the ever-increasing pressure of business, the concentration of people was probably greater than in any English town, except for parts of London, and there were one or two concessions to the climate, like the clothes worn by servants and slaves, or the midday business break.[124] But in most other respects Mr. Pepys would have felt perfectly at home in Port Royal.

NOTES

1. B.M. Harleian 3361, fo. 41r. The general development of the town is also discussed in chapter 7.
2. B.M. Add. MSS. 11410, fo. 1.
3. *J.H.A.* i (Statistical Papers, p. 20); these round figures must of course be approximations.
4. This was the survey of 1673 (*J.H.A.* i, Statistical Papers, p. 40); that of 1671 (B.M. Add. MSS. 11410, fo. 209) gave slightly higher totals.
5. According to Richard Blome, *A description of the island of Jamaica* (London, 1672) p. 31.
6. Taylor gives the figure of 1,200 (Taylor MS., p. 492) and Sir Hans Sloane that of 1,500; see his *Voyage to the islands*, i. lviii.
7. Figure quoted by Leslie, *History of Jamaica* (3 vols., London, 1774), ii. 139.
8. Preserved in P.R.O. C.O. 1/45/97-109.
9. According to the minister, Francis Crow, Port Royal in 1687 had 'five Blacks to one White' (see Henry J. Cadbury, 'Conditions in Jamaica in 1687', *J.H.R.*, iii. 2 (1959), 54). Taylor says that slaves and free were roughly equal in number (Taylor MS., p. 499), but both of them seem to exaggerate the number of 'blacks'.
10. Taylor's figure of 10,000 inhabitants is surely exaggerated; on this see Dunn, *Sugar and slaves*, p. 184. However, the 1680 census figure is certainly low, since it did not include mariners at sea.
11. See, for instance, Bridenbaugh, *No peace beyond the line*, p. 201.
12. The abundance of children at Port Royal was one of the things which particularly struck Dr. Thomas Trapham; see his *Discourse of the state of health of the island of Jamaica* (London, 1679), p. 13.
13. See for instance, Clinton Black, *Port Royal* (Kingston, 1970), pp. 22-3, for an account of Mary Carleton, the 'German princess' shipped to Jamaica in 1671. According to A. E. Smith, by the 1680s Jamaica was the main receiving-point for felons; see *Colonists in bondage* (Gloucester, Mass., 1965), p. 103.
14. *J.H.A.* i. 84; Long mention that some convicts also came after the Rye House plot of 1683 (*A history of Jamaica*, i. 625).
15. P.R.O. C.O. 138/5, fo. 84, 'His Majesty's letter touching the transportation of rebells'.
16. Taylor MS., p. 177.
17. As he termed them; they were in fact convicts, which he (like Captain James) had acquired from Captain Richardson, keeper of Newgate Prison in London.
18. See also *C.S.P.* 1689, 295 of 26 July 1689, the Council and Assembly's address to the king: '... again, when planters have gone on board to buy Negroes ...'.
19. We learn his name and that of the ship (the *Port Royal Merchant*) from the customs records, P.R.O. C.O. 142/13, fo. 3.
20. Royal Society MSS., George Ellwood, Jamaica, 15 June 1672.
21. Hanson, *The laws of Jamaica* (Spanish Town, 1792), p. ix.
22. Coventry Papers, vol. 104, fo. 249.
23. Two interesting cases are cited by Dunn, *Sugar and slaves*, p. 307.
24. Bridenbaugh, *No peace beyond the line*, pp. 193-4.
25. In *A voyage to the islands*, i. xc-cliv.
26. See the National Library of Jamaica transcript, 'P.R.O. captains' journals 68' under this date.
27. Ellwood (Royal Society MS.) and Trapham (*A discourse of the state of health in the island of Jamaica*, p. 13) are agreed on this; as we shall see, the site of Kingston was at first found much less salubrious. According to the 1680 census, in the previous two years there had been 130 births and 90 deaths among the 'whites', and 72 births and 48 deaths among the 'blacks'.
28. By Hans Sloane; see *A voyage to the islands*, p. x.
29. Cadbury, 'Conditions in Jamaica in 1687', *J.H.R.* iii. 2 (1959), 54.
30. Taylor MS., p. 494.
31. Royal Society MSS., George Ellwood, Jamaica, 15 June 1672.
32. See chapter 6 concerning these imports.
33. Taylor MS., p. 500.
34. Sloane, *A voyage to the islands*, p. xv.
35. Taylor MS., p. 494.
36. Royal Society MSS., George Ellwood, Jamaica, 15 June 1672.
37. Jamaica Archives, Inventories, liber I.
38. See above, pp. 127-9.

[39] Taylor MS., p. 503.
[40] Jamaica Archives, Inventories, liber I.
[41] This is mentioned by Bridenbaugh, *No peace beyond the line*, p. 329.
[42] According to Francis Hanson, *The laws of Jamaica*, p. 26.
[43] Jamaica Archives, Inventories, liber II.
[44] Coventry Papers, vol. 75, fo. 234.
[45] See the articles by Frank Cundall in *The Connoisseur* of 1925 and 1929, both called 'Tortoiseshell carving in Jamaica'.
[46] C.S.P. 1672, 773 of 2 March 1673.
[47] I.R.O. Deeds, liber XI, p. 104.
[48] See chapter 6; we owe the reference to William Clifton to W. A. Claypole's unpublished Ph.D. thesis, 'The merchants of Port Royal 1655-1700', submitted to U.W.I. in 1972, p. 135.
[49] These rings are now preserved at the National Library of Jamaica.
[50] See the *Report* of the Jamaica National Trust Commission (1968).
[51] Taylor MS., p. 492.
[52] Which were made of white kaolin clay and imported in huge quantities from London and Bristol.
[53] Taylor MS., p. 504.
[54] See, for instance, I.R.O. Deeds, liber XII, pp. 30 and 56.
[55] These small, separate brick houses are still to be seen in many islands, particularly those of the Bahamas.
[56] See Ivor Nöel Hume, *Historical archaeology* (New York, 1966), p. 139.
[57] Jamaica Archives, Inventories, liber I.
[58] See above, pp. 122-3 for information about later prisons; the tower in Fort Cromwell had been used as a prison for a brief period during the 1650s.
[59] I.R.O., Deeds, liber XII, p. 64.
[60] Jamaica Archives, Inventories, liber I.
[61] Jamaica Archives, Inventories, liber I.
[62] Jamaica Archives, Inventories, liber I.
[63] Gimp or gymp was a 'silk, worsted or cotton twist with a cord or wire running through it'.
[64] P.R.O. C. 110/152, Brailsford Papers.
[65] Surely Captain Thomas Stubbs, whose *Richard and Sarah* arrived back in Port Royal on 21 November 1688; see above, p. 97.
[66] Taylor MS., p. 500.
[67] A linen from Ghent in what is now Belgium.
[68] A stout cotton, woven with raised stripes and often used for beds and bedroom hangings.
[69] A linen from Silesia.
[70] A dress material woven from a mixture of wool and linen.
[71] A kind of double camlet, used for dress and upholstery.
[72] Coventry Papers, vol. 74, fo. 56.
[73] Taylor MS., p. 497.
[74] Coventry Papers, vol. 74, fo. 56.
[75] Taylor MS., p. 578-87.
[76] Concerning this long delay, see Cundall, *Governors of Jamaica in the 17th century*, p. 111.
[77] The Spanish factor was in fact James Castillo (see below, p. 158); 'senior Alverious' may be David Alvarez (appendix 4).
[78] B.M. Add. MSS. 12430, fo. 36r.
[79] P.R.O. Adm. 51/345 under this date.
[80] See the National Library of Jamaica transcript, 'P.R.O. captains' journals 68', under this date.
[81] Brilliantly described by Johan Huizinga in *The waning of the middles ages* (London, 1955).
[82] *J.H.A.,* i. (Statistical Papers, p. 37).
[83] For an account of the legal structure see E. H. Watkins, 'A history of the legal system of Jamaica 1661-1900', Ph.D. thesis, Sheffield, 1968.
[84] B.M. Sloane 1599, fo. 45r. 'Charles Barree' is of course Charles Barre.
[85] Taylor MS., p. 493.
[86] Cundall, *Governors of Jamaica in the 17th century*, p. 39.
[87] Taylor gives a figure of 2,000 (p. 496), but this must be too high, as the 1680 census gives only half that number.
[88] Taylor MS., p. 497.

[89] P.R.O. Adm. 51/3870 under 8 July 1679.
[90] There had been slave-revolts on plantations in 1673, 1675, and 1678. Taylor affirms that the Port Royal slaves had a plot about 1685 to fire the town, but this does not seem to be confirmed by any other source. Indeed, it is curious, given the nature of the site, that there was no fire until the disastrous one of 1703 (see below).
[91] See Hanson, *The laws of Jamaica*, p. 31.
[92] B.M. Add. MSS. 11410, fo. 425, letter of 29 November 1671 from Sir Thomas Lynch to Lord Arlington.
[93] See Cundall and Pietersz, *Jamaica under the Spaniards*, p. 84.
[94] According to Sloane, *A voyage to the islands*, p. lxxxvi.
[95] John Oldmixon, *The British empire in America* (2 vols., London, 1708), ii. 285.
[96] B.M. Sloane 1599, fo. 10r.
[97] On this postal history see Thomas Foster, *The postal history of Jamaica 1662-1860* (London, 1968). There was a scheme in 1670 for the marshal to collect ships' letters and post a list of them 'at the market-place' (Council minutes, N.L.J. M.S.T. 60, p. 187), but this probably did not work.
[98] I.R.O., Deeds, liber XXI, p. 101.
[99] See F. J. Osborne, S.J., 'James Castillo - asiento agent', in *J.H.R.*, viii (1971), 9-18.
[100] Only twelve Catholics could be found in 1689 to sign a petition to Albemarle; see B.M. Add. MSS. 12429, fo. 160.
[101] Osborne, 'James Castillo', p. 16.
[102] Coad, *A memorandum of the wonderful providences of God*, p. 46.
[103] See, for instance, Henry J. Cadbury, 'Conditions in Jamaica in 1687', *J.H.R.*, iii. 2 (1959) 52-7. Crow is also mentioned in Coad, *A memorandum*, p. 96.
[104] Captain Thomas Southey, *Chronological history of the West Indies* (3 vols., London, 1827), ii. 23.
[105] See Henry J. Cadbury. 'Quakers and the earthquake at Port Royal, 1692', in *J.H.R.*, viii (1971) 19-31, and Harriet F. Durham, *Caribbean Quakers* (n.p., 1972).
[106] Cadbury 'Conditions in Jamaica in 1687', pp. 29-30.
[107] Ibid., p. 54.
[108] Quoted by Samuel and Edith Hurwitz in 'The New World sets an example for the Old; the Jews of Jamaica and political rights 1661-1831', in *American Jewish Historical Quarterly*, lv (1965), 37-56. See also P.R.O. 1/28/159, a petition against the Jews whose only prominent signatory appears to be Anthony Swymmer.
[109] Jacob Andrade, *A record of the Jews in Jamaica* (Kingston, 1941), p. 136.
[110] *J.H.A.*, i. 114.
[111] See, for instance, *C.S.P.* 1661-8, 374 of 10 October 1662 and 664 of 18 February 1664.
[112] Taylor MS., p. 504.
[113] *C.S.P.* 1681-5, 902 of 19 January 1683.
[114] B.M. Add. MSS. 12429, fo. 166v.
[115] 'Silabubus, cream-tarts and other quelque choses', according to the Taylor MS., p. 503.
[116] Ibid.
[117] Ibid.
[118] Jamaica Archives, Inventories, liber I.
[119] I.R.O., Inventories, liber II, p. 78; see Roderick Cave, 'Thomas Craddock's books' in the *Bulletin* of the Jamaica Library Association, January 1973.
[120] Taylor MS., p. 502.
[121] Taylor MS., p. 504.
[122] See Black, *Port Royal*, pp. 22-3.
[123] *Sugar and slaves*, p. 181.
[124] Taylor MS., p. 502.

CHAPTER NINE

The Earthquake and the Passing of Commercial Primacy 1692–1722

On Wednesday, 7 June 1692, the Anglican rector Dr. Emmanuel Heath went after the morning service to drink a glass of 'wormwood wine' with John White, president of the Council, 'as a whet before dinner'. They sat together in a 'place hard by the church', perhaps a wine shop near the Merchants' Exchange, but they never ate dinner that day. About twenty minutes to twelve, Dr. Heath felt the ground 'rowling and moving' under his feet. White assured him that it was only another earthquake, and nothing to fear, but another shock succeeded the first, and then another, after which whole buildings began to crash down. The church itself, standing at the east end of the town, rapidly descended into the sea, its tower collapsing in the process. At the northern edge of the town the wharves and at least two rows of houses slid into the deep water of the harbour; Dr. Heath's preprandial drink had been interrupted by the geological calamity described in chapter 1.[1]

In the rest of the island, the shock was felt as a kind of 'wave',[2] but at Port Royal the rolling sensation was succeeded by a general 'trepidation or trembling',[3] and the ground seemed to open up in several places at once. As one witness put it:

> The sand in the street rose like the waves of the sea, lifting up all persons that stood upon it, and immediately dropping down into pits; and at the same instant a flood of water rushed in, throwing down all who were in its way; some were seen catching hold of beams and rafters of houses, others were found in the sand that appeared when the water was drained away, with their legs and arms out.[4]

Many were imprisoned in the ground, which seem to close up again after bursting open in this way. Dr. Heath did his best to escape by running towards what he calls 'Morgan's Fort', where the ground was open.⁵ However, as he ran southwards he saw the sea 'mounting in' over the forts in that direction; many who escaped the initial crash on the north and on the east must have succumbed to this tidal wave from the south, particularly if they had the misfortune to be trapped in the ground or in the wreckage of buildings.

In fact, once Dr. Heath reached his house he found that it was still standing. No doubt it was built towards the eastern end of the underlying coralline mass, whose burden of structures survived largely intact; at Fort Charles, for instance, the central tower housing the powder did not suffer at all.⁶ However, outside this area the damage was very extensive, the more so since the brick houses built by the English were more vulnerable than the simpler wooden structures favoured by the Spaniards would have been.⁷ To the north, all the wharves fell into 30 or 40 feet of water, and were followed by the houses on the streets as far back as Jew (or 'New') Street.⁸ These houses descended rather than toppled, as has been explained in chapter 1, so that the roofs of the ones nearer shore were plainly visible, and some indeed were half out of the water. All the wealth of the greatest storehouses was sunk, as were Forts James and Carlisle. To the east, there was now an expanse of water where once Fort Rupert had stood, and to the south Morgan's Line was severely damaged. The sea continued to encroach for some time after the initial shock,⁹ until the shoreline was eventually held at the position shown on figure 4.

About 2,000 people perished in the earthquake itself,¹⁰ and as we shall see many more died in its aftermath. Among the 'persons of note' who were killed were Attorney-General Simon Musgrave, Provost-Marshal Reeves, Colonel Reade, Captain Ruden, and Naval Officer Reginald Wilson.¹¹ The mortality at Port Royal was much greater than in the rest of the island, where only about 50 people were killed. No doubt this was because Port Royallers were in danger not only from their treacherous sand, but also from falling buildings and the tidal wave. There were, of course, many narrow escapes and miraculous deliverances, of which the best known is that of Lewis Galdy, first swallowed up and then spewed out by the earth; this Huguenot refugee's tombstone may still be seen outside Saint Peter's church (figure 26). The escape of one woman is described thus:

> when she felt the house shake, she ran out, and called all within to do the same; she was no sooner out, but the sand lifted up, and her Negro woman grasping her they both dropped into the earth together, and at

the same instant the water coming in rolled them over and over, till at length they caught hold of a beam, where they hung till a boat came from a Spanish vessel and took them up.[12]

There were some heroic acts, like that of Thomas Norris's 'Negro man', who after rescuing a sea-captain perished while trying to save his master,[13] but on the whole the earthquake and its sequel did not bring out the best in the Port Royallers. The president and Council did their best to keep order, holding their sessions on board the *Richard and Sarah* in the harbour,[14] and the worthy Dr. Heath worked hard among the survivors:[15]

> burying the dead, christening of children, preaching and praying with the bruised, wounded and dying people, going from ship to ship to do his office, as well as on shoar . . . he is much to be commended, and deserves praise from everyone, having discharged his duty like a good shepherd.

Figure 26 Tombstone of Lewis Galdy at Port Royal (Photo by Buisseret)

The Earthquake 167

But for many of the inhabitants the earthquake was a splendid opportunity to loot and even, it was said, to murder if necessary. As the vicar of Withywood put it:

> immediately upon the cessation of the extremity of the earthquake, your heart would abhorr to hear the depredations, robberies and violences that were in an instant committed upon the place by the vilest and basest of the people; no man could call any thing his own, for they that were strongest and most wicked seized what they pleased ... even the very slaves thought it their time of liberty, wherein they committed many barbarous insolencies and robberies, till they were suppress'd by the death of some, and punishment of others ... .[16]

To crown this horrible scene, there floated on the water not only the corpses of those recently killed, but also of those previously buried in the cemetery; this had been severely shaken in the earthquake, and had yielded up some of its inhabitants. The authorities did their best to sink what they described as 'floating carcasses', but some eluded them, as did the bodies of some unfortunates trapped in inaccessible places. The result of this, and of the fact that the survivors were often wet, ill-lodged, and short of both medicines and water,[17] was that almost half of them died of malignant fevers,[18] bringing the total number of dead at Port Royal up to about 4,000, slaves and free.

This loss of life meant that the defences of the town were very ill-manned, and in any case only Fort Charles and part of Morgan's Line remained more or less intact.[19] Many ships had been 'overset and lost' in the harbour,[20] including H.M.S. *Swan*, which 'careening close by the wharf was so damnified by the fall of the houses that upon view since she is condemned as unfit for further service'.[21] It is possible, as we shall see in chapter 11, that her hull has since been found by archaeology. The island was thus very vulnerable to foreign invasion, and there was in addition a lively expectation that the remaining slaves might revolt; the vicar of Withywood goes so far as to write that:

> Our first fears were concerning our slaves, those irreconcilable and yet intestine enemies of ours, who are no otherwise our subjects than as the whip makes them, who seeing our strongest houses demolisht, our arms broken, and hearing of the destruction of our greatest dependency, the town of Port Royal, might in hopes of liberty be stirred up to rise in rebellion against us ... .[22]

However, neither the French nor the slaves took their chance. The French tried an invasion, but were ignominiously repulsed, and the slaves did not make any concerted attempt at a revolt, partly no doubt because the earthquake took them by surprise, and partly perhaps because their condition in the island was not yet as bleak as it would be when the plantation system was more fully developed.

All the same, the situation as Port Royal was now desperate. The town had lost more than half of her inhabitants, and had been reduced to an island of 25 acres, on which the sea constantly encroached. Some of her residents lost all faith in her future, and persuaded the Council to agree:[23]

> upon another place, called the Rock, whereon to build a town for the reception and accomodation of merchants . . . it being capable to receive ships of the greatest burden very night to the shore, which may be much advantaged in a small time by the building of wharfs etc. for the benefit of lading and unlading of ships, as at Port Royal before. From thence it is but a short way to Ligania, the first and principal place for planting . . .

It does not seem, however, that this settlement at the Rock (now Rockfort) ever prospered, and little by little life flowed back into Port Royal. Trade revived, and Fort Charles was reconstructed, following the plan shown on figure 27. The new governor, Sir William Beeston (whose logs we used in chapter 5), proved a dynamic leader, and devoted much energy to restoring the fortunes of Port Royal. Thus in May 1701 he was able to write to the Council of Trade and Plantations that:

> We are now building and will soon be finished a round tower of 60 foot diameter at the east end of Port Royal, which will carry 12 or 16 guns, which we build in that figure to hinder a surprize, there being no dore nor ascent but by a ladder.[24]

This structure, which replaced the sunken Fort Rupert, was designed to protect the eastern end of the island, and to prevent entry to the harbour by the channel which had been opened up there (see figure 4); it was completed in 1701 and named 'Fort William'.[25] Alas for Beeston's hopes; in 1713 the new fort was dismantled, and four years later it was 'quite decayed'.[26] For many years its very site was lost, having been covered by the successive buildings of the naval dockyard (see chapter 11).

Fort William was no doubt allowed to fall into decay because the channel which it covered was filling up, as a result of both natural accretion and of the boats which were sunk in the gap to encourage this. However, Port Royal as a whole went through a very perilous

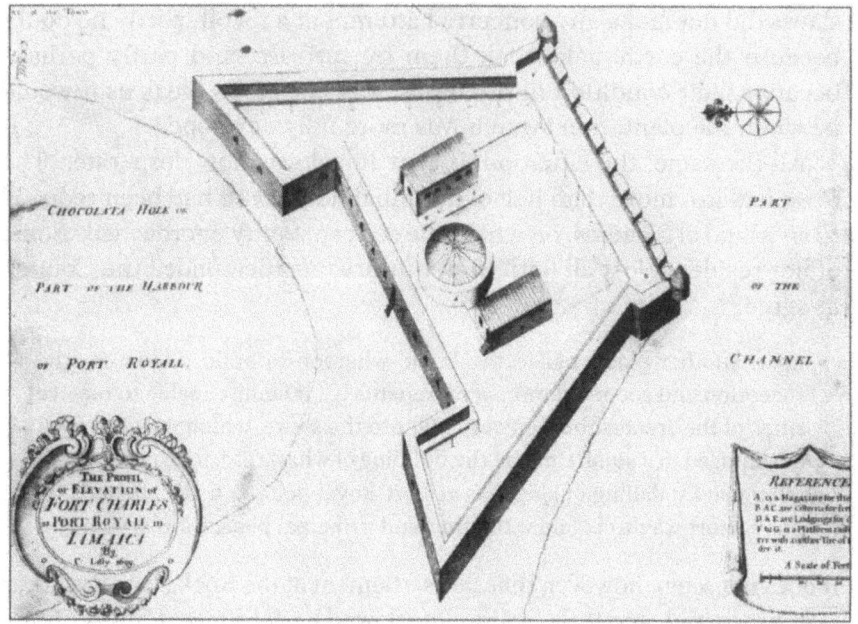

Figure 27 'The profil or elevation of Fort Charles . . . 1699' (Public Record Office)

phase in the early eighteenth century, for the catastrophe of 1692 was followed in 1703 by a disastrous fire. Twenty-five acres was not nearly room enough for all the merchants who still wished to do business in Jamaica; the houses had become very densely packed together, and once the fire started it spread with devastating effect and rapidity. Almost the whole town was consumed; as the master of a packet-boat laconically noted in his log, 'Arr. Jamaica 29 [January 1703]. Port Royal burnt, all but the Castle.'[27]

At once there was a strong movement to shift the chief seat of trade to the growing town of Kingston (as the old settlement of 'Ligania' or 'Ligonee' was now called), and to prohibit the resettling of Port Royal; 13 days after the fire a bill to this effect was sent up to the Council and, the governor strongly favouring it, was made law. A debate now ensued between those who advocated the claims of Kingston, and those who remained loyal to Port Royal.[28]

The Kingston faction claimed that Port Royal was vulnerable to fire and earthquake, and could not cover the new channel into the bay which had been opened up by the earthquake; moreover, they said, Kingston was a healthy site and easily defended by land and sea. To these arguments the supporters of Port Royal replied that Kingston was difficult of access for sailing vessels, that it was open to amphibious assault, and that it was very unhealthy (mortality was certainly very high there during the early years of settlement). On the whole the seamen preferred Port Royal, whose harbour was so convenient, whereas the most influential merchants favoured Kingston, where their warehouses were more secure. After many arguments and appeals to London, the Kingston Act was disallowed, and the two centres were permitted to develop side by side.

Port Royal for a time seemed to be holding its own as a commercial centre; as we shall see, it was also becoming a considerable naval base. Successive governors carried on with the strengthening of the defences, to which the Hanover Line was the most noteworthy addition (see chapter 10). However, there had been a severe hurricane on 28 August 1712, which did much damage to shipping in the harbour, and this proved a portent of worse things to come. Exactly ten years later, on 28 August 1722, there was 'a most dreadful storm',[29] which in the words of Governor Sir Nicholas Lawes was so destructive that:

> most of the shipping in our harbours is destroyed and many hundreds of people, particularly at the town of Port Royal, have lost their lives by the fall of houses and inundation of the sea.... The newly-erected line on Port Royal called Hanover Line stood it the best, and as I have been informed has been of great security to the remaining part of that town, which otherwise might have been destroy'd...

It seems that about 400 people were killed, and half the town destroyed; in the words of John Atkins, a naval surgeon on a visit at the time, the hurricane 'split the castle [and] lay the church and two-thirds of the town flat, burying three or four hundred people in the ruins'.[30] This time the blow was fatal; three major disasters in 30 years deterred even the most determined settlers, and for the rest of the century Port Royal flourished only as a naval station, whose history is recounted in the next chapter.

NOTES

[1] Most of the accounts of the earthquake used in this chapter are listed by Cundall in *Governors of Jamaica in the 17th century*, pp. 134-6; to these should now be added the numerous documents printed in vol. viii (1971 Port Royal) of *J.H.R.*, and also the curious letter in Thomas Foster's *The postal history of Jamaica* (London, 1968), p. 4.

[2] See Sloane's account in *The Philosophical Transactions of the Royal Society of London*, iii. 625.

[3] According to Captain Crocket's account, printed in the *Journal of the Institute of Jamaica*, i (1891), p. 148.

[4] *Philosophical Transactions*, p. 627.
[5] This must be the 'back seaside' referred to by the author of *The truest and largest account of the late earthquake* (London, 1693), p. 7.
[6] Ibid., p. 12.
[7] This weakness had been forseen by Sloane; see his *Voyage to the islands,* p. 625.
[8] *The truest and largest account,* p. 4.
[9] For some time it even looked as if the whole site might disappear into the sea: *A true and particular relation of the dreadful earthquake* (London, 1748), p. 332.
[10] This is the figure given by most of Cundall's sources, and confirmed by the log of H.M.S. *Guernsey* (P.R.O. Adm. 52/30) for 22 June 1692: 'The people that were kil'd and drown'd were about 2,000'.
[11] See Captain Crocket's account, and also the letter from Edmund Edlyne to Blathwayt, unknown to Cundall and published in *J.H.R.*, viii (1971), 60-2.
[12] *Philosophical Transactions,* p. 627.
[13] *J.H.R.*, viii (1971), 23-4.
[14] See their letter to the Lords of Trade and Plantations, *C.S.P.* 1689-92, 2278 of 20 June 1692.
[15] Captain Crocket's account, p. 150.
[16] *The truest and largest account,* pp. 5-6.
[17] Ibid., p. 9.
[18] This is the figure given in *A true and particular relation*, and supported by other contemporary estimates.
[19] Beeston to the Lords of Trade and Plantations, *C.S.P.* 1693-6, 209 of 23 March 1693.
[20] *Philosophical Transactions,* p. 627.
[21] *The truest and largest account,* p. 7.
[22] Ibid., pp. 11-12.
[23] Ibid., p. 8.
[24] *C.S.P.* 1701, 486 of 30 May 1701.
[25] Beeston to the Council of Trade and Plantations, *C.S.P.* 1701, 963 of 20 October 1701. There is an account of this tower in the 'Description de l'isle Jamaique' preserved at the Newberry Library, Chicago, Ayer Collection no. 293 (II).
[26] *J.H.A.*, ii. 116 and 248.
[27] Quoted by Cundall, *The governors of Jamaica in the first half of the eighteenth century* (London, 1937), p. 29.
[28] This debate is well described by Cundall, *The governors of Jamaica in the first half of the eighteenth century*, pp. 30-3.
[29] See the letter from Lawes to the Council of Trade and Plantations quoted below; *C.S.P.* 1722-3, 295 of 20 September 1722.
[30] *A voyage to Guinea, Brasil and the West Indies* (London, 1737), p. 236.

CHAPTER TEN

Port Royal as a Naval Station 1692–1900

INTRODUCTION

As we have seen in chapter 5, some kind of naval force was based on Port Royal from 1668 onwards, even if it only consisted at times of one or two frigates. After 1692 this force was normally very much more powerful, for the Royal Navy was expanding rapidly and Jamaica's economy becoming more and more valuable to England. There is of course a great mass of archival material concerning naval activity in eighteenth- and nineteenth-century Port Royal; so much, indeed, that this chapter can take account of only a very small part of it.[1]

Four main chronological divisions suggest themselves: from 1692 to the peace of 1713, from 1713 to the Peace of Paris (1763), from that date until the end of the Napoleonic Wars in 1815, and finally from 1815 until the closure of the dockyard in 1905. During the first three of these periods, from 1692 until 1815, many operations were mounted from Port Royal, which became by far the most important British base in the Caribbean. Until about 1740, on the other hand, the administrative framework lagged far behind the tactical requirements. Under Vernon (1739-42) this weakness was largely remedied; his administrative innovations and those of his successors will be described separately from our account of the naval operations.

ADMINISTRATIVE ORGANIZATION, 1692-1715

During this period there seems to have been little improvement on the distinctly makeshift arrangements of the period before the earthquake.[2] When a naval vessel needed to careen, it was still sometimes necessary to 'press' merchant ships in order to heave her down.[3] True, the *Lewis* hulk was deliberately sunk in the Chocolata Hole, where she could be used for small vessels on the careen, but larger ones still had no proper careenage or yard, and had to find a convenient spot somewhere along the Palisadoes spit.[4] This must have resulted in much loss of time, not to mention pilferage of stores.

Most of the naval vessels at Port Royal in the early eighteenth century soon fell into a lamentable state of disrepair, for they often arrived battered from the transatlantic crossing, and once in tropical waters fell victim to the teredo worm, which swiftly riddled their hulls. The Admiralty had established supply-agents at Port Royal (and at Lisbon), but their efforts do not seem to have been very successful.[5] In the absence of adequate supplies, and lacking any proper place for careening, whole squadrons were often more or less incapacitated. The Admiralty did not have the resources necessary for mounting a large-scale base, and the local authorities were often uninterested in helping.

Governor William Beeston, who in effect ruled the island during a crucial period between March 1692 and January 1702, was more concerned with the defences of Port Royal than with repairing and provisioning the naval ships. By October 1693 he had recovered what he could from the wreckage of the earthquake; Fort Charles mounted 38 guns and Forts Morgan and Walker about half a dozen each.[6] It was at this time that Fort Charles was drastically remodelled, and began to assume something like its present shape. By April 1694 a 'second new bastion' was largely completed,[7] and the fort soon began to look as it is shown in figure 27. This new work was carried out in well-laid brick, which contrasts sharply with the crude stone-work of the earlier structure, still visible in the foundations of the fort.

At the eastern end of the town, several hundred yards of shallow water separated Port Royal from the mainland.[8] This channel of course made the town very vulnerable, and a large round tower with twelve 18-pounders, called 'Fort William',[9] was built in 1701 to command it. This tower, whose foundations were revealed by the excavations carried out by Mayes in 1969-70,[10] soon became useless, as the channel was before long filled in both by nature and by artifice, the Port Royallers sinking old boats in the gap to encourage accretions of sand and gravel. In the late 1690s, Christian Lilly drew what he called 'the ichnography of Port Royal in Jamaica', and this plan, reproduced as figure 28, gives us a good idea of the town's appearance at the turn of the century. It had been reduced in area from about 60 to 25 or so acres; most of the commercial area had disappeared, and so had what Lilly calls 'the best buildings'.

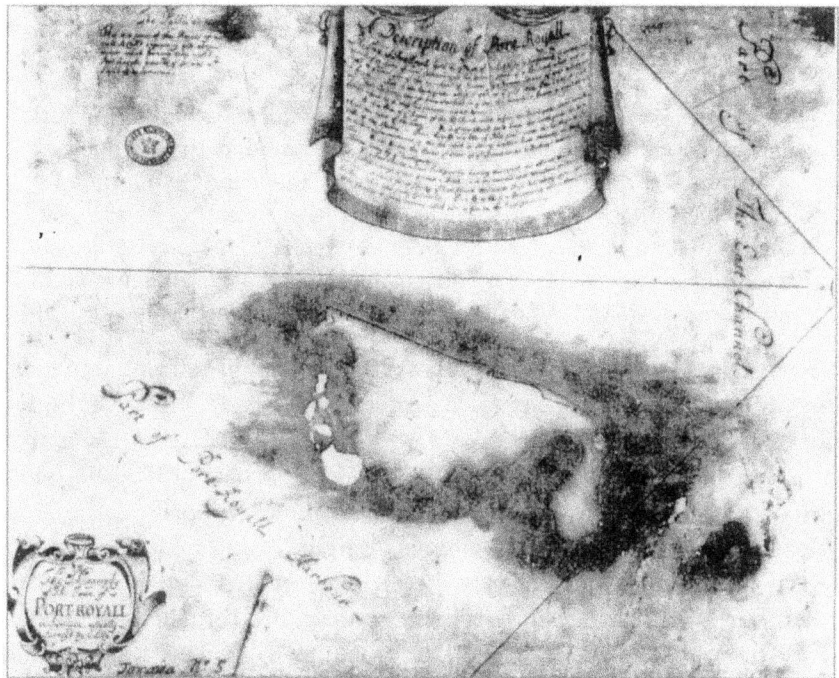

Figure 28 Christian Lilly, 'The Ichnography of the Town of Port Royall',
c. 1700 (Public Record Office)

OPERATIONS, 1692-1715

The fragile and defective administrative structure which we have described above sustained many naval operations, some of which were tactical triumphs, and all of which contributed to the general strategic aim of denying the island to the French or Spaniards. At the time of the earthquake there were two naval vessels based on Port Royal: H.M.S. *Guernsey* and *Swan*. The latter, as we have seen, was cast ashore in the town, 'suckt amongst the houses'[11] and wrecked; *Guernsey* was cruising at the time, and hurried back to find, as her log puts it, ' the Point almost down'.[12] On 28 June 1692 H.M.S. *Mordaunt*, Captain Francis Maynard, joined *Guernsey* at Port Royal, and the crews of both vessels helped in the rescue work, particularly in the task of 'weighing guns'; in May 1693 *Mordaunt*'s crew also weighed H.M.S. *Swan*, though she never served again.

By that time *Mordaunt* herself was getting rather unseaworthy, and so was ordered back to England. In September 1693 she stocked up with provisions at Kingston, the new town over the water, and in

The Naval Station   175

November set sail. However, *Mordaunt* never reached England. As her log puts it:

> [We] run aground upon the north-west part of the Collovados [the Colorados archipelago, north-western Cuba], and at the third stroke sunke. Before daye we cutt our masts down and launched our pinnace and yoall [yawl?]. At day we made a raft of our masts and yards, but finding that we could not tow it ashore we concluded to land what people we could in our boats, who carried them to the island Bonavista 12 miles from the ship. All day we kept landing of our people . . .[13]

Eventually Captain Maynard and his crew got ashore in Cuba; to judge by previous examples they were probably detained for a while, but we have no further news of them.

That left *Guernsey* on the station. In February 1693 she had a thorough refit, putting 'our sails and all our rigin on bord the grate Spaniard hulk which was Sir James Castello',[14] and in June sailed for 'ould England' as her log calls it, arriving in Deptford Dock late in October. The previous March, H.M.S. *Falcon* had returned to Jamaica, but she was captured by the French in June 1694, after a stout resistance by Captain Bryan.[15] The ships which captured *Falcon* were part of the great fleet with which the French in the summer of 1694 threatened the whole island, and ravaged parts of it. In June they were in Saint Thomas, mercilessly plundering the area around Port Morant, and early in July they sailed westwards along the south coast. Their commander, Admiral Jean Du Casse, was in favour of an attack on Port Royal, where Beeston was furiously organizing what defence he could, but some of the French captains advised against the venture, and the fleet of 22 ships, carrying 3,000 men, sailed on to be repulsed at Carlisle Bay.[16]

Beeston seems to have had only H.M.S. *Advice* to help defend Port Royal at this critical juncture, but by the end of the year she had been joined by H.M.S. *Hampshire*, 46 guns, and H.M.S. *Experiment*, 32 guns. The sources do not permit any very accurate account of how many ships were at Port Royal at any given time in these years, but it does look as if the mid-1690s saw a significant increase in the number of those assigned to Jamaica. Two or three of them would normally come out from England early in the year, escorting merchant vessels. After unloading and reloading at Port Royal and Kingston, the latter would leave during March, escorted by such naval vessels as were now due to return to England. In July 1696, for instance, H.M.S. *Hampshire* had been two years in Jamaica, and had been joined by H.M.S. *Southampton*, 48 guns, *Reserve*, 48 guns, and *Lincoln*, 50 guns.[17]

As well as the vessels which came on this rotating system, there were others which came out as part of squadrons, sent with some offensive purpose in mind. The first of these seems to have been that commanded by Sir Francis Wheeler, which consisted of 11 third-, fourth-, and fifth-rates, a bomb [a small vessel carrying mortars], and three fireships, and sailed from England in January 1693.[18] His instructions ordered him to attack and devastate Martinique, and then, basing himself on Jamaica, to attack Hispaniola. In the event Wheeler carried out a short but damaging raid on Martinique and then, finding that his men were falling sick, and apprehending the hurricane season, he hurried northwards, touching at Port Royal before going on to Boston and thence back to England.

The next sizeable squadron to reach Jamaica was that commanded by Vice-Admiral John Benbow. In December 1701 his two third-rates and eight fourth-rates came to anchor in Port Royal harbour, where he was reinforced the following May by several more vessels under the command of Commodore William Whetstone.[19] Hostilities with France, suspended by the Treaty of Ryswick (1697), had now broken out again, and Benbow's cruisers were very active off both Cuba and Hispaniola. Thinking that Du Casse had gone to Cartagena, Benbow then led the bulk of his squadron into the southern Caribbean. There, on 19 August 1702, he sighted Du Casse's ships off Santa Marta, in what is now Colombia.

Thus began what Clowes calls 'one of the most painful and disgraceful episodes in the history of the British Navy'.[20] The French squadron was inferior both in firepower and in number of ships to the British, but of the six ships supporting Benbow in H.M.S. *Breda*, 70 guns, only H.M.S. *Ruby*, 48 guns, showed any inclination to get to grips with the enemy. The result was that H.M.S. *Breda* was severely damaged, Benbow was wounded - mortally as it turned out - and Du Casse escaped into Cartagena. One of the timorous captains died at Port Royal on his return, two were shot for cowardice at Plymouth on their return to England, and one was cashiered.[21] For some time after this incident the French enjoyed maritime supremacy in the Caribbean, though they made little use of it.

Meanwhile the strength of the vessels at Port Royal on the rotating system varied between three and five; in 1704, for instance, the sizeable naval ships were H.M.S. *Norwich* and *Anglesey* (fourth-rates),

Experiment (fifth-rate) and *Seahorse* (sixth-rate). The latter was a handy little vessel of only 20 guns, well suited for chasing pirates. In 1704, in fact, she was wrecked upon a rock in Manchioneal Harbour while chasing a French privateer.[22] In the spring of 1706 another squadron came out, under the command of Captain William Kerr. This consisted of H.M.S. *Breda, Windsor*, 60 guns, *Sunderland*, 60 guns, and *Assistance*, 50 guns, and its chief object was 'to attempt the Spanish galleons'.[23] However, this venture failed and Kerr, disappointed in his hope of prize-money, began recouping his lost expectations by taking bribes for 'permitting and protecting contraband trade, and for sparing the property of the enemy'.[24] Returning in 1707, he was dismissed the service in 1708.

Meanwhile Commodore Charles Wager had arrived at Jamaica in 1707, and he too aimed at capturing some of the Spanish galleons. Sailing from Port Royal on 14 April 1708 with four ships, he eventually sighted 17 sail of Spaniards near Cartagena. In the ensuing battle the main Spanish ship, the *San Josef*, 64 guns, was sunk, and a 44-gun ship captured. In fact the bulk of the treasure had been on the *San Josef* and on another ship, of 64 guns, which had escaped into Cartagena. Wager felt that two of his captains had not pursued this ship with sufficient zeal; they were tried by court-martial on board H.M.S. *Expedition* in Port Royal Harbour on 23 July 1708 and were dismissed their ships.[25]

Wager returned to England in 1709, and was succeeded at Port Royal by Commodore James Littleton (1710-12). He too aimed at capturing part of the plate fleet, but was decoyed away from Cartagena by a groundless report that a large French fleet had arrived in the West Indies; in his absence the galleons safely reached Havana and thence Spain. The last of the commanders to operate out of Port Royal before the Treaty of Utrecht (1713) was Rear-Admiral Sir Hovenden Walker, whose 'Journal of a residence in Jamaica' is preserved among the manuscripts of the National Library of Jamaica. His period of command (1712-14) was marked chiefly by violent quarrels with the Governor and by the freedom with which he used H.M. ships for private trading ventures. He was recalled in 1714.

The period between 1692 and 1715 thus saw a steady growth in British naval of power at Port Royal, and a corresponding change in its tactical objectives. Whereas until then the vessels had been used chiefly for diplomatic missions and for the suppression of pirates, in this period Port Royal began to shelter large fleets destined for extensive offensive operations. These operations were not as yet very successful, but the very presence of such fleets greatly reduced the fear which haunted Jamaica's British rulers - that the island would be either recovered by the Spaniards or seized by the French.

Of course, such large fleets were not assembled merely on the off-chance that they might fall in with the plate-fleet, even though that was surely the most persistent dream of the naval commanders. In the early eighteenth century the trade of Jamaica was beginning to assume sizeable proportions in the general British pattern, even alongside the older intra-European trades; the fleets came not only to ensure safe passage to and from Jamaica and England but also, paradoxically enough, to protect the vessels trading from Jamaica to the Spanish Main.[26] By 1701, nearly a third of the British navy's cruiser and convoy vessels were guarding the commerce of the West Indies.[27] Ogle, commander-in-chief on the station since 1732, had forwarded plans for 'a careening-place proposed to be made at Port Royal' to the Admiralty, and these were approved the following December. The work was costed as follows:[28]

```
- for a drift wharf for careening
  (50 feet by 120 feet by 20 feet by 116 feet) .................. £942
- for a capstan house
  (37 feet by 133 feet square) ........................ £1,209
- two bays for masts ............................................. £886
- smith's sho ........................................ £81. 10s. 0d.
- pitch-house ........................................... £10
- for a wall round the yard, 756 feet in length and 12 feet high
  from the foundation ................................. £664
                                                        ─────────
                                                        £3,792. 10s. 0d.
```

Ogle had also proposed a new hospital at Port Royal; this does not seem to have been built in his time, but by May 1735 the little 'drift wharf' had been constructed, and so had the smith's shop and capstan house (see figure 29). The maps and correspondence concerning the yard are rather scanty for the next 30 years, but it looks as if about 1739 a further burst of activity occurred, after which the yard looked something like figure 30. There was now a handsome careening-wharf, backed up by the necessary ancillary services, all contained within a properly walled enclosure.[29] At the other end of town, too, building went on in the early part of the period. Here the work centred on Fort

Charles, to which were added in the 1720s Hanover Line to the north, and the Town Line to the south-east (see figure 31); both these works survive virtually intact.

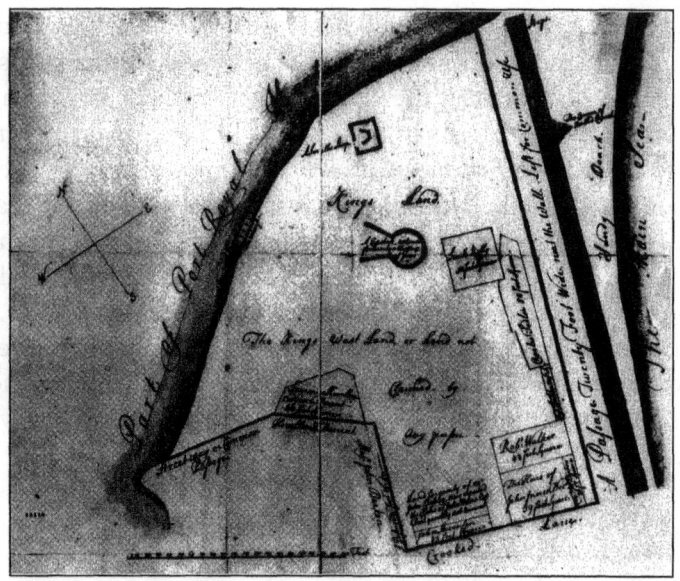

Figure 29 Anon. Sketch of the dockyard in 1735 (Library of Congress)

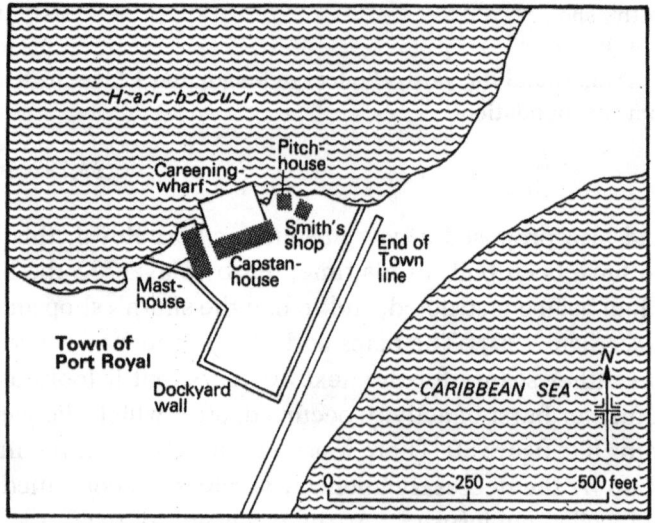

Figure 30 The dockyard in 1739

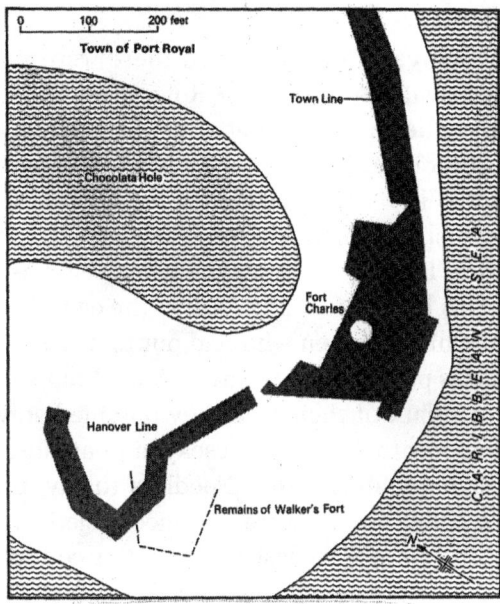

Figure 31 The work of the 1720s by Fort Charles

When Vice-Admiral Vernon reached Port Royal, in the autumn of 1739, the yard was able to undertake the refitting of his squadron; as he wrote in May 1740 to the duke of Newcastle, 'I believe I may say never more work was done in less time, and with fewer hands, than what has been done since my coming in . . .'.[30] There was still no hospital, and sick seamen were boarded out in rented houses in Port Royal, from which they often deserted.[31] Vernon pressed for a proper hospital, with an 'internal piazza' for security's sake, and by the beginning of 1743 this seems to have been ready; three fine new storehouses stood in its grounds, which occupied the former site of Axtell's Pen, a mile or so west of Kingston. This new complex received the name of 'Greenwich'.[32] The other considerable work undertaken by Vernon was the establishment of a proper watering-place at 'the Rock'. Here, near present-day Rockfort, he constructed a 'bridge' (i.e. a wharf) and three pumps, which as he wrote 'gave a dispatch even beyond my expectations, as we could fill three longboats together and all in twenty minutes'.[33]

By 1750, then, the major improvements were complete, and the dockyard had assumed the general appearance which it would retain for the next century. It was now well equipped to receive ships after the transatlantic crossing, re-victual them, water them, refit them, and send them out on those Caribbean operations which were mounting in intensity.

The Naval Station

OPERATIONS, 1715-1763

For the first ten years of this period there were no major engagements, and the naval vessels at Port Royal were largely employed in chasing pirates. The most celebrated of these malefactors was Jack Rackham, who after beginning his career in the crew of Captain Charles Vane (who eventually was hanged at Port Royal) graduated to the command of his own ship, which was in 1720 captured in Negril Bay by Captain Jonathan Barnet, R.N. Rackham himself was hanged at Gallows Point, and his body later exhibited on the cay which still bears his name; the two of his crewmen who had put up the most spirited resistance to the sailors proved to be women - Anne Bonney and Mary Read. As both were pregnant at their trial they obtained stays of execution, and Anne seems eventually to have escaped punishment, though poor Mary died in Spanish Town gaol. Needless to say, the efforts of the naval vessels to catch pirates were not encouraged by the inhabitants of Port Royal, and on one occasion in 1716 a condemned man 'was from under the gibbett rescued by the mobb at Port Royal'.[34]

Towards the middle of the 1720s, that calm which the Treaty of Utrecht had brought to European relations began to be disturbed by an offensive *rapprochement* between Austria and Spain. The British reacted in part by sending to the West Indies a large fleet under Vice-Admiral Francis Hosier. This force arrived at Porto Bello in June 1726, and began to blockade the Spanish treasure-fleet. Hosier's blockade turned out disastrously, for he lost through fevers as many men as had originally come out from England, and was only able to remain barely operational by drawing on the seamen of Port Royal. Eventually he himself succumbed to fever, as did his successor Vice-Admiral Edward Hopsonn; the whole campaign was long remembered as a horrible example by other naval commanders.

The next decade was reasonably quiet in the Caribbean, but then in October 1739 Vice-Admiral Edward Vernon arrived at Port Royal with five sizeable ships and a determination to strike at the Spaniards. The following November he sailed for Puerto Bello and captured it with surprising ease; perhaps indeed the Spanish commander surrendered prematurely. Vernon then returned to Port Royal, where in February 1740 he furiously refitted his ships in order to assault Cartagena. Finding the following March that this city was far too strong for an attack by his small squadron, he sailed on to Chagres, which was easily captured and yielded much loot.[35]

Vernon then returned to Port Royal, where he was joined in January 1741 by Rear-Admiral Sir Chaloner Ogle with a truly formidable force, by far the largest which had been seen in Jamaica until that time. Combining his fleet with his own vessels, Vernon was able to sail for Cartagena at the head of 124 sail, of which nearly 30 were third- and fourth-rates. The assault began on 9 March 1741, but a month later it was clear that the necessary progress was not being made, and following mutual recriminations between Vernon and General Wentworth, commanding the land-forces, the surviving elements of the great fleet sailed back to Port Royal, where they arrived on 19 May 1741. Vernon and Wentworth were not yet convinced of their incompatibility, and once again set forth, this time against the much less ambitious target of Santiago de Cuba. Again they failed, and again in December 1741 Port Royal witnessed the return of a defeated and demoralized force.[36]

It was from the time of the arrival of Ogle's fleet in 1741 that Port Royal permanently boasted up to fourteen naval ships of various sizes, often including five to seven line-of-battle ships.[37] However, these much more powerful fleets did not achieve the successes which might have been expected of them. Captain Charles Knowles, for instance, failed in February 1743 against La Guaira, and again the following April against Puerto Cabello. Provided shore-defences were well sited and resolutely handled, they could at this time often repulse even powerful fleets. Knowles discovered this again in February 1748, when after capturing Port Louis in Hispaniola he was repulsed before Santiago de Cuba.[38]

In the second phase of the great European wars of the mid-eighteenth century, the so-called Seven Years' War, the outstanding feat of the Port Royal-based forces was undoubtedly the capture of Havana in Cuba. This time the fleet under Admiral Sir George Pocock numbered about 200 sail, including 30 ships of the line. The Spanish commander Don Luis de Velasco put up a brave resistance, and the shore-batteries severely damaged several British ships, but in the end the main defences were carried by a land attack, and the great city fell in August 1762. The following month negotiations for peace were actively undertaken in Europe, and in November 1762 the preliminaries were signed of the Peace of Paris, which restored Hispaniola to the Spaniards, at the cost of Florida.[39]

The Peace of Paris also marks a convenient point at which to summarize this account of operations based on Jamaica. The period 1715-63 saw a constant and considerable growth in the number and size of the vessels based on Port Royal and, as we have seen, a corresponding development of the dockyard facilities there. Consequently there emerged a pattern of naval operations quite different from that of the French, who had virtually no overseas bases and so had to send their fleets out fresh from France for each season.[40] Each of these systems had its advantages; the British seamen were better seasoned, and their ships were available much longer on station, while on the other hand the French ships were generally in better repair, and were not so vulnerable to the hurricane season. On the whole, the British system seems to have been marginally more advantageous, particularly for routine tasks like blockading Santo Domingo and convoying merchantmen home. The Port Royal base was of course central to this system; without its dockyard facilities the British would have had to adopt the same pattern of operations as the French, and the whole course of the wars might have been different.

ADMINISTRATION ORGANIZATION, 1763-1815

This period witnessed a steady expansion of the dockyard, in response to the need to service more and larger ships. Some time during the mid-1760s a new careening-wharf was built to the west of the existing one; the dockyard wall was expanded westwards to accommodate it, and a capstan-house was built to serve it (figure 32). A little later, about 1770, the wall round the yard to the east was also extended, until it encompassed a large area within which a smith's shop was built (also see figure 32).

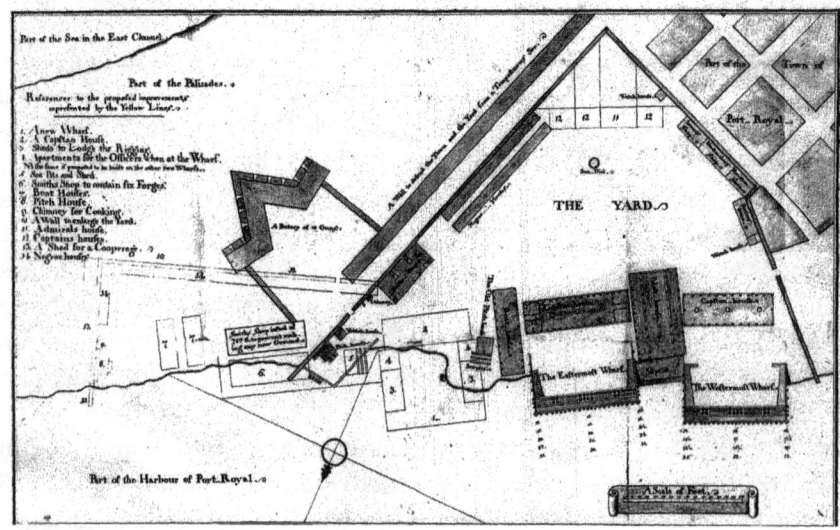

Figure 32 The dockyard in 1770

Rear-Admiral Sir George Rodney came out to Port Royal as commander-in-chief in 1771, and in September of that year had to report to the Admiralty a severe earthquake,[41] in which:

> His Majesty's dockyard has suffered considerably. The pitch-house is split up the middle of the arch, the chimney thrown down, the coppers and chimney where the people cook while at the wharf are rendered useless; the smith's shop split in several places, and so shaken as to be quite unserviceable. The foundations of the capstern- and mast-houses have likewise received much damage.
>
> His Majesty's hospital at Port Royal seems to have suffered more than any other building, the chimneys shaken down, the walls shattered; the partition walls and gable end of the northern wing and a southern wall next the dispensary greatly damaged.

No doubt the smith's shop and the capstan- and mast-houses were patched up so as to restore them to service; certainly there was no considerable rebuilding at this time. It is rather surprising to read of an evidently extensive hospital at Port Royal since, as we have noted above, a large new hospital had been built at Greenwich in the 1740s. However, this latter establishment had proved to be 'remarkable for its bad air and the mortality which always prevailed there';[42] it was henceforward reserved for French prisoners and for soldiers, while sailors seem to have used the hospital at Port Royal.[43]

During his period as commander-in-chief (1771-4) Rodney was particularly concerned with the problems of buoying and pilotage in the approaches to Port Royal. He had a survey made by the cartographer George Gauld, and the latter's 'Directions for the harbours of Port Royal and Kingston' survive among Rodney's papers.[44] Gauld is particularly interesting when he writes about land-accretion at the point:

> Port royal point has of late years gained considerably on the sea, and in all probability it will extend as far as the inner knoll. There are several people now living, who remember the water coming close to the walls of Fort Charles, and ships at that time used to sail over what is now dry land. The traces of the successive beaches are plainly to be seen all the way from the fort to the point.

Eventually he incorporated his observations into the printed *Map of the harbour of Kingston*, for which the manuscript original survives in the (British) Hydrographic Office.[45] Gauld mentions that Rodney ordered all the most dangerous shoals to be buoyed, and figure 33,

Figure 33 Leading-marks for the South Channel (Hydrographic Office, Taunton)

which may well be in Gauld's hand, shows 'the Portuguese buoy' and the leading-marks for the southern channel, which was the route by which ships often left Port Royal. The seagull floats immediately above a 'notch in mountain', which in turn has to be lined up with the eastern tip of Fort Augusta; these marks are perfectly identifiable to this day.

Rodney's name has also become associated with the lookout on Port Henderson Hill.[46] This enjoyed a very extensive view to eastward, whence hostile fleets would surely come, and was in line of sight with the signal-station on the beach by the Salt-Ponds, in Saint Thomas. On receiving an alarm, the officers on 'Rodney's Lookout' would notify both the army (regular and militia) and the navy. The lookout was built in 1778, when Rodney was away in the Leeward Islands; no doubt it was named after him when he visited Jamaica in triumph in 1782 (see below). Finally, Rodney was active at Rock Spring; Vernon's watering-place had fallen into disrepair, and it was rebuilt.[47]

The reader will recall that in its early days Port Royal was protected to the east by Fort Rupert, and then, after the earthquake of 1692, by Fort William. By 1780, however, the expansion of the dockyard eastwards had bypassed these earlier sites, and the base had virtually no defences on the Palisadoes side. During the period of command of Sir Peter Barker a large battery was therefore built to the east of the yard, and named 'Prince William Henry's Polygon' in honour of the third son of George III, who visited the island in 1783 during his service as a midshipman.[48]

This battery was severely damaged in the hurricane of 1787, but in any case it had been sited without due thought, for again in the 1790s the base had to expand eastwards, far beyond the place where the ruins of Polygon stood. This time the land was acquired in order to establish a victualling stores, built in 1799. By then the naval base had assumed the shape shown on figure 34; it was nearly half a mile long, and had reached its greatest extent. Figure 35 shows how it then looked from Apostles' Battery, on the opposite side of the harbour. Working from the right, we first see the great flag hanging limply above Fort Charles, in front of which the land has been considerably built up. Then may be seen the town itself, behind the medium-sized vessel, and after that, to the left of the other flag, the naval dockyard starts. The two capstan-houses are plainly visible, and to the left of them stretch the ancillary buildings. Just offshore is moored a ship of about 70 guns, whose upper pennant shows the land breeze to be just getting up.

While all this expansion was going on at the eastern end of the town, in Port Royal itself life was coming more and more to revolve around the navy's requirements. We have no statistics to show how the population and economic activity declined after the hurricane of 1722, but we may be sure that both were sharply reduced. Such men as remained found employment either as seamen or as fishermen, while the women of Port Royal helped the sailors, not only in providing the dubious entertainments of a naval port, but also in operating lodging-houses where sailors could be cared for when they were sick. Couba

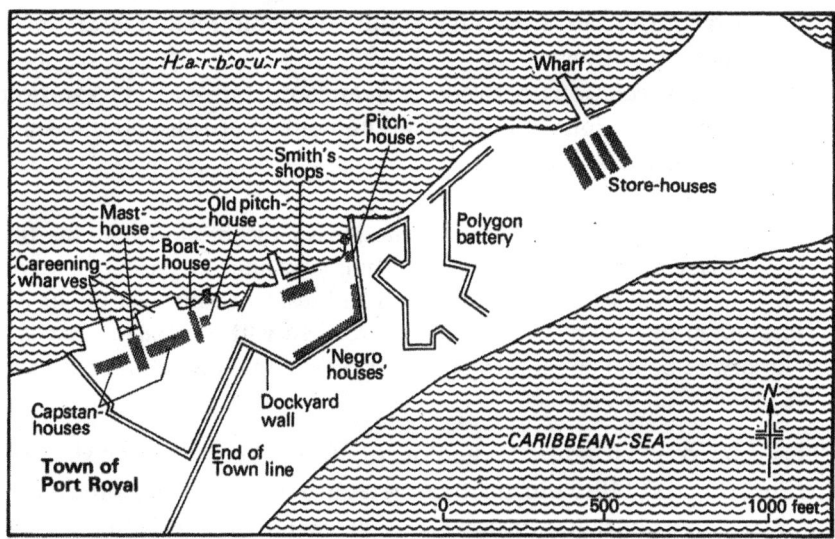

Figure 34 The dockyard in 1799

Figure 35 Anon. Port Royal from Apostles' Battery (National Library of Jamaica)

Cornwallis is the best-known of these lodging-house keepers; she became 'a favourite nurse with naval officers'[49] and looked after Nelson as well as many others.

In general, relations between Africans and Europeans were probably more harmonious at Port Royal than anywhere else on the island. As James Kelly observed:

> Sailors and Negroes are ever on the most amicable terms. This is evidenced in their dealings, and in the mutual confidence and familiarity that never subsist between the slaves and resident whites. There is a feeling of independence in their intercourse with the sailor, that is otherwise bound up in the consciousness of a bitter restraint, that no kindness can overcome . . .[50]

This relatively harmonious relationship was reflected, as we shall see, in Port Royal's ability during the nineteenth century to become a town of distinctive character, producing a disproportionate number of men who left their mark on Jamaican life.

OPERATIONS, 1763-1815

This stretch of years between the Peace of Paris and the Treaty of Vienna was the one which saw the most intense naval activity at Port Royal; it is full of interest for the naval historian, though it has so far been neglected. The commander-in-chief between 1771 and 1774 was Rear-Admiral Sir George Rodney, whose period of command was marked chiefly by intemperate displays of strength on the Spanish Main, the French remaining quiescent.[51] The situation was altogether more serious by 1778, when Vice-Admiral Sir Peter Parker became commander-in-chief. In North America the colonists were inflicting severe losses on the British forces, and in Europe Great Britain was soon at war not only with France but also with Spain and Holland. In the summer of 1779 the French admiral Charles-Hector, comte d'Estaing arrived in the West Indies with a very powerful fleet, and it seemed only a question of time before Jamaica was attacked.

It was during this crisis that the young Horatio Nelson was for a time appointed to command the batteries of Fort Charles.[52] These formed part of a defensive system in which anchored ships played a considerable part; the larger ones were lined up so as to block the channel off Fort Charles, and the smaller ones were so disposed as to command various vulnerable points within the harbour. Figure 36 shows the defensive scheme of Port Royal in 1782 as imagined by Major General

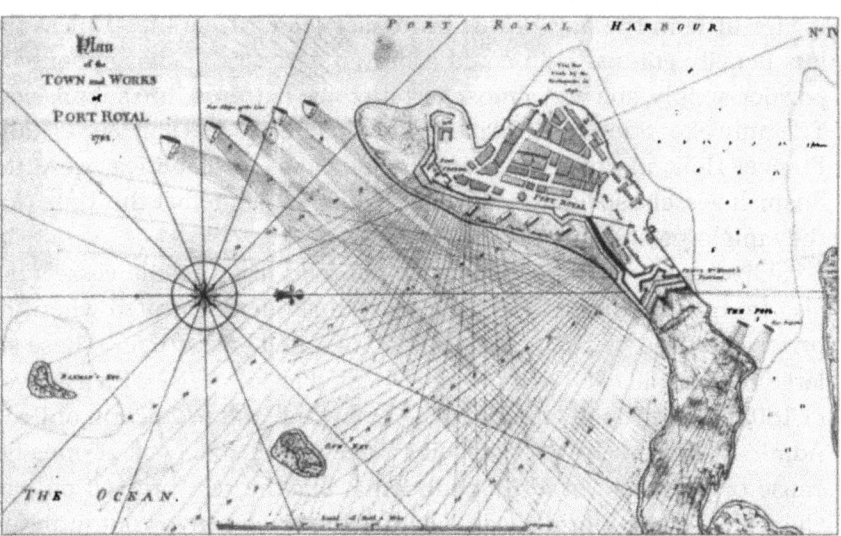

Figure 36 Archibald Campbell, 'Plan of the town and works of Port Royall, 1782' (British Library)

The Naval Station 189

Archibald Campbell, lieutenant-governor at the time; his maps are often a little fanciful, but this one seems to give a good impression of the defensive arrangements.

Early in 1780 Rodney returned to the West Indies, and for the next two seasons was engaged in the eastern Caribbean against powerful French fleets. Many inconclusive engagements of great tactical interest were fought between these evenly-matched antagonists,[53] until in April 1782 Rodney gained a decisive victory at the Battle of the Saints. The French admiral de Grasse was captured on board his flagship the *Ville de Paris*, 110 guns, and Rodney bore away for Port Royal with this and other prizes.[54]

Meanwhile the ships based on Port Royal were encountering varying fortunes. The young Nelson, in command of H.M.S. *Hinchinbrooke*, 28 guns, made a highly successful cruise between September and December 1779, capturing 'four sail, for which I shall share about £800 stirling', as he wrote at the time.[55] Others were not so lucky. Captain Robert Manners Sutton, for instance, was in command of H.M.S. *Sphinx*, 20 guns, when she fell in with the 32-gun French frigate *Amphitrite*. The latter opened fire first; 'her superior weight of metal soon brought down the *Sphinx's* main-topmast and cut her sails and rigging to pieces; and after a two hours' fight Captain Sutton hauled down his flag'.[56] In general, single-ship engagements of the 1770s and 1780s were decided by weight of metal, size and nautical qualities counting for little in the face of this brute fact of maritime life. Unless the less heavily gunned ship could score an early hit on her opponent's powder-supply, she was almost certain to be battered into submission. The only exception to this rule, which applied to the ships of Britain, France, Holland, and the infant United States of America, were the Spanish vessels, so wretchedly equipped and manned at this time that they might be easy prey.

Ships were in danger, of course, not only from hostile vessels but also from the elements, This was strikingly demonstrated when the prizes captured by Rodney at the Saints sailed for Europe. These six large vessels - all of 64 guns or more - sailed in July 1782 with a convoy of 180 merchantmen, all under the command and protection of Rear-Admiral Thomas Graves.[57] One or two ships turned back at once because of leaks and other impediments, but the rest pressed on past Cuba and up the Florida coast. Perhaps half the convoy put into New York, but in September the fleet still numbered about 90 sail when it was caught off the banks of Newfoundland in a fierce gale from the

ESE, which suddenly and even more terrifyingly shifted into a violent squall from the NNW. This shift of wind was disastrous; the British flag-ship had to be abandoned, and both the *Ville de Paris* and the *Glorieux* sank with almost all hands. In those northerly waters, seamen who had to take to such fragile and exposed boats had little chance of survival.

In 1783 the peace of Versailles was concluded, and there was a respite of nearly a decade in the hostilities between France and Britain. In 1793, though, war broke out again, and rapidly spread to the West Indies. Three years later Vice-Admiral Sir Hyde Parker became commander-in-chief at Port Royal, where between 1796 and 1800 he presided over a truly remarkable campaign against French commerce; between February and October of 1799, for instance, the British fleet took 47 armed and 225 merchant vessels,[58] all of which were disposed of in the normal way through the island's Vice-Admiralty court.[59]

The Port Royal commander, Vice-Admiral James Dacres (1804-8), was of course closely concerned with those manoeuvres in 1804 and 1805 which ended in the Battle of Trafalgar; indeed, for a time it looked as if he might have to resist a major French assault on the island. After Trafalgar the possibilities of French attack receded, and the only other incident worthy of mention is the capture in 1807 of Curaçao by Captain Charles Brisbane.[60] In general, the French ships suffered during the Revolutionary and Napoleonic Wars from their tactic of laying off and shooting at their opponents' masts and rigging; the British on the other hand tended to engage more closely, so that their murderous caronnades, heavy short-range weapons, could be brought into play.[61]

Figures 37, 38 and 39 show the different sizes of ships based on Port Royal at this time. The smallest of them is H.M.S. *Racoon*, a brig of 16 guns, which under Commander Austin Bissell was very active off Cuba and Santo Domingo in the summer of 1803. She is seen entering Port Royal with her prize, whose *tricolor* is aptly surmounted by the Union Jack. This prize may well be the *Lodi*, captured on 11 July 1803 in Leogane Road;[62] they are just passing Gun Cay (surprisingly with the gibbet) before rounding the point and bearing up into the harbour. The mountains in the background do not seem to be very accurately drawn, but the general impression of Port Royal, with the tall masts standing high above the rather low houses, seems very faithful.

Figure 38 shows a larger vessel, H.M.S. *Shark*, of about 20 guns. This ship does not ever seem to have distinguished herself, but she has at least been exceptionally well drawn. Note the dense mass of ship-

Figure 37 Anon., H.M.S. *Raccoon* returning to Port Royal Harbour (National Library of Jamaica)

Figure 38 Anon., H.M.S. *Shark* at Port Royal (National Library of Jamaica)

ping off Kingston, whose church-spire is plainly visible, and also part of the dockyard at Port Royal. The mountains are shown with considerable fidelity, and include patches of cultivation where none now exist.

Figure 39 is a rather naive delineation of an altogether larger ship, H.M.S. *Hercule*, which in June 1803 had been involved in an abortive action off Cape Saint Nicholas.[63] The *Hercule* was a standard 74-gun

Figure 39 Anon., H.M.S. *Hercule* at Port Royal (National Library of Jamaica)

ship, the largest size in common use. She is shown at anchor off Port Royal, with Apostles' Battery visible on the right, and the point on the left. Round the point is coming another vessel of similar size, dwarfing the land-installations just as close-sailing vessels to this day dwarf the buildings of Port Royal; this is a very striking visual experience which has hardly changed over the centuries. It was on board *Hercule* that in 1804 a 'grand breakfast' was offered to Lady Nugent and her party by Vice-Admiral Dacres;[64] he was the last commander-in-chief to operate sizeable fleets out of Port Royal.

ADMINISTRATIVE ORGANIZATION, 1815-1905

Although the dockyard did not take in any new ground during this period, much building-work was done, chiefly to enable new types of ship to be serviced. One improvement, which survives intact, was the building of a new wall at the western end of the yard. The town of Port Royal had in 1815 suffered from a disastrous fire, which had burned a few buildings at the edge of the yard; after the building of this wall the latter was separated from the town by a fire-gap about fifteen yards wide (see figure 40).

The main work of these years was however the construction of a new naval hospital. Begun about 1817, this building was largely supported by prefabricated cast-iron units brought from England. The

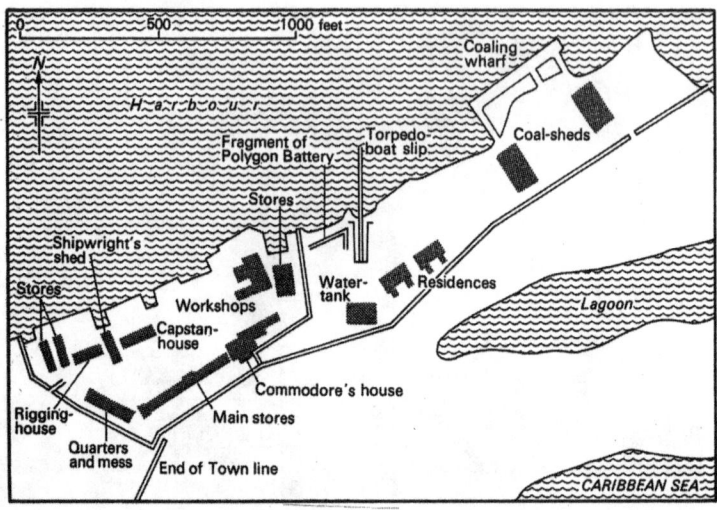

Figure 40 The dockyard in 1900

skill with which it was constructed is shown by its present condition, for even after the earthquake of 1907, as well as many other lesser shocks, it is almost as true over its 400-foot length as when it was first built. Among its earliest patients was Captain J. H. Boteler, R.N., who interestingly describes his time in the recently completed hospital and his ultimate recovery.[65] Down the years the comments on the hospital are uniformly favourable;[66] it was well designed and well maintained.

Figure 41, one of the remarkable series of lithographs executed by J. B. Kidd in the late 1830s, shows the hospital just to the left of the central ship. Its long low outline is unmistakable to this day, though most of its outbuildings have been demolished. This plate has several other features of interest; to the left of the hospital may be seen the waterfront of the town and the dockyard, while to the right of the ship is Fort Charles, under the newly planted palms. A very speedy-looking island boat is just putting out with the land breeze of the evening, and a small boat with a furled lateen sail is edging its way homeward in the left foreground.

In 1838 Port Royal's naval status changed, when it ceased to be an independent command and became the headquarters of the Jamaica Division of the North America and West Indian station, commanded by a commodore. This did not prevent further material growth; on the contrary the middle years of the nineteenth century saw the completion of very extensive buildings in the heart of the dockyard. A very large new stores-block was built, crowned with a conspicuous clock-tower, and a new boat-slip was constructed (see figure 40). The photograph reproduced as figure 42 shows part of the yard shortly after the completion of this work. The long stores-block with its tower is in the centre; a covered way leads from this stores to the wharf. On the left is part of the mast-house, and left of centre is the conspicuous flagstaff. On the left-hand (eastern) end of the stores was built the Commodore's house, which generations of naval officers remembered with nostalgia, especially for the excellence of its billiards-table and baths.[67]

Figure 43 reproduces a delightful anonymous water-colour, painted no doubt in the 1850s. The tower and flagstaff of the dockyard are at once recognizable, as are its various wharves; on the left a merchantman is inching her way up to Kingston in the calm air, while a man-of-war lies off the yard. In the foreground are some of the mooring-buoys at which naval ships were normally secured. This scene may well have been painted from the receiving-ship, which was moored just off Port Royal and used both to hold stores and as a prison-ship.[68] For many years the ship assigned to this duty was the *Urgent*, sold out of service as late as 1903.[69]

In the early 1860s the dockyard was further improved by the addition of coaling-sheds and coaling-wharves at the eastern end, near the

Figure 41   Joseph Kidd, View of Port Royal about 1830 (National Library of Jamaica)

Figure 42 Photograph of the dockyard about 1865 (National Library of Jamaica)

Figure 43 Anon. Watercolour of the dockyard about 1865 (National Library of Jamaica)

Figure 44 Albert Huie, The eastern end of Port Royal (National Library of Jamaica)

victualling-yard. A supply of about 10,000 tons of coal was kept here,[70] and great sheds formed a distinctive feature of Port Royal, well captured by Albert Huie (figure 44), before their dismantling in the 1950s. They also, of course, enabled the yard to deal with the latest naval vessels, which increasingly used coal.

In the closing decades of the nineteenth century it was becoming apparent that this modern base could no longer be adequately defended by the guns of Fort Charles, of the Hanover Line, and of the Town Wall, all built nearly two hundred years earlier. A great new battery was therefore installed to seaward of Fort Charles, and named after the reigning sovereign. Victoria Battery held two 9.2-inch guns and two 6-inch guns, all housed in a formidable series of bunkers. The whole installation was much shaken by the earthquake of 1907, but its remains may still be seen.

About 1900 the final improvements were made to the yard, when a torpedo-boat slip was installed just to the north-east of the site of Polygon Battery, and the wall was extended to include the area of the coaling-wharves (see figure 40). By then, though, Port Royal's days as a naval base were numbered. The later nineteenth century had seen the rise of the so-called blue water school of British imperial strategists, advocating very powerful fleets operating out of the United Kingdom, supported by a small number of strongly fortified overseas bases. The Port Royal yard was too small to rank as one of these, and so in 1905, following the reorganization directed by Admiral Sir John Fisher, her last commodore hauled down his flag.[71]

The dockyard rapidly fell into decay; many of its buildings were intentionally demolished, and others collapsed of neglect, so that today, as we shall see, it is hard to identify even some of the most recent structures. Meanwhile the town had been enjoying a certain quiet prosperity.[72] Visiting naval officers were uniformly appalled by its appearance,[73] but the relations of the seamen with the inhabitants continued to be good. Captain Boteler, who had been nursed in the new naval hospital by a certain Dolly Johnson, a bumboat-woman, gives this account of his last sight of that admirable lady:

> I ought not to leave out the bumboat woman, and who washed for me, Dolly Johnson, a jet-black Negress, a splendid figure, supple and most graceful in all her movements . . . We had just cleared the harbour's mouth when Dolly paddled alongside, and standing up, swaying and bending over the vessel's side, 'may Goramighty bless you and de kooner, and send you good luck and plenty ob dollar, and I bring you yam, plantain and banana for de cruise', and away she went, scouting any payment.[74]

Operations, 1815-1905

During the decade following the treaty of Vienna, the smaller naval ships at Port Royal were kept busy chasing pirates, who often made their bases on the southern coast of Cuba. The *Recollections* of Captain Boteler describe two interesting chases of this kind, which were often perilous for the seamen concerned, since they usually had to land and pursue their dangerous quarry across very rough and unfamiliar country. Brought back to Port Royal, the pirates would be tried and then often hanged. Boteler describes one of these occasions:

> At the end of May (1823) they were hung at Gallows Point on the Palisades, a long neck of sand connecting the town of Port Royal with the main island of Jamaica, and forming the snug and roomy harbour. I witnessed the execution; early in the morning the *Gloucester*'s boats, manned and armed and with a guard of marine drums and fifes, went up to Kingston, returning in procession towing the launch with the captain (Aragonez) and nine pirates, the drums and fifes giving out the

'Dead March in Saul', 'Adeste Fideles' etc. The following morning the other ten were also executed - a fearful sight. No men could go to their death with less apparent concern. Before the captain first went up the ladder he called upon his men to remember they were before the foreigners and to die like Spaniards . . .[75]

As the century wore on, quite different types of vessel began to make their appearance at Port Royal. Figure 45 reproduces a lithograph of about 1855 by Adolphe Duperly, the early Kingston photographer. The ships are improbably close together, but he gives a good idea of the types. On the right may be seen H.M.S. *Cumberland*, a conventional sailing man-of-war very similar to the one shown in Kidd's lithograph (figure 41). The vessel to the left of her is the paddle-wheel steam sloop *Buzzard*, with 6 guns and engines developing 300 horse-power. To the left of *Buzzard* are two 12-gun brigs, followed by H.M.S. *Imaum*, 72, which for many years was the depot-ship at Port Royal. In front of *Imaum* and to her left is H.M.S. *Devastation*, another of the new steamships; she too was a paddle-wheel steam sloop, whose engines developed 400 horse-power.[76] In the background, between *Devastation*'s fore- and main-masts, may be seen the newly completed clocktower of the dockyard, and finally on the left are two more small paddle-steamers. Duperly has of course arranged all these ships with a certain artistic licence, but the selection of vessels gives us a good idea of the appearance of the Port Royal anchorage in the years when sail was giving way to steam.

Figure 45 Adolphe Duperly, Naval vessels at Port Royal about 1855 (National Library of Jamaica)

Many of the political events of the nineteenth century left their mark on Port Royal. In May 1864 the Archduke Maximilian called there, *en route* to his ill-fated Mexican venture.[77] In 1865 the Confederate commerce-raider *Alabama* put in there, and Captain Semmes enjoyed a trip ashore, where he was particularly captivated by the Port Royal mountains.[78] In the same year, it was from Port Royal that H.M.S. *Wolverine* set out, on her terrible mission of reprisal following the Morant Bay Rebellion. Eight years later, Port Royal saw the hasty departure and triumphant return of H.M.S. *Niobe*, which successfully rescued some British subjects unjustly held as pirates at Santiago de Cuba.[79] With the economic decline of Jamaica, however, the importance of Port Royal as an operational base was also declining. Considerable numbers of naval vessels continued to frequent her harbour, and her commodores continued to preside over their large shore-establishment, but its *raison d'être* was fading away. Eventually the time came when the British were content to regard the Caribbean as 'an American lake', and once that time came Port Royal's larger strategic significance had passed away.

Epilogue

Just after the turn of the century, then, Port Royal lost the dockyard on which so much of her prosperity was based. When he was writing *Historic Jamaica*, in 1915, Frank Cundall hoped that the completion of the Panama Canal would restore her importance,[80] but things did not work out like that. On the contrary, when the coastal artillery units withdrew in the 1950s, Port Royal had become less significant than ever before.

Since then there have been hopeful signs. The establishment of the Police Training School for a time offered a livelihood to a number of Port Royallers, and the transfer to Port Royal of the naval units of the Jamaica Defence Force has given employment to others. The old naval dockyard has in part been converted to the requirements of an hotel and marina, and increasing numbers of tourists may be expected to visit Port Royal as the years go by. Within the town itself the formation of the Port Royal Brotherhood, precipitated by the hurricane of 1951, testified to the emergence of a new community spirit. Meanwhile the life of many of the inhabitants continues to centre on the sea, whether as fishermen, customs officers, or absent seamen. Emerging from a dismal recent past, and encumbered with memories of distant febrile activity, Port Royal now seems due to enter upon a period of moderate prosperity.

Notes

1. It is no longer possible, for instance, to to consider studying the logs of all the ships on the station; these are preserved in great numbers at the Public Record Office and in the National Maritime Museum.
2. For a detailed discussion of naval administration, see Ruth Bourne's *Queen Anne's navy in the West Indies* (New Haven, Conn., 1939).
3. See, for instance, *C.S.P.* 80 of 13 February 1693. *C.S.P.* 1702-3, 1082 of 10 September 1703.
4. *C.S.P.* 1702-3, 1082 of 10 September 1703.
5. The orders to Joseph Gyde, supply agent at Port Royal in the early eighteenth century, are preserved in the Bodleian Library, Rawlinson A 232.
6. *C.S.P.* 1693-6, 635 vi of 19 October 1693.
7. Ibid., 1004 of 5 April 1694, Beeston to the Lords of Trade and Plantations.
8. See Plate 7 in Buisseret, *The fortifications of Kingston*.
9. *C.S.P.* 1701, 486 of 30 May 1701, Beeston to the Council of Trade and Plantations.
10. *Port Royal Jamaica: excavations 1969-70* (Kingston, 1972), pp. 53-4.
11. Cundall, *Governors of Jamaica in the 17th century*, p. 135.
12. P.R.O. Adm. 52/30 under 21 June 1692.
13. P.R.O. Adm. 52/68, date 21 November 1693.
14. P.R.O. Adm. 52/38, date 2 February 1693.
15. *C.S.P.* 1693-6, 1484 of 6 November 1694.
16. See Cundall, *Governors of Jamaica in the 17th century*, pp. 149-52, and also David Buisseret, 'The French invasion of Jamaica in 1694', *Jamaica Journal* 16/3 (1983), 31-3.
17. See the *Twelfth Report of the Historical Manuscripts Commission*, p. 342.
18. See Clowes, *The Royal Navy*, ii. 469-71 for this paragraph.
19. Ibid., ii. 368.
20. Ibid., ii. 372.
21. On this whole affair Ruth Bourne amplifies and to some extent corrects the version given by Clowes; see her *Queen Anne's navy*, pp. 154-61.
22. *C.S.P.* 1704-5, 295 of 4 May 1704; Governor Handasyd to the Council of Trade and Plantations.
23. *C.S.P.* 1706-8, 279 of 20 April 1706.
24. Clowes, *The Royal Navy*, ii, 509.
25. Ibid., ii. 376.
26. See Curtis Nettels, 'England and the Spanish-American trade, 1680-1715', *Journal of Modern History*, iii (1931), 1-32.
27. Bourne, *Queen Anne's navy*, p. 58.
28. National Maritime Museum, Ad/A2233 (no folio-numbers).
29. See the map of Port Royal (unnumbered) preserved at the Naval Library, Ministry of Defence, London.
30. *The Vernon Papers*, ed. B. McL. Ranft (London, 1958), p. 97.
31. Ibid., p. 324.
32. Ibid., p. 356. See also P.R.O. C.O. 700/14, a map by Archibald Bontein of 1748.
33. *The Vernon Papers*, p. 177.
34. *C.S.P.* 1716, 203 of 12 June 1716, Governor Hamilton to the Council of Trade and Plantations.
35. Clowes, *The Royal Navy*, iii. 61-2.
36. Ibid., iii. 76-7.
37. Richard Pares, *War and trade in the West Indies 1739-1763* (Oxford, 1963), p. 266.
38. Clowes, *The Royal Navy*, iii. 132-5.
39. On the Havana expedition see Clowes, op cit., iii. 245-50.
40. On the two systems see Pares, *War and trade in the West Indies*, pp. 278-85.
41. This letter is quoted by Frank Cundall in *Historic Jamaica* (London, 1915), p. 67.
42. According to Edward Long, *A history of Jamaica*, ii. 107.
43. Described by Long (op cit., ii. 147) as 'a large, airy and well-contrived building'. On the hospitals, see Jean and Oliver Cox, *The naval hospitals of Port Royal, Jamaica* (J.N.H.T., 1995).
44. P.R.O. 30/20, vol. 18 ('Rodney papers').
45. Hydrographic Office (Taunton, England), D961 16N.
46. For a plan and brief description see Buisseret, *The fortifications of Kingston*, pp. 38-9.
47. On this work see David Spinney, *Rodney* (London, 1969), p. 252.

⁴⁸ For a plan and brief description see Buisseret, *The fortifications of Kingston*, pp. 42-3.
⁴⁹ According to Cundall, *Historic Jamaica*, p. 72.
⁵⁰ Quoted by Edward Brathwaite on p. 301 of *The development of creole society in Jamaica 1770-1820* (Oxford, 1971).
⁵¹ On this command see Spinney, *Rodney*, p. 250-68.
⁵² See his letter of 12 August 1779 to Captain Locker, printed in *The dispatches and letters of vice-admiral Lord Viscount Nelson*, ed. Sir Nicholas Harris Nicolas (7 vols., London, 1845-6), i. 31-2.
⁵³ Amply described in Clowes, *The Royal Navy*, iii. 448-537.
⁵⁴ Two of the guns from the *Ville de Paris* may still be seen at the Rodney Memorial in Spanish Town.
⁵⁵ Clinton Black's *Port Royal* quotes this, in an interesting section on 'Lord Nelson' (pp. 62-5).
⁵⁶ Clowes, *The Royal Navy*, iv. 31.
⁵⁷ Clowes, *The Royal Navy*, iv. 86 ff.
⁵⁸ According to Frank Cundall's *Chronological outlines of Jamaica history* (Kingston, 1927), p. 26.
⁵⁹ See Michael Craton's 'The role of the Caribbean Vice-Admiralty courts in British imperialism' in *Caribbean Studies*, xi (1971), 5-20.
⁶⁰ Clowes, *The Royal Navy*, v. 236-8.
⁶¹ This sentence relies on the very interesting observations made by Clowes, op. cit., iv. 543-4.
⁶² See Clowes, op cit., v. 555-6.
⁶³ Clowes, op. cit., v. 317-18.
⁶⁴ See *Lady Nugent's journal*, ed. Philip Wright (Kingston, 1966), p. 200.
⁶⁵ See *Recollections of my sea life from 1808 to 1830* (London, 1942).
⁶⁶ See, for instance, N. B. Dennys, *An account of the cruise of the Saint George . . . 1861-2* (London, 1862), p. 76, and Captain W. R. Kennedy, R.N., *Sport, travel, and adventure* (Edinburgh and London, 1875), p. 281.
⁶⁷ See, for instance, W. H. Watts, *The commission of H.M.S. Retribution* (London, 1904), p. 135 and J. N. Dalton (ed.), *The cruise of H.M.S. Bacchante 1879-82* (2 vols., London, 1886), i. 147.
⁶⁸ See Kennedy, *Sport, travel and adventure*, p. 281, for a sketch of this ship.
⁶⁹ Cundall, *Historic Jamaica*, p. 79.
⁷⁰ Watts, *The commission of H.M.S. Retribution*, p. 126. The dredging operations for the coaling-station were particularly destructive of parts of old Port Royal; see Robert Marx, *Pirate Port* (London, 1968), p. 87.
⁷¹ By an ironic twist, this last commodore was F. W. Fisher, Sir John's brother.
⁷² See H. P. Jacobs, 'Port Royal in decline', *J.H.R.*, viii (1971), 34-59.
⁷³ See, for instance, Kennedy, *Sport, travel and adventure*, p. 281, and Paul Thompson (ed.), *Close to the wind; the early memoirs of Admiral Sir William Creswell* (London, 1965), p. 48.
⁷⁴ Boteler, *Recollections*, p. 124.
⁷⁵ Boteler, op. cit., p. 114. See also Clowes, *The Royal Navy*, vi. 234-5 for an account of two similar engagements.
⁷⁶ Some of these technical details may be found in the (annual) *Jamaica Almanacks* which sometimes list the vessels on station.
⁷⁷ See C. V. Black, 'When Maximilian visited Kingston', *Bulletin of the Jamaican Historical Society*, ii (1957), 2-4.
⁷⁸ See F. L. Casserly, 'A great sea-raider's links with Jamaica', in the *Bulletin of the Jamaican Historical Society*, ii (1957), 108-12.
⁷⁹ See Clowes, *The Royal Navy*, vii. 238-42.
⁸⁰ Op. cit., p. 80.

CHAPTER ELEVEN

Archaeological Investigations at Port Royal

The recovery of items from sunken houses at Port Royal began almost before the earthquake was over. Many of the buildings lay in water so shallow that they could be entered and searched; for some time there was, as we have noted in chapter 9, such a collapse of law and order that many of the structures were thoroughly plundered. Other buildings lay as deep as 50 feet under water, but these too were quite accessible to the Port Royallers who, as we have seen, included a large number of skilful divers accustomed to working on wrecks. The houses were in general so thoroughly picked over that Robert Marx, who led the underwater project of 1966-8, rarely discovered objects of interest except when a collapsed structure had covered them.[1]

For many decades after 1692 the sunken houses remained clearly visible, and authors described the curious sensation of floating over them in boats. In course of time, however, the heavier small objects sank deep into the seabed, and even large buildings came to be obscured under layers of silt and coral. By 1835, when Lieutenant B. Jeffrey, R.N. carried out a survey in the area, only the tops of many houses were visible, though the water was still often clear enough for these 'traces of houses' to be 'especially distinct'.

Perhaps the most interesting nineteenth-century description of the drowned city was that written by Jeremiah Murphy in 1859. Murphy, who was a naval diver attached to the dockyard, wrote a letter to the *Falmouth Post* describing his experiences:[2]

> I first went down on the remains of old Port Royal on the 29th August (1859), and found that what I had heard with regard to some of the buildings being seen when the water was clear was correct. I landed among the remains of ten or more houses, the walls of which were from 3 to 10 feet above the sand. The day was rather cloudy and I could only get a view of a small portion at a time.

After repairing H.M.S. *Valorous*, I went down again on the 9th instant, at what is called at Port Royal 'the Church Buoy', but which ought to be called 'the Fort Buoy', it being placed on the remains of old Fort James; but the day was unfavourable, the water being muddy - so that I could not see much; and being impressed with the idea that it must have been the remains of the church on which I was, my explorations that day were not satisfactory.

About 12 o'clock (being then down four hours) the water cleared a little, and getting a better view I concluded that the ruins which I was on must have been those of a fort. But soon after I found a large granite stone somewhat the shape and size of a tombstone, which was covered with a coral formation, so that I could not tell whether it had an inscription or not. Fancying this stone to have been a tombstone, thereby indicating the vicinity of a churchyard, I was not satisfied what the character of the building could have been.

I came to the surface about 1 o'clock determined to wait a more favourable day. In the meantime Mr de Pass was so good as to obtain for me, from the collection of Henry Hutchings, Esq., a map of the old town as it stood before the earthquake, by which I learnt that the ruins, of the nature of which I had all along had my doubts, were in fact the ruins of Old Fort James, and that the church stood about the east end of the present dockyard . . .

I am of opinion, from what I have seen of old Port Royal, that many of the houses remained perfect after the earthquake, though sunk in the water, and that the sand has been thrown up, and the mud settled around and in them from time to time, until all [but] the largest buildings are covered over, so that the remains of the houses which I have seen may have been the top part of the highest buildings; which is apparently the case from the irregularity of the heights . . .

During the following hundred years various divers worked in the area, but the next considerable discovery appears to have been that made in May 1954 by Mr. and Mrs. Alexis Dupont, accompanied by Mr. Cornel Lumiere. Diving in the same area as Murphy, they came across an arched doorway with a flight of steps, though on their return they were unable again to find this site.[3]

Two years later Mr. Edwin Link, engineer and inventor (the 'Link trainer') from the United States, visited Port Royal, and made a preliminary survey of the area round Fort James. Here he discovered and raised a cannon,[4] but soon decided that his equipment was not equal to an extensive investigation. Returning in June 1959 with the specially equipped *Sea Diver*, Link and his group tried a number of sites, including the one near Fort James and another in the king's warehouse.[5] They recovered considerable quantities of pewter, clay pipes, and glass, and also found a most curious watch, made by Paul Blondel about 1686.[6]

In 1960 Mr. Norman Scott, also from the United States, led another team to Port Royal, this time concentrating on the area round Fort Carlisle, off Morgan's Harbour. Here they found a wooden wheel, possibly from a gun-carriage, and the usual bottles and clay pipes, but on the whole their excavation was not very rewarding.[7]

Early in 1966 there began what had certainly been the most intensive and fruitful underwater investigation until then. This was conducted by Mr. Robert Marx, who for about two years worked chiefly in the area off the naval hospital, where there was some danger of a deepwater pier being constructed. Here Marx found enormous quantities of artefacts - too many, indeed, for the available conservation facilities. There was the usual haul of pewter, copper, brass, and glassware, as well as mounds of bricks. The two most spectacular items recovered by Marx were a hoard of Spanish-American coins and a pocket-watch. The coins, which were in remarkable condition, had been minted between 1653 and 1690 in Latin America; their recovery was all the more curious, as they lay in an area apparently accessible to earlier divers. The watch was remarkably well restored, and proved to have been made by Aron Gibbs of London.

When Marx returned to the United States in 1968, the Jamaica National Trust Commission secured the services of Mr. Philip Mayes, an English archaeologist whose interests lay rather in land than in underwater archaeology. His attention centred on the site of the early naval dockyard, menaced by the proposed construction of an hotel, but the two years which he spent at Port Royal also marked a decisive step forward both in the identification of various sites and in the organization of facilities for conservation and preservation.[8] Mayes's task was made much easier by the chance discovery in 1968 of the remains of Fort Rupert, in the lagoon to the east of the Port Royal Primary School (see figure 47).[9] With this site identified, it was for the first time possible to accurately plot the position of many features in the town, using Fort Rupert in the east and Fort Charles in the west as points of reference.[10]

Mayes was able to work out a whole comparative sequence of scaled maps, which permitted him in particular to identify the different phases

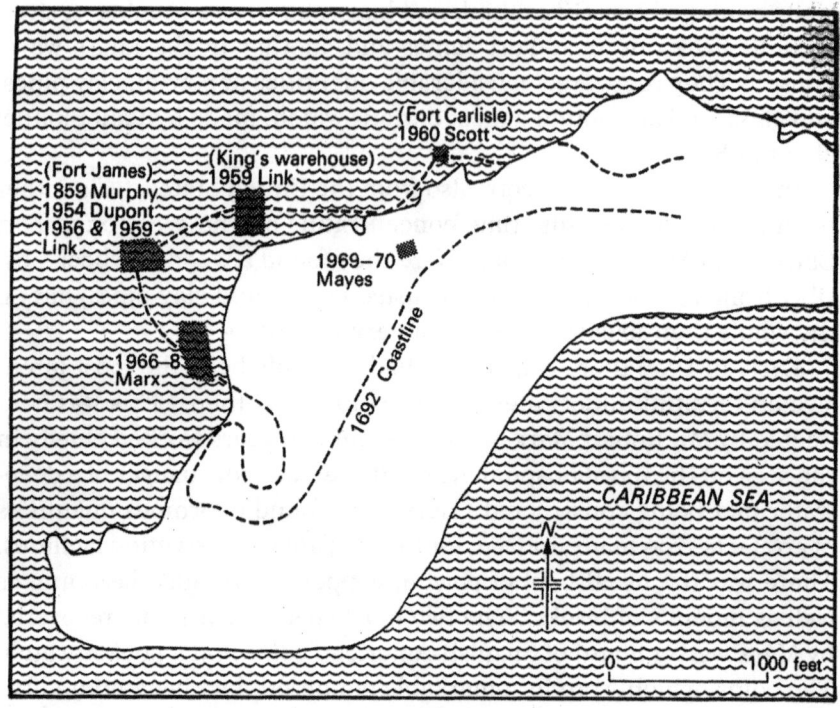

Figure 46 Areas of archaeological investigation

in the development of the dockyard.[11] When he came to excavate there, the technical problems were considerable. The various buried buildings could generally be identified, even though they were in an extremely complex sequence, by using the series of maps, but the excavation could only be kept reasonably dry by the installation of an extensive wellpoint system, with a pumping capacity of 6,000 gallons of water per minute. In fact, Mayes found that to keep a hole about 10 x 30 x 40 feet dry, he had to pump constantly at a rate of about 4,500 gallons per minute.[12]

With this considerable installation functioning, it was possible to investigate a promising area in the dockyard, which in fact proved to contain the pre-earthquake Anglican church (see appendix 3). The south-east corner of this structure was fully exposed, and a good deal of timber was recovered from it, including fragments of four pews and much decoration-work.[13] The relative shortage of time and of funds precluded the extension of the investigation to the potentially even more interesting eastern end of the church, but even without this further work the investigation had been remarkably fruitful. Mayes also did a great deal to organize the conservation in the old naval hospital, where very well-equipped laboratories were established and manned by local staff.

Mayes left in 1971, and was succeeded by Anthony Priddy, who for two seasons worked on the area facing New Street between Love and Dove Streets. The plats indicated that the lot was conveyed in one piece to John Fletcher in 1661, but over the next 30 years it was constantly sub-divided into eight or more dwellings. Priddy's work enabled the English architect, Oliver Cox, to make faithful and highly suggestive images of this central area (figures 18 and 24), where the overcrowding was worst. Indeed, looking at these drawings we are surprised that no major fire occurred before 1703.

There was an interval after Priddy's departure, and then in 1981 Professor Hamilton, of Texas A & M University, began a series of yearly investigations, carried out under his direction by students of his university's underwater archaeology field school. Their work, which lasted until 1990, was concentrated on a relatively small area, at the intersection of Queen Street and Lime Street, immediately north of the investigation carried out by Marx (figure 46), and the yearly progress was recorded in successive numbers of the *INA Newsletter*.[14] Probably the most remarkable result of this long series of digs derived from the use of SHARPS, introduced in 1987. This Sonic High Accuracy Ranging and Positioning System used high frequency sound to measure distances with very great accuracy. When the system was used in conjunction with known and unmoved landmarks, such as Fort Charles and Fort Rupert, it allowed Hamilton to determine that at the time of the earthquake there had been very little lateral movement of the buildings, which had simply sunk into the ground. This meant not only that structures could be identified even more accurately than before, but also that the streets were in effect still on much their old alignment, and fundamentally changed our understanding of the catastrophe of 1692.

At least 14 students made substantial contributions to the *INA Newsletter*, and it would be impossible to note all their contributions. Many, though, bore on problems that we have already discussed, in many cases corroborating our conclusions. Janice Carlson and Shirley Gotelipe-Miller, for instance, worked on the great collection of pewter which had been recovered by various archaeologists. In the absence of a catastrophic event like the one in 1692, ancient pewter is often absent from archaeological sites, since it was so often melted down and re-used. The Port Royal collection is the largest assembly of seventeenth-century pewter ever recovered from a single site, and an invaluable resource for comparative and dating purposes. It has even permitted the partial reconstruction of the work of Simon Benning, pewterer, whose touch mark included his initials and a pineapple, symbol of Jamaica.[15]

Port Royal's silver was studied by Laurel Anne Breece, under the direction of Merrick Posnansky, of the University of California at Los Angeles.[16] She was able to work on 16 items, including spoons, a porringer, a wine-taster and a tooth-pick. Curiously, only one piece, a spoon, had a hallmark, and this was from London. The most unusual item was the tooth-pick, for it was most intricately carved, with a pineapple on one end. Since the pineapple was a motif closely associated with early Jamaica, it seems very likely that this piece was made on the island. Breece also checked 22 inventories of Port Royal residents among the probate records of Spanish Town, finding that there was no discernible correlation between the total value of the estate and the occurrence or absence of silver; it must have been a matter of personal taste.

Returning to Professor Hamilton's students, we have the work by Helen Dewolf on Chinese porcelain. Curiously, of 3,912 seventeenth-century shards, no less than seven per cent was Chinese porcelain, much of it still intact. These pieces included a medallion bowl, small cups and bowls, and two Dog of Fo figurines. The latter are particularly interesting, as well as beautiful, for we know that they went into production in China in 1645. The figurines show a male and a female dog, the latter having a puppy at her paw. These porcelain pieces suggest that Port Royal was a prosperous and cosmopolitan society, supported by extensive trade networks, and this is also the impression derived from Patricia McClenaghan's work on drinking-glasses, whose fragments came from an exceptionally wide range of sources.

Pipes were studied by Becky Jobling, using a huge deposit of over 5,000 fragments. She determined that most came from England, the majority from Bristol but some from London and Broseley, and even a few from Holland. Maker's marks were frequently preserved, as was the decoration, but much of the craftsmanship was poor and it is possible that many seconds were being shipped to Port Royal.[17] Yabba ware, studied by John Bratten, was also relatively crude, but then this was primarily a kitchen ware, suitable for cooking such meals as stews. Tommy Hailey, however, studied the lead content of the various lead-glazed ceramics, and found that this was particularly high in yabba ware, though it was also often high in other ceramics, exceeding as much as forty times the recommended level set by the U.S. Food and Drug Administration for large hollow-ware. Such an excess can apparently have bad effects on the reproductive, immunological, digestive, cardiovascular and nervous systems, without necessarily producing the sort of symptons that would have been noticed by contemporary physicians.

As we have noticed, the excavators discovered the wreck of a large ship, perhaps H.M.S. *Swan*; an assessment of this vessel was given by Sheila Gifford.[18] Diana Thornton concentrated not on the material culture, but on "The probate inventories and the wealth of seventeenth-century Port Royal".[19]

She took 160 Port Royal probate inventories, aware both that these were only a sample and that they created a bias towards movable goods. Still, some trends were clear: the merchants were the most prosperous, but during the seventeenth century substantial assets were being accumulated not only by tradesmen and artisans, but also by people like fishermen. Houses generally seem to have had eight rooms, fully furnished; the beds were particularly lavish. People wore elegant clothes, few of which were ready made, though this was common in England by the late seventeenth century. Sir Henry Morgan was particularly well clothed: as Gifford puts it, 'Port Royal was definitely an early center of conspicuous consumption'. This lavishness extended in particular to what was called 'coyned money', both English and Spanish. It would appear that many Port Royallers held more in loose change than the average estate value in Boston in 1688; the town reminds one of the kind of free-wheeling financial operations associated in our day with offshore financial havens.

A great deal of archaeological work, then, was accomplished between 1959 and 1990. However, a glance at the map shows that the part explored is very small in comparison with the total area of interest (see figure 46); as Marx wrote in the conclusion to his *Pirate Port*, 'the majority of old Port Royal's secrets still lie buried under the sea'. They seem safe for the time being, since the Port Royallers are well aware of the importance of not allowing them to be looted. However, it is rather difficult to see the way forward, since Hamilton has demonstrated the remarkable amount of time and effort that is needed to fully investigate even a small part of the sunken area. Perhaps we should rest content for the time being with the satisfaction that the archaeological finds so far seem to fully confirm what had been discovered from the documents.

NOTES

1. See his book, *Pirate Port*, passim.
2. Quoted in extenso by Frank Cundall, *Historic Jamaica*, pp. 58-9.
3. See Philip and P. A. Mayes, 'Port Royal, Jamaica the archaeological problems and potential', in *The International Journal of Nautical Archaeology and Underwater Exploration*, I (1972), 101.
4. See Marx, *Pirate Port*, p. 89.
5. Their expedition is described in Marion C. Link's 'Exploring the drowned city of Port Royal', *National Geographic*, 117 (1960), 151-83.
6. This watch aroused an interesting learned controversy; see the 'Notes on a 17th-century watch found at Port Royal' in the *Bulletin*, v (1970), 71-5.
7. See Marx, *Pirate Port*, p. 92.
8. See the Jamaica National Trust Commission's *Port Royal Jamaica: excavations 1969-70* (Kingston, 1972).
9. See the short article by M. Pawson, 'Fort Rupert rediscovered', in the *Bulletin of the Jamaican Historical Society*, iv (1968), 311-16.
10. See for instance, the aerial photograph in *Jamaica Journal*, iv. 2 (1970), 3.
11. We should like here to express our gratitude to Mayes for making this sequence of maps available to us; it was particularly useful for chapter 10.
12. Philip and P. A. Mayes, 'Port Royal, Jamaica', p. 108.
13. See *Port Royal Jamaica: excavations 1969-70*, passim.
14. Published by the Institute of Nautical Archaeology, College Station, Texas.
15. See Professor Hamilton's 'Simon Benning, pewterer of Port Royal' in *Text-aided archaeology*, ed. Barbara Little (Boca Raton, 1992).
16. See '17th-century silver: the Port Royal collection', MA dissertation University of California at Los Angeles (1992).
17. See also Karen Gardner, 'Abundant pipe remains attest to the popularity of smoking' and Kenen Heidtke, 'Crude red pipes reflect local traditions', both in the *INA Newsletter*, 14/1-2 (November, 1987), 12-13.
18. See her article 'The Port Royal ship' in the *INA Newsletter*, 17/2 (Summer 1990), 8-10.
19. *INA Newsletter*, 14/2 (November 1987).

CHAPTER TWELVE

Port Royal Today

The visitor will normally approach Port Royal by land, driving along the Palisadoes road, only opened in 1936. Figure 2 gives a good idea of the fragility of this link, which can easily be cut by storms, at least temporarily. Past the airport, the extensive mangrove swamps on the harbour side, and the dunes covered with scrub and cactus on the seaside all must look much as they did in 1655.

The first sign of Port Royal is the naval cemetery, which lies on the right-hand side of the road about half a mile out of the town; its site cannot be far from that of the graveyard destroyed in 1692 (see chapter 9). This collection of nineteenth-century tombstones testifies to the prevalence of yellow fever, and also takes us into the more obscure corners of Port Royal's history; the visit of the Royal Netherlands' corvette *Soembina*, for instance, in 1869, when the captain and two seamen were drowned in Kingston Harbour. There is also one particularly pathetic memorial to '—, a little still-born child, daughter of Commodore and Mrs. de Horsey, b. at Admiralty House, Port Royal, 30 Dec., 1872'.[1]

Continuing on the Port Royal road, we next come to Fort Rupert, on the left. On dry ground may be seen what looks very much like the remains of an octagonal tower, while about 20 yards out in the lagoon is a large fragment of the brick battery wall, part of Fort Rupert. The lagoon is clear and the water harmless; the visitor armed with a diving-mask can easily inspect this curious relic. About 100 yards past Fort Rupert, with the nineteenth-century wall running close by the road on the right, is a marked rise in the road. Here the visitor is in fact driving up what remains of the southern rampart of Polygon Battery, whose largely complete northern horn lies inside the dockyard area, just by the place where light craft are now beached. Here too may be seen the torpedo-boat slip, still used for launching and recovering small vessels.

Morgan's Harbour, a club and hotel, next appears on the right. Here some attractive brick storehouses, which probably date from the eighteenth century, may be seen beside the pool. Working westwards within the dockyard area, we come first to the site of the church excavated by Mayes in 1970-1, and then to the walls and buildings by the entrance to the dockyard from New Street in the town of Port Royal. Here is one stone store-building from the eighteenth century, protected by the double walls, with some fine angled brickwork around the gate in the inner wall. Working back southwards, the visitor leaves the dockyard by the southwestern-gate, near which are the foundations of an early wall.

Tower Street may then be seen running off to the south-west, protected from the sea by the massive Town Wall.[2] This street soon changes its name to Church Street, after Saint Peter's church.

This is a much-restored structure originally built in 1725-6; it contains some interesting commemorative art[3] and a remarkable eighteenth-century organ-loft. The visitor may also be shown the communion plate, which is alleged to have been a gift by Sir Henry Morgan from his Spanish plunder, but which in fact appears to be early eighteenth-century North American silverware. In the graveyard is one particularly interesting tomb, which was transferred here from Green Bay, across the harbour. It commemorates Lewis Galdy, whose remarkable escape in 1692 has already been mentioned in chapter 9.

Continuing past Saint Peter's, the visitor enters the old Police Training School, and eventually arrives at Fort Charles. This, as we have seen, is the oldest surviving monument of the British occupation of Port Royal - and indeed of Jamaica - and remains much as it was left after the remodelling of 1725 (see chapter 10). At the entrance the visitor will note the section of very early walling at the ground level, as well as the massive anchors, one of which was accidentally recovered in 1935 by the anchor of a Canadian freighter in the harbour.

To the south of Fort Charles are the remains of the Victoria Battery, which was built in the later 1880s and wrecked by the earthquake of 1907.[4] West again of Fort Charles may be seen the very interesting fragment of wall known as the Hanover Line, which dates from the 1720s and is substantially unchanged. Emerging from the old Police Training School, the visitor does best to strike off down Dove Lane and then down Gaol Alley. Here may be seen the Old Gaol, repaired about 1990 by Peter Francis of the Urban Development Corporation. Examination of the building revealed carpenters' marks characteristic of the seventeenth century, and the high quality of the workmanship indicated to British experts that the building might be due to shipwrights

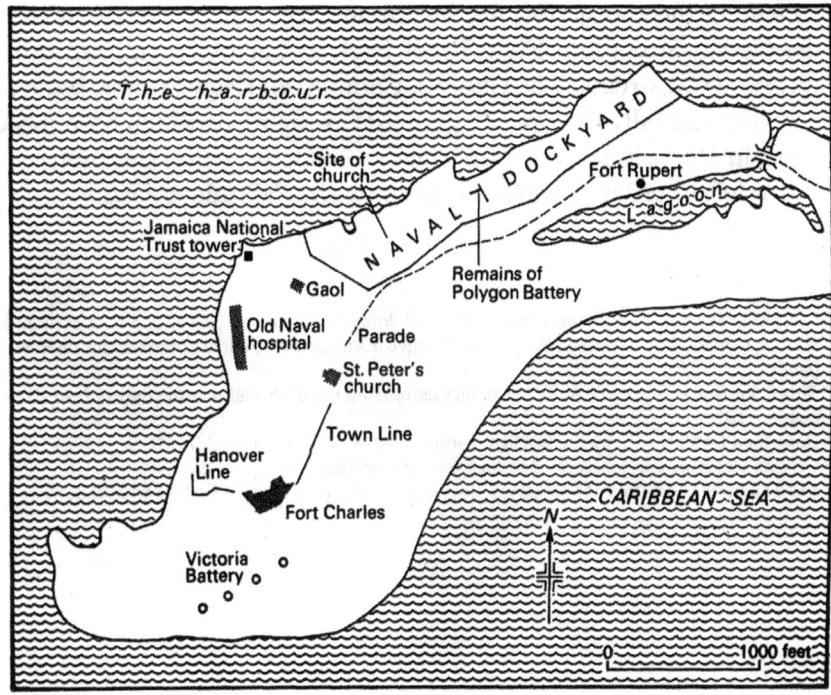

Figure 47 Surviving sites of interest

rather than 'housewrights'. Proof of its solidity is that it has survived over 14 hurricanes, 6 earthquakes and two disastrous fires.

To the west will then be seen the old naval hospital, whose remarkable history has been recounted by Jean and Oliver Cox.[5] It might be better known as the 'cast iron hospital', for like the Iron Bridge in Spanish Town, it exemplifies a very early use of that material. It was designed by Edward Holl, a naval architect who worked in partnership with such engineers as Marc Isambard Brunel and John Rennie. For the hospital, Holl collaborated with John Sturges, of the Bowling Iron Works in Bradford, Yorkshire, England. This was a very innovative works, which from the early 1790s was producing the steam engines patented by James Watt - without Watt's knowledge, as it happened. The hospital is thus a monument from a remarkably fertile time of innovation, at a crucial time in the English Industrial Revolution. It is at present in a state of some disrepair, but should on no account be allowed to deteriorate further, given its remarkable place in the history of industrial architecture.

Leaving the Naval Hospital by Broad Street, the visitor can then take Queen Street and High Street back to Cagway Road, reflecting that these two streets, like Church, Cannon, and New Streets, seem to be on substantially the same alignments as the roads which bore those names in 1692. Emerging from Cagway Road, the visitor has then only to turn left in order to leave the town by the Palisadoes road.

NOTES

[1] See Philip Wright, *Monumental inscriptions of Jamaica* (London, 1966), p. 53. Algernon de Horsey, Commodore between 1872 and 1875, gave his name to the shoal known as the 'de Horsey patch'.

[2] This is known as 'Morgan's Wall', but in fact dates from the early eighteenth century (see above, chapter 10).

[3] Described by Mrs. L. Lewis in 'English commemorative art in Jamaica', *J.H.R.*, ix (1972).

[4] On this structure see Buisseret, *The fortifications of Kingston*, pp. 47-8.

[5] See *The naval hospitals of Port Royal*, Jamaica (1995), on which I relied for what follows.

Conclusion

Port Royal today is an unspectacular little town, and a considerable effort of the historical imagination is needed to visualize it at the various periods of its history. In a certain sense, this task is made easier by its present obscurity; Fort Charles, for instance, is not imprisoned by skyscrapers as are the early monuments of, say, Boston, to name Port Royal's seventeenth-century associate. At the point of the spit it is very easy to imagine how things looked in 1654, before the English came. There is the same kind of pebbly beach, steeply shelving underwater and constantly replenished by the action of waves and currents. The cays, of course, have also changed very little since the Spaniards brought their vessels past them in order to heave down on the *cayo de carena*. Behind the beach-area, with its striated layers, comes a mass of prickly bush, with a good deal of cactus; the appearance of this too would have been well known to Spaniards and indeed Taino Indians.

Slightly more effort is required to imagine how Port Royal looked in 1660, the year of Ysassi's departure. Five years earlier he had given an account of its appearance from what is now Port Henderson Hill; in 1660 this view would have revealed the main lines along which the new settlement would develop. Towards the sea, on the right, was Fort Cromwell, with its round tower conspicuous above its rather pitiful gun-lines. This fort was of course lapped by the sea on one side and by Chocolata Hole on the other. In Chocolata Hole one or two small vessels probably moored habitually by 1660, and there would have been a few ships off the harbour proper, where the earliest settlers had built their crude wooden houses.

These stretched in a line along the gentle sandy curve of the bay, from the state's large storehouse to King's House, surrounded by its palisade. A little to the right of King's House, towards the south, was the wooden church, Christchurch, and behind the row of houses facing on to the harbour were already other rows of houses, though the whole area was as yet far from full. The whole settlement still had a very open look, since there were no forts apart form Fort Cromwell and the line of palisades across the spit, past King's House.

Things would be very different 30 years later, towards the peak of Port Royal's commercial prosperity. By then the crude wooden buildings had given way to those brick town-houses which Sloane so much mistrusted, and though the streets were still sandy they were wide - without pavements, of course - and gave into well-stocked shops. By then, a visitor observing the town from the market-place would have seen a cross-section of the various happenings which we have described, perhaps too analytically, in chapters 4 to 8. Just after daybreak the guards would make their last rounds, and while they were dispersing to their houses the 'flesh and turtle' market would be getting under way, down at the other end of the High Street, on Fishers' Row. Slowly the shops would open, following a time-table less fixed, no doubt, than ours, and then towards mid-morning the land-breeze (never very strong) would drop, and it would get hot. About then, too, such ships as had been lying off for the night would begin to come into the harbour, bringing eagerly awaited goods and news. Just as is the case in small islands to this day, news of a particularly interesting shipment would soon spread, and housewives would lay in stocks of the new material, or of the new season's wine.

Sometimes the ships would bring important persons, to be saluted repeatedly by forts and ships; on days like that the noise must have been deafening, and the town particularly animated, as members of the House of Assembly and others hurried to Port Royal to make their mark with the new man. Some of these figures would have become very familiar to the town's by-standers. Reginald Wilson, for instance, was not only naval officer but also merchant (in a small way), assemblyman, and churchwarden; he must have hurried many times about the streets, from one duty to another. Among the inhabitants, free and unfree, there would also mingle the visitors, many of them seamen of one kind of another, though there would also be a few passengers, like John Taylor; Port Royal must have seemed a home from home to them after the relatively crude establishments of the smaller eastern Caribbean islands.

Once the midday sun began to take its toll, the shops would be closed and Port Royal would relapse into a Mediterranean torpor. By then the markets would have sold their stuffs, and the stall-holders would have dispersed, some no doubt returning across the harbour to smallholdings on the mainland. Not many people would now be left on the streets, until the town began to come to life again about three in the afternoon. Then the bustle would slowly work up again, until by six or so the shops brought their shutters down, and the taverns began to do brisk business. By then too the sea breeze would be dying away, and in the cool of the evening the inhabitants would walk by the sea, or venture out along the spit to the east.

Nothing is now left on the ground from that opulent period but Fort Rupert and parts of Fort Charles. Since 1692 the handsome brick houses have disappeared, and with them the town's teeming life. Some of the views of the middle of the eighteenth century, taken from high in the hills above the Liguanea plain, capture this change in visual emphasis at Port Royal. Now the town has assumed the modest appearance which it has retained to the present day, and the chief signs of activity are around the naval yard. Here the great ships dwarf the land-installations, even after the extensions of the middle and end of the century.

Port Royal offered a case history of naval development between 1760 and 1860, as the ships became radically different and the dockyard much larger. By then, as Duperly has shown us, many of the vessels were steam-driven, and the dockyard held considerable stores of coal, as well as mechanical workshops and a handsome new stores-building. In the town itself there was some interesting building of characteristically Jamaican town-houses, with their verandahs and jalousied windows; some examples of this style survived right down to the hurricane of 1951. After 1900 the naval activity diminished year by year, and the naval installations became increasingly decrepit, if they were not actually destroyed. Perhaps the last events of naval significance occurred during the Second World War, in the memory of people still living. Then they would look from their homes on the Kingston plain out to Port Royal, to see what ships from the Royal Navy might be anchored there.

Some were engaged in hunting German submarines, which sank many oil tankers in the Caribbean and Gulf of Mexico. Others were part of larger schemes, like the aircraft-carrier H.M.S. *Indomitable,* which grounded in the South Channel on the way to the Pacific theatre in 1942. It was lucky for her, since otherwise she surely would have been sunk along with the *Prince of Wales* and *Repulse* off Malaysia.

By the 1960s the largest vessels operating out of Port Royal were the power-boats of the marlin-fishermen, and nearly all the naval buildings had collapsed. So we come to our own days, when Port Royal is a modest fishing-village and a base to the Jamaica Defence Force's naval wing, with its fast patrol boats. By now little of the historic past is visible on the site, but Port Royal has become, as we hope to have shown, a splendid place for the use of the historical imagination.

Appendix 1
Privateers frequenting Port Royal 1659-60
(Extracted from D'Oyley's Journal, B.M. Add. MSS. 12423)

Name	Ship	'Lett Passe' date
Jaque Le Paine (Lepene)	*Bonaventure*	17 September 1659
Capt. Thomas Gregge	*Aimé*	28 September 1659
Capt. Richard Guy[1]	*Hopewell Adventure*	24 November 1659
Capt. Lewis Alford	?	7 November 1659
Capt. Bonidell	?	24 November 1659
Capt. Bequell	?	3 December 1659
Capt. Peterson	?	31 December 1659
Capt. Laques	A barque	31 December 1659
Capt. Allen	*Thriver*	1 April 1660
Capt. Wade	*Sea Horse*	4 April 1660
Capt. James	*America*	16 May 1660
Capt. Mansfield[2]	?	4 December 1660

[1] Captured a prize in May, 1660, with 14,775 pieces of eight on board, and a further prize in the following month for which he was paid '133 lbs. 9 oz of bullion, being the tenths of bullion brought in'.

[2] Later became 'admiral' of the Port Royal privateers

APPENDIX 2

'An account of the private ships of warr belonging to Jamaica and Turtudos [Tortuga] in 1663 (B.M. Add. MSS. 11410, fo. 10)

	Men	Gunns
Sr. Thomas Whetstone, comdr. of a Spanish prize	60	17
Capt. Smart, comdr. of the *Griffon*, frigott	100	14
Capt. Guy, cmdr. of the *James*, frigott	90	14
Capt. James, cmdr. of the *American*, frigott	70	6
Capt. Cooper, his frigott	80	10
Capt. Morris, comdr. of a beganteene	60	7
Capt. Brenningham, his frigott	70	6
Capt. Mansfield's breganteene	60	4
Capt. Goody, a pincke	60	6
Capt. Blewfield belonging unto Cape Grace Deos living amongst the Indians, a barke (being manned with English, Dutch and Indians)	50	3
Capt. Hardue, a frig. Spanish prize	40	4
11 ships; these 740 men are English, Dutch and French with many more	740	81

There are 4 more belonging to the island of Jamaica which I cannot give an accompt of.

Of forraigners:

Capt. Senolve, a Dutchman having 3 small ships full of men from Jamaica which have transported themselves to the River	100	12

Ships belonging to Turtudos having the govr.'s commissions:

Capt. David, a Dutch ship and Portugall comdr.	40	6
A flyboate belonging to the governor of Turtudos, the captain's name I know not	80	9 All French
Capt. Buckell, a French frigott	70	8
Capt. Clostree, a French commission (most Frenchmen)	68	9
	358	44

This information I have received from credible persons; most of the English private ships and captns. are very well known to myself, wch. I did think convenient to give you an accompt of.

APPENDIX 3

The sites of the Anglican churches before 1692

One of the most perplexing problems in the topography of early Port Royal has been the siting of the Anglican church, or rather churches, since 'Saint Paul's' and 'Christchurch' are known to have existed simultaneously. The only way to resolve this problem is to set out the surviving evidence chronologically, and that is the aim of this appendix.

D'Oyley's oak church or 'market house', completed towards the end of 1658,[1] was no doubt small but adequate for the needs of the embryonic town. It must surely be to this church that the patent acquired by Mr. John Loving on 16 October 1661 refers: his plot bounded 'north to the High Street, 74 feet, west 66 feet on land now or late of Henry Tryon, and eastward to the church 60 feet'.[2] This places the church on the south side of High Street, not far from King's House - a likely spot.

Between 1661 and 1672 the surviving records make only passing mention of churches in Jamaica - or more usually to the lack of them. As early as June 1661, though, the Council must have had another structure in mind for Port Royal, for a revenue minute of that date provides for the reserving of 150 pounds towards the cost of a church and court-house. The ensuing decade was one of general consolidation in Jamaica, and many areas began to make provision for churches; as Modyford wrote in his 'View of the condition of Jamaica' (1664), 'they are now levying contributions to raise churches in some of the richest parishes'.[3] At Port Royal, D'Oyley's old church was probably becoming inadequate for the growing town, and in any case it stood on unpatented land. Consequently, on 9 May 1672 Lieutenant-Governor Lynch ordered that a plot of land be surveyed and laid out for a church, and this was duly accomplished on 10 June 1672.[4] The land bounded 'north on High Street, 80 feet, south by Church Lane 92 feet, west on Mr. John Loving, and east 70 feet', on what has been transcribed from the plat books as 'Church Lane' but is more probably 'church land'. In this case land on which the old church was still standing.

This plot is the one directly to the east of the one granted in 1661 to Loving, when it was noted that to Loving's east was already a church. The new church plot also bounded southward on to 'Church Lane' (or perhaps 'Church Street'), further evidence to suggest that D'Oyley's church was probably on the eastern boundary of this site. The case is clinched by the sale in 1663 by Henry Sweeting, merchant of London, to his son John, of 'all those four messuages or tenements near the sea shore of Cagway, joining to the east end of the church or churchyard of the said parish of Cagway, now or late in the several tenures or occupations of Captain Thomas Morgan, Susan Gillian and the said Henry Sweeting or their assigns . . .'.[5]

Work probably began on the new church in the latter half of 1679, apparently to the design of William Beeston.[6] In 1680, an observer noted that Port Royal 'has a mean house belonging to the King, and a worse church. But in Sir Thomas Lynch's time [1671-5] divers gentlemen contributed towards building a good one, and they are now about it'.[7] In the same year, another report mentioned that 'the church is now finished to the steeple outward',[8] and Morgan wrote about 'the church, which is now almost finished. It is all finished but the plastering of the chancell, which will be done next week, and the rest of the windows glazed'.[9]

Shortly before the dedicatory service in the new church, William Jackson, mariner of Port Royal, conveyed to Charles Penhallow and Reginald Wilson, 'churchwardens of the parochial church of Port Royal called Christchurch' and to 'John Longworth, clerk, parson and present incumbent of the church' a small fragment of his land onto which Christchurch intruded, for the sum of six pounds.[10] Almost immediately afterwards the new church - Saint Paul's - was opened, and Mr. Longworth preached on the text 'put off thy shoes from thy feet, for the place where thou standest is holy ground' before Sir Henry Morgan and a gathering of the elite of Port Royal.[11]

This new church was described by John Taylor in his manuscript, and was partially excavated by Philp Mayes (chapter 11). From the latter's report of his findings it is clear that Taylor's account of the church was faulty in several respects, which is not surprising since Taylor is unreliable on topographical and architectural details. However, our analysis of the documents has at any rate made plain the sequence of Anglican churches. D'Oyley's oak church, eventually named 'Christchurch', stood and was used until about 1682, when it was replaced by Saint Paul's, 'the handsomest church in America'.

1 See above, p. 13
2 N.G. cards 589 and 592.
3 *J.H.A. Statistical Papers*, p. 21.
4 N.G. card 225.
5 I.R.O. Deeds, liber XIV, p. 183.
6 P.R.O., C.O. 1/50, Lynch to the bishop of London, 23 October 1683.
7 N.L.J., MS. A1, fo. 51.
8 B. M. Sloane 2724, fo. 239.
9 Bodleian, Rawlinson D 843, fo. 187, 18 August 1680.
10 I.R.O. Deeds, liber XIII, p. 64.
11 See Cruikshank, *The life of Sir Henry Morgan*, p. 310.

APPENDIX 4

List of craftsmen and tradesmen in Port Royal before 1692

Architect	Snead, Robert (1684)
Baker	Wingar, William (1683)
Barbers	Alcocke, William (1676)
	Books, Charles (1680)
Blacksmiths	Davidson, William (1679)
	Hanson, William (1679)
	Jackson, Henry (1673)
	King, Edward (1676)
Bricklayers	Richardson, Samuel (1683)
	Smelling, William (1683)
Butchers	Dennis, John (1676)
	Elkins, George (1668)
	Elkins, Isaac (1673)
	May, Augustin (1668)
	Walker, Robert (1677)
Carpenters, cabinet-makers and joiners	Albert, John (1675)
	Avis or Aves, Robert (1666)
	Bartaboa, Peter (1666)
	Bradford, Edward (1680)
	Brock, Richard (1657)
	Budden, John (1672)
	Budden, Julian (1677)
	Coxshott, Abraham (1683)
	Gale, John (1680)
	Gardener, Samuel (1676)
	Germayne or Jermayne, Robert (1672)
	Goodall, Richard (1674)
	Gray, Thomas (1673)
	Hallett, John (1675)
	Homes, Thomas (1668)
	Jones, Griffith (1675)
	Perkins, Henry (1670)
	Perkins, William (1675)
	Small, Henry (1665)
	Smith, Robert (1676)
	Thompson, Richard (1674)
	Typton, Thomas (1677)
	Watkins, Moses (1689)
	Winde, Thomas (1677)
	Yonge, Stephen (1675)

Chandler	Bates, William (1674)
Chyrurgeons	Axtell, William (1674)
	Baskerfield Dr. (1674)
	Cartwright, Anthony (1675)
	David Dr. (1674)
	Doggett, Nathaniel (1677)
	Ellett Dr. (1674)
	Fisher Dr. (1674)
	Hardson, Robert (1668)
	Homes or Holmes, George (1664)
	Jackson Dr. (1676)
	Sperry, Francis (1673)
	Trapham, Thomas (1678)
	Widall, Robert (1672)
Combmaker	Bennett, Paul (1673)
Coopers	Hall, James (1676)
	Holloway, Richard (1685)
	King, Thomas (1688)
	Mercer, Thomas (1679)
	Moore or Moire, William (1679)
	Niele, Joseph (1683)
	Pullin or Pullein, Henry (1675)
	Trissell, Nicholas (1680)
	Tull, John (1679)
	Watson, Thomas (1680)
	White, Joel (1674)
Cordwainers	Barnard, George (1675)
	Becke or Berke, Peter (1674)
	Fox, N. (1689)
	Greene, Edward (1676)
	Griffith, John (1679)
	Hobby, Thomas (1679)
	Hudson, George (1671)
	Landerson, Garrett (1670)
	Nelmes, John (1679)
	Pearce, Crispin (1683)
	Pearce, John (1663)
	Skannon, Edward (1680)
	Stevenson, John (1674)
	Wade, John (1684)
	Waller, John (1675)
	Weight, John (1677)
	Wilmott, John (1673)

Drugster	Mathews, William (1682)
Fishermen	Collingwood, Richard (1674)
	Hall, Daniel (1680)
	Norris, Henry (1675)
	Russell, James (1680)
Glazier	Hudson, Thomas (1684)
Goldsmiths	Lord, Richard (1677)
	Pingart, James (1679)
	Watson, Henry (1680)
	Westbrooke, Caleb (1681)
Gunsmiths	Massey, Stephen (1664)
	Philpott, John (1680)
	Pocock, Thomas (1684)
	Pym, Jonathan (1689)
Hatmaker	Rosewell, John (1683)
Ivory turner	Clifton, William
Labourers	Dennis, John (1674)
	Maloane, Hugh (1673)
	Martin, Thomas (1669)
Limeburner	Hardwick, John (1675)
Mariners	Bailing, Alexander (1680)
	Bird, Richard (1675)
	Bowtell, Thomas (1675)
	Bradley, Joseph (1670)
	Brewer, Adam (1673)
	Burley, John (1679)
	Cave, William (1677)
	Claiton, Peter (1675)
	Cooper, William (1668)
	Coxen, John (1674)
	Cupid, Joseph (1672)
	Dunn, Michael (1675)
	Farnandoes or Fernandez, Joseph (1678)
	Fitchwilliam or Fitzwilliam, Thomas (1677)
	Gage, Stephen (1673)
	Gardener, Henry (1670)
	Gardener, Phillip (1674)
	Gomerford, Mathew (1675)
	Hall, Jacob (1675)
	Harris, Lewis (1679)
	Jackson, George (1672)

Jarman, John (1677)
Jules, William (1687)
Keene, Robert (1675)
King, John (1663)
Knight, William (1675)
Lewis, David (1675)
Lyndy, William (1675)
Martin, David (1672)
Mayes, William (1672)
Morris, John (1674)
Morris, William (1669)
Ripley, Richard (1671)
Rogers, Richard (1673)
Russell, William (1675)
Rysby, James (1678)
Sawkins, Richard (1681)
Shepheard, Andrew (1668)
Smith, James (1680)
Smith, Morgan (1668)
Stickalorum, Jasper (1668)
Stone, Edward (1666)
Taylor, Mathew (1670)
Taylor, Robert (1664)
Tompson or Thompson, Peter (1677)
Turpin, James (1670)
Vines, Walter (1666)
Watts, Alexander (1682)
White, John (1684)
Whiting, William (1668)
Williams, Patrick (1680)
Williams, Robert (1680)
Willis or Wyllis, Edward (1664)

Masons Stone, John (1673)
Weston, Robert (1668)
Wheeler, Michael (1675)
White, Robert (1670)

Merchants Agard, John (1680)
Allen, Samuel (1679)
Alvarez, David (1677)
Alveringa, Joseph d'Acosta (1674)
Aristioguetta, Francisco de (1674)
Ashurst, Jonathan (1671)
Atterbury, Edward (1678)

Ayleward, Lawrence (1674)
Bach, Samuel (1674)
Barker, Samuel (1679)
Bathurst, Joseph (1670)
Beeston, William (1666)
Belfield, John (1666)
Bird, Richard (1670)
Blatt, James (1670)
Bodkin, Henry (1669)
Bodley, James (1674)
Bowman, James (1677)
Bolton, Randolph (1680)
Bragge, William (1664)
Bray, Thomas (1679)
Buckler, Alexander (1673)
Burnside, Andrew (1671)
Burton, John (1680)
Carter, Isaac (1671)
Cecill, James (1668)
Cole, George (1682)
Cole, James (1670)
Cooke, Edward (1672)
Cordova, Moses Jesurum (1675)
Coward, William (1675)
Crane, William (1667)
Crosse, Epinatus (1662)
David, Alexander (1672)
Delion, Jacob (1671)
Desalina, Diego Clement (1674)
Desosamendes, Abraham (1671)
De Silva, Mordakay (1678)
Downes, James (1670)
Ellbridge, Aleworth (1674)
Ellis, Edward (1680)
Fawsett, James (1673)
Feake, Josua (1663)
Gabay, Solomon (1674)
Gerrard, Samuel (1674)
Gibbon, William (1672)
Gleed, Henry (1672)
Gomez, David (1670)
Gutoros, Jacob Mendes (1675)
Hall, Francis and William (1687)
Halstead, William (1674)

Harding, James (1670)
Hayes, John (1676)
Hayn, Joachim (1666)
Hazle, Edward (1680)
Head, John (1673)
Henriquez, Jacob Bueno (1672)
Hicks, Nicholas (1673)
Hill, Roger (1672)
Holloway, Andrew (1675)
Hoveden or Howeden, N. (1664)
Hudson, Thomas (1674)
Hunt, Joseph (1672)
Hutchinson, William (1680)
Jennings, Joseph (1682)
Jordain, Daniel (1672)
King, Thomas (1670)
King, William (1668)
Kinder, John (1689)
Knight, Charles (1680)
Langford, Abraham (1675)
Ledsham, N.
Lewis, Samuel (1670)
Lockyer, Thomas (1674)
Loving, John (1664)
Lucas, Isaac (1670)
Man, Francis (1686)
Man, Samuel (1686)
Martin, James (1666)
Martyne, Thomas (1675)
Mason, Stephen (1681)
Mathews, Thomas (1673)
Mohun, John (1673)
Moone, John (1676)
Moulder, Edward (1677)
Narbona, David Lopez (1674)
Neale, Thomas (1678)
Newton, Isaac (1674)
Niclaes, John (1686)
Palmer, Henry (1672)
Penhallow, Charles (1677)
Perera or Peryia, Abraham Messiah (1671)
Pinhorne, Edward (1666)
Povey, Edward (1667)
Pugh, Peter (1666)

Pullin or Pullein, John (1666)
Putford, William (1672)
Quadman, Peter (1670)
Raymond, Edward (1674)
Roe or Rowe, James (1679)
Rutton, Mathias (1667)
Saunders, Christopher (1673)
Short, Jerome (1667)
Southern, Elias (1672)
Stanton, Edward (1672)
Stephenson, Edmond (1674)
Swanley, Robert (1672)
Sweeting, John (1675)
Swymmer, Anthony (1674)
Tilley, Thomas (1688)
Torras, Jacob (1671)
Tritton, Robert (1667)
Turner, Edward (1684)
Vandananker, Cornelius (1670)
Walker, John (1669)
Ward, Henry (1679)
Watson, Thomas (1682)
Wells, John (1682)
Whitfield, Charles (1665)
Williams, Rowland (1679)
Willia, Banjamin (1673)
Willis, Edward (1680)
Wilson, Reginald (1670)
Wills, Samuel (1673)
Wyatt, William (1679)

Pewterers	Benning, Simon (1667)
	Childermas, John (1670)
	Luke, John (1679)
Pipemaker	Pope, John (1680)
Porter	Paul, George (1670)
Poulterer	Jeffreys, Richard (1677)
Sailmakers	Brewer, Adam (1671)
	Clark, Thomas (1665)
	Philips, Robert (1677)
	Selcombe, Francis (1677)
Schoolmaster	Bird, Peter (1677)

Shipwrights	Cavell or Cadell, William (1676) Freeman, Marmaduke (1686) Rollerson or Rollenson, Jacob (1675)
Tailors	Case, William (1676) Crane, William (1669) Daniel, Shadrack (1671) Ducker, John (1668) Ebden, Pewter (1683) Hawkins, Edward (1668) Martin, David (1670) Stone, John (1677) Ware, Thomas (1686) Warriner, George (1665)
Watermen	Adams, Barnaby (1668) Brocke, William (1674) Clements, Joel (1668) Dalton, John (1674) Gomersall, John (1671) Hancock, Nicholas (1674) Jones, John (1671) Saunders, Sydrack (1680) Smith, John (1675) White, Joel (1674)
Wherrymen	Grant, John (1669) Morgan, Edward (1680)
Victuallers, vintners and tavern-keepers	Adams, Barnaby (1675) Adkins, Gabriel (1668) Baldwin, John (1670) Barbar, Jonas (1680) Barre, Charles and Mary (1685) Bassett, John (1668) Carter, Caesar (1664) Clifton, William (1677) Cook, Thomas (1675) Copeland, William (1675) Dayton, Mary (1664) Eayres, John (1670) Ells, John (1672) Finne, Thomas (1680) Fist, Anthony (1681) Fitch, Richard (1677) Gage, Anne (1670)

George, Francis (1677)
Gray, Samuel (1678)
Hay, John (1673)
Hill, Thomas (1674)
Hoveden, John (1663)
Howett or Howell, William (1669)
Lenham, George (1679)
Lyssons, Nicholas (1671)
Manderson, Francis (1674)
Martine, James (1667)
Mapeley, Richard (1670)
Mayham, Christopher (1671)
Mills, Thomas (1681)
Mussett or Muffett, James (1671)
Parker, William (1670)
Payne, Thomas (1672)
Pitts, John (1663)
Seaman, Edward (1688)
Stockley, Edward (1688)
Taylor, Thomas (1674)
Tompson, Richard (1673)
Turpin, James (1679)
Walker, John (1664)
Ward, John (1680)
Wildish, John (1670)
Wills, Captain Henry (1679)
Yates, Edward (1674)

Notes about appendix 4
The dates provided after each name are intended as an indication of the year in which the person concerned is known to have lived in Port Royal; of course, they usually lived there both before and after that year. Some names appear in more than one list, probably because the person changed his or her occupation. The lists cannot pretend to be complete, but they do provide some indication of the diversity of occupations. Readers will notice old friends among many categories, such as Simon Benning the pewterer, or Thomas Trapham the doctor. The list is also useful for such purposes as identifying the extent of the Jewish community, or calculating the number of women operating their own business. Many of the names, too, belong to a wider Jamaican history: the victualler Nicholas Lyssons, for instance, gave his name to a community that still thrives.

APPENDIX 5
A list of Port Royal Taverns
(from the I.R.O. deeds)

	Location
The Black Dogg (1682)	?
The Blue Anchor (1679)	?
The Catt and Fiddle (1676)	Figure site 3
The Cheshire Cheese (1684)	'Fronting north on New Street'
The Feathers (1681)	Figure site 49
The Green Dragon (1674)	Figure site 22
The Jamaica Arms (1677)	'Lying on Yorke Street'
The King's Arms (no. 1) (1677)	'Facing the Parade'
The King's Arms (no. 2) (1682)	Figure site 20
The Salutacon (1680)	Figure site 52
The Shipp (1674)	'Fronting north on Queen Streete'
The Sign of Bacchus (1673)	'On Yorke Street'
The Sign of the Mermaid (1685)	Figure site 49
The Sign of the George (1682)	'Fronting to the old market place'
The Sugar Loaf (1667)	?
The Three Crownes (1673)	Corner of High Street and Lime Street
The Three Mariners (1677)	Figure site 50
The Three Tunns (1665)	Figure site 49
The Windmill (1684)	'Fronting s/e on Cannon Street'

APPENDIX 6

Anglican ministers and churchwardens at Port Royal before 1692

Ministers	1661-4	George Johns ('an old army preacher')
	1668-71	John Maxwell ('a Scotchman')
	1674-5	Jacob Hane (or Hayne or Haine)
	1681-4	John Longworth
	1688	Dr. More ('an ancient man')
	1692	Dr. Emmanuel Heath
Churchwardens	1667	Caesar Carter and Samuel Stretton
	1669	John Davenport and Dennis McCragh
	1674	Henry Ward and John Waite
	1681	Charles Penhallow and Reginald Wilson
	1684	Reginald Wilson and John White
	1685	Henry Ward and Joseph Jennings

The terminal date for each minister represents the latest date his name occurs in the records and therefore not necessarily the date at which his Port Royal ministry ended. Among the churchwardens, eight of the eleven names appear on appendix 4, giving some notion of the extent of its coverage.

Bibliography

1 Manuscripts

Bodleian Library, Oxford

Rawlinson, A171, fo. 199, "Commissions and instructions of the naval officer in Jamaica"

Rawlinson, A 232, Orders to Joseph Gyde, supply agent at Port Royal, c. 1710

Rawlinson, A300, "Journal of H.M.S. *Boneta*" 1683-6

Rawlinson, B250, fo. 59-63, "Goods exported from Jamaica to England", 1680-1712

Rawlinson, D843, fo. 187, letter of Sir Henry Morgan, 1680

British Library (formerly "British Museum")

Additional Manuscripts 5414-5, William Hack maps dedicated to the duke of Albemarle

Additional Manuscripts, 11410, "Papers relating to the West Indies", 1654-82

Additional Manuscripts, 12423, The journal of Colonel Edward D'Oyley

Additional Manuscripts, 12424, "1671 journal of William Beeston in the Assistance" etc.

Additional Manuscripts, 12427, Journal and letter-book of Colonel Christian Lilly, 1720-1734

Additional Manuscripts, 12429, "A collection of tracts relating to the island of Jamaica"

Additional Manuscripts, 12430, "A journal kept by Colonel William Beeston . . ." (1655-1680)

Additional Manuscripts, 12431, "Miscellaneous papers relating to Jamaica, etc."

Additional Manuscripts, 16371, John Man's map, 1662

Additional Manuscripts, 18986, fo. 257-61, report on Jamaica c. 1657 by Tobias Bridge

Additional Manuscripts, 24,546 and 34,015, Those who left London for the colonies, 1655

Egerton Manuscripts, 2395, The papers of Thomas Povey, 1627-1699

Egerton Manuscripts, 2648-9, The papers of the Barrington family, 1643-1660

Harleian Manuscripts, 3361, "A brief survey of Jamaica"

Harleian Manuscripts, 6922, An account of the 1692 earthquake by Edward Heath

King's MSS, 214, Archibald Campbell, A memoir relative to the island of Jamaica, 1782

Sloane Manuscripts, 1599, fo. 106, "Minutes of the Council in Jamaica, 1687-9"
Sloane Manuscripts, 1831A, Log of the *Gilliflower*
Sloane Manuscripts, 2724, "Papers concerning the Earl of Carlisle in Jamaica"
Sloane Manuscripts, 2902, "Papers relating to trade, etc."
Sloane Manuscripts, 3918, An account of Jamaica by Henry Barham, c. 1722
Sloane Manuscripts, 3984, fo. 201-7, List of ships visiting Jamaica, 1687-8
Stowe Manuscripts, 747, Account of 1692 earthquake
Stowe Manuscripts 305, Account of French attack in 1694
Stowe Manuscripts 427, Report on HM ships in Port Royal harbour, 1771

Huntington Library, California
The papers of William Blathwayt, 1646-1717

Island Record Office
Deeds, liber I etc.

Jamaica Archives
Inventories, liber I etc.
Patents, liber I etc.

Longleat House (papers seen only on microfilm)
Coventry Papers, volumes 74-75; despatches to Henry Coventry, 1672-1679

National Library of Jamaica
MS A1, "History and state of Jamaica under Lord Vaughan"
MST 41, List of rebels to be transported
MS 60, Transcripts of the minutes of the Council of Jamaica, 1661-1672
MST 96, "Entry book of letters . . . written by Thomas Povey, 1655-60"
MS 159, Jamaica under the Earl of Carlisle
MS 288, Logs of H.M.S. *Assistance* etc.
MS 391, Some letters of Cary Helyar
MS 982, Patents and accounts of Sir Thomas Lynch
MS 1658, State of Jamaica in 1664 and 1670

National Maritime Museum (Greenwich)
ADM/Y/PR/1 and ADM/Y/PR/2, Plans of the dockyard, about 1768
JOD/4 Edward Barlow, Journal of his life and voyages, 1656-1703

Newberry Library, Chicago
Ayer MS 293 (II) "Description de l'isle Jamaique", c. 1700

Pepysian Library, Cambridge
MS 2867, fo. 325, "Instructions to Captain Talbot"
MS 2873, fo. 487, "Considerations worthy of Your Majesty's knowledge"
MS 2867, "Naval and Admiralty precedents"

Public Record Office
30/20, vol. 18, Rodney Papers
Adm 51/3870, log of H.M.S. *Hunter* (1678)
Adm 51/3926, log of H.M.S. *Norwich* (1680-82)
Adm 51/345, logs of H.M.S. *Boneta* (1683) and *Falcon* (1686)
Adm 52/30, log of H.M.S. *Guernsey*, 1692
Adm 52/68, log of H.M.S. *Mordaunt*, 1692
C 110/152, "Correspondence and accounts of Thomas Brailsford"
CO 1.19, fo. 125, "The scituacion of the island" about 1665
CO 1/32, fo. 194, "The disposall of the fleet" in June 1656
CO 1/45/59, The Jamaican militia in 1680; population of Port Royal in 1680
CO 138/5, fo. 84, "His Majesty's letter concerning the transportation of rebells"
CO 139/1/55-8 [slave codes]
CO 142/13, "Shipping returns, 1680-1705"
CO 700/14, Map of Kingston Harbour by Archibald Bontein, 1748
CO 700: Jamaica 5, Map of Port Royal by Christian Lilly

Royal Society, London
Misc. MSS, 83.12, Letter by George Ellwood concerning Jamaica, 1672

2 Printed material

Acts of Assembly passed in the island of Jamaica from the year 1681 to the year 1754 inclusive (Saint Jago de la Vega, 1769)
Acts of the Privy Council
Anderson, W.W., ed., *An account of America* (1671) (Kingston, 1851) includes chapter by John Ogilby
Andrade, Jacob, *A record of the Jews in Jamaica* (Kingston, 1941)
Andrews, C.M., *Guide to materials for American history to 1783* (2 vols., Washington 1912 and 1914)
Anon., *Interesting tracts relating to the island of Jamaica* (Spanish Town, 1800)
Anon., *The truest and largest account of the late earthquake* (London, 1693)
Ashley, Maurice, *Financial and commercial policy under the Cromwellian Protectorate* (London, 1934)

Atkins, John, *A voyage to Guinea, Brasil and the West-Indies* (London, 1737)
Battick, John F. (ed.), "Richard Rooth's sea journal of the Western Design", *Jamaica Journal*, 4 (1971) 3-22
Bennett, J. Harry, "Cary Helyar, merchant and planter of seventeenth-century Jamaica", *William and Mary Quarterly* xxi (1964) 53-76
Birch, Thomas, ed., *A Collection of the State Papers of John Thurloe* (7 vols., London, 1742)
Black, Clinton de V., *Port Royal* (Kingston, 1970)
Black, Clinton de V., "When Maximilian visited Jamaica", *Bulletin of the Jamaican Historical Society*, ii (1957) 2-4
Blome, Richard, *A description of the island of Jamaica* (London, 1672)
Boteler, Captain J.H., RN, *Recollections of my sea life from 1808 to 1830* (London, 1942)
Bourne, Ruth, *Queen Anne's navy in the West Indies* (New Haven, 1939)
Brathwaite, Edward, *The development of creole society in Jamaica 1770-1820* (Oxford, 1971)
Breece, Laurel Anne, *Seventeenth-century silver: the Port Royal collection* (MA dissertation for the University of California at Los Angeles, 1992)
Bridenbaugh, Carl, *Cities in the wilderness* (New York, 1960)
Bridenbaugh, Carl and Roberta, *No peace beyond the line* (New York, 1972)
Bridges, G. W., *The Annals of Jamaica* (2 vols., London, 1827-8)
Buisseret, D.J., *The fortifications of Kingston 1655-1914* (Kingston, 1972)
Buisseret, D.J., "Edward D'Oyley, 1617-1675", *Jamaica Journal*, v (1971) 6-10
Buisseret, D.J., "A pirate at Port Royal in 1679", *The Mariner's Mirror* lvii (1971) 303-5
Buisseret, D.J., "The loss of H.M.S. Norwich off Port Royal in June 1682", *The Mariner's Mirror,* liv (1968) 403-7
Cadbury, William J., "Conditions in Jamaica in 1687", *JHR* iii.2 (1959) 52-57
Cadbury, William J., "Quakers and the earthquake at Port Royal in 1692", *JHR* viii (1971) 19-31
Calendar of State Papers, Domestic Series
Cappon, L.J., "The Blathwayt Papers of Colonial Williamsburg, Inc.", *The William and Mary Quarterly* iv 3 (1947) 321-31
Casserly, F.L., "A great sea-raider's links with Jamaica" in the *Bulletin* of the Jamaican Historical Society, ii (1957) 108-12
Cave, Roderick, "Thomas Craddock's books" in the *Bulletin* of the Jamaica Library Association, January 1973.
Claypole, William, "Land settlement and agricultural development in the Liguanea plain, 1655-1700", MA thesis UWI (1969)
Claypole, William, "The merchants of Port Royal", PhD thesis UWI (1972)

Claypole, William and David Buisseret, "Trade patterns in early English Jamaica", *JCH* v (1972) 1-19

Clowes, W.L., *The Royal Navy* (7 vols., London, 1897-1903)

Craton, Michael, "The role of the Caribbean Vice-Admiralty courts in British imperialism", *Caribbean Studies* xi (1971) 5-20

Coad, John, *A memorandum of the wonderful providences of God* (ed. London, 1849

Cox, Jean and Oliver, *The naval hospitals of Port Royal, Jamaica* (report for the Jamaica National Heritage Trust, 1995)

Cox, Oliver, *Upgrading and renewing a historic city: Port Royal, Jamaica* (1984: report commissioned by the Overseas Development Administration of the British Government, and now held at the National Library of Jamaica)

Cruikshank, E.A., *The life of Sir Henry Morgan* (Toronto, 1935)

Crump, Helen, *Colonial admiralty jurisdiction in the seventeenth century* (London, 1931)

Cundall, Frank, *The governors of Jamaica in the first half of the eighteenth century* (London, 1937)

Cundall, Frank, *The governors of Jamaica in the seventeenth century* (London, 1936)

Cundall, Frank, *Historic Jamaica* (London, 1915)

Cundall, Frank, "Tortoise shell carving in Jamaica", *The Connoisseur* (1925 and 1926)

Cundall, Frank and Joseph Pietersz, *Jamaica under the Spaniards* (Kingston, 1919)

Dalton, J.N., ed., *The cruise of H.M.S. Bacchante 1879-82* (2 vols., London, 1886)

Davies, P. Spencer, "Seventeenth-century pewter from the sunken city of Port Royal, Jamaica", *The Connoisseur* (February, 1975) 136-41

Davis, Ralph, *The rise of the English shipping industry* (London, 1962)

Davis, K.G., *The Royal African Company* (London, 1957)

Dennys, N.B., *An account of the cruise of the Saint George . . .* (London, 1862)

Dunn, Richard, *Sugar and slaves* (Chapel Hill, 1972)

Durham, Harriet F., *Caribbean Quakers* (n.p., 1972)

Esquemeling, John, *The buccaneers of America* (London, 1911)

Feiling, Keith, *British foreign policy 1660-1772* (London, 1930)

Finch, A.G., see Historical MSS Commission

Firth, Sir Charles H., *Cromwell's Army* (London, 1912)

Firth, Sir Charles H., ed., *Narrative of General Venables* (London, 1900)

Foster, Thomas, *The postal history of Jamaica 1662-1860* (London, 1968)

Goreau, Tom and Kevin Burke, "Pleistocene and holocene geology of the island shelf near Kingston, Jamaica", *Marine Geology* iv (1966) 207-25

Grassby, Richard, "English merchant capitalism in the late seventeenth

century", *Past and present* xlvi (1970) 92.
Hamilton, D.L., "Simon Benning, pewterer of Port Royal", in Barbara Little, ed., *Text-aided archaeology* (Boca Raton, 1992)
Hanson, Francis, *The laws of Jamaica* (Spanish Town, 1792)
Haring, C.H., *The buccaneers in the West Indies in the 17th century* (London, 1910)
Historical MSS Commission: report on the MSS of A.G. Finch (London, 1913)
Hume, Ivor Noël, *Historical archaeology* (New York, 1966)
Hurwitz, Samuel and Edith, "The New World sets an example for the Old; the Jews of Jamaica and political rights, 1661-1831", *American Jewish Historical Quarterly* lv (1965) 37-56
Jamaica National Trust Commission, *Port Royal Jamaica: excavations 1969-70* (Kingston, 1972)
Journals of the House of Assembly of Jamaica, 1663-1826 (14 vols., Kingston 1811-29)
Kennedy, Captain W.R., RN, *Sport, travel and adventure* (Edinburgh/London, 1875)
Knight, Franklin and Peggy Liss, eds., *Atlantic port cities: economy, culture and society in the Atlantic world, 1650-1850* (Knoxville, 1991)
Lewis, Mrs. L., "English commemorative art in Jamaica", *JHR* ix (1972)
Link, Marion C., "Exploring the drowned city of Port Royal", *National Geographic*, 117 (1960) 151-83
Long, Edward, *A History of Jamaica* (3 vols., London, 1774)
Marx, Robert, *Port Royal* (London, 1968)
Mayes, Philip, *Port Royal, Jamaica: excavations 1969-70* (Kingston, 1972)
Mayes, Philip and P.A. Mayes, "Port Royal, Jamaica: the archaeological problems and potential", *The international journal of nautical archaeology and underwater exploration*, i (1972)
McGrath, P., ed., *Records relating to the Society of Merchant Adventurers of the city of Bristol in the 17th century* (Bristol, 1952)
McPherson, David, *Annals of commerce* (4 vols., London, 1805)
Nettels, Curtis, "England and the Spanish-American trade, 1680-1715", *Journal of modern history*, iii (1931) 1-32
Newton, A.P., *The colonizing activities of the English Puritans* (Oxford, 1914)
Nicholas, Sir Nicholas Harris, ed., *The dispatches and letters of vice-admiral Lord Viscount Nelson* (7 vols., London, 1845-6)
Ogilby, John, see W.W. Anderson
Oldmixon, John, *The British Empire in America* (2 vols., London, 1708)
Osborne, Francis, SJ, "James Castillo - Asiento agent", *JHR* viii (1971) 9-18
Pares, Richard, *Merchants and planters* (Cambridge, 1960)
Pares, Richard, *War and trade in the West Indies 1739-1763* (Oxford, 1963)

Pares, Richard, *Yankees and Creoles* (London, 1956)
Pietersz, Joseph and H.P. Jacobs, "Two Spanish documents of 1656", *JHR* ii 2 (1952) 24
Ranft, B. McL., ed., *The Vernon papers* (London, 1958)
Sheridan, Richard, *The development of the plantations to 1750* (Barbados, 1970)
Sloane, Sir Hans, *A voyage to the islands Madeira, Barbados...and Jamaica* (2 vols., London, 1707 and 1725)
Smith, A.E., *Colonists in bondage* (Gloucester, MA, 1965)
Southey, Captain Thomas, *Chronological history of the West Indies* (3 vols., London, 1827)
Spinney, David, *Rodney* (London, 1969)
Spurdle, F.G., *Early West Indian government* (Palmerston North, New Zealand, 1962)
Tanner, J.R., *Catalogue of the Pepysian manuscripts* (4 vols., Cambridge, 1902-1922)
Taylor, S.A.G., *The Western Design* (Kingston, 1965)
Tedder, A.W., *The navy of the Restoration* (Cambridge, 1916)
Thompson, Paul, ed., *Close to the wind: the early memoirs of Admiral Sir William Creswell* (London, 1965)
Thornton, A.P., *West-India policy under the Restoration* (Oxford, 1956)
Thornton, A.P., "The Modyfords and Morgan", *JHR* ii (1952) 48
Thornton, A.P., "Some statistics of West Indian produce, shipping and revenue 1660-1685", *CHR* iii-iv (1954) 251-80
Trapham, Thomas, *Discourse of the state of health of the island of Jamaica* (London, 1679)
Ward, Estelle, *Christopher Monck, Duke of Albemarle* (London, 1915)
Watkins, E.H., "A history of the legal system of Jamaica, 1661-1900", PhD thesis, Sheffield, 1968
Watts, W.H., *The commission of H.M.S. Retribution* (London, 1904)
Whitson, Agnes, *The constitutional development of Jamaica, 1664-1729* (Manchester, 1929)
Wright, Philip, ed., *Lady Nugent's journal* (Kingston, 1966)
Wright, Philip, *Monumental inscriptions of Jamaica* (London, 1966)
Yates, G.S., "J. Belfield, a Port Royal merchant", *Bulletin* of the Jamaican Historical Society, iii (1961) 243-5
Zahediah, Nuala, "The merchants of Port Royal, Jamaica, and the Spanish contraband trade, 1655-1692," *The William and Mary Quarterly*, 43 (1986) 570-93
Zahediah, Nuala, "Trade, plunder and economic development in early English Jamaica, 1655-1689", *The Economic History Review*, 39 (1986) 205-22

INDEX

Albermarle, duke and duchess of, 74, 79-80, 151-154, 158
Alexander, Nicholas: land grant to, 16
Anglican church, 130, 158; artefacts from, 206. *See also* St. Peter's
Anglican ministers, 233
Apostle's Battery, 187, 188
Arawaks. *See* Taino Indians
Archbould, Lieutenant-Colonel, 19; land grant to, 125
Archeological investigations, 203-209, 212
Architects, 223
Architecture: in Port Royal, 131; in Spanish Town, 131
Arnold, Jeremiah (member of Merchants' Royall Company), 136
Artefacts: recovered by Link expedition, 127, 142-144, 205, 208, 209. *See also* Pewter, Pipes, Chinese Porcelain, Ceramics, Ivory
Artisans. *See* Craftsmen
Atkins, John (naval surgeon), 171
Attorneys: responsibilities of, 86

Bach, Samuel (merchant), 86, 130, 138, 155, 156, 158
Baker, Captain, 100-101
Bakers, 223
Bannister, Captain Joseph (pirate), 65, 69-73
Barbers, 223
Barre, Charles and Mary: property owned by, 127-128, 160
Barry, Captain Samuel: land grants to, 14
Bartaboa, Peter (carpenter), 115, 156
Battle of the Saints, 190
Battle of Trafalgar, 191
Bay of Campeche: raid against, 30
Beckford, Peter, 115
Beeston's journal, 34
Beeston, William (merchant), 63-64, 86, 156, 169, 174, 176
Belfield, John (merchant), 86, 116, 157
Benbow, Vice-Admiral John, 177
Bennett, Paul (craftsman), 144
Benning, Simon (pewterer), 144, 208, 231

Bird, Richard (merchant), 124
Bissell, Commander Austin, 191
Blacksmiths, 223
Blackthorne, Robert (secretary to the Admiralty commanders), 21
Blathwayt Papers, xiv
Blondel, Paul (watch maker), 205
Board of Survey: report on the loss of the *Norwich*, 78; responsibilities of, 65
Bonham's Point, 50-51, 127
Bonney, Anne (pirate), 182
Boteler, Captain J. H., 194, 198
Brass artefacts, 205
Bratten, John: on yabba artefacts, 208
Brailsford, Thomas (merchant), 102
Brayne, Governor, 12, 19, 125
Breece, Laurel Anne: on silver artefacts, 208
Bridewell: prison for women criminals, 117, 156
Brickmakers, 223
Brickmaking industry, 13
Brisbane, Captain Charles, 191
British invasion: of Jamaica, 7
British Museum, xiii, xiv
Brock, Richard (carpenter), 11, 116-117
Brunel, Marc Isambard (engineer), 213
Buccaneers. *See* Privateers
Building specifications, 121
Burrough, Captain Cornelius (steward general), 17, 18, 20, 21, 25, 115
Butchers, 223
Byndloss, Major Robert, 32, 42

Cagway. *See* Port Royal Point, fortifying of
Calendar of State Papers, xiii
Campbell, Major General Archibald (lieutenant-governor), 189
Careening facilities, 10, 173-174, 179; lack of, 130
Caribbean: trade within the, 90, 92
Carleton, Mary: the German princess, 161, 162n
Carlisle, Earl of, 43
Carlson, Janice: on pewter artefacts, 207
Carpenters, 223

Index 241

Cartagena, 35; attack on, 182-183
Carter, Ceasar (churchwarden), 119
Cartwright, Dr. Anthony, 119
Cary, Colonel Theodore, 32, 51, 53
Castillo, James, 158
Catholic church, 130, 158; suppression of, 160
Cayo de carena, 6, 7
Cemetery. *See* Naval cemetery
Ceramics, 209
Chandlers, 224
Charles I: death of, 154-155
Charles II, 28, 37
Childermas, John (pewterer), 144
Chinese porcelain, 208
Chitty, William (engineer), 53
Chocolata Hole, 109, 215
Churches, 129-130
Churchill, Father Thomas (chaplain), 158
Churchwardens, 223
Clifton, William (ivory turner), 144
Climate, 140
Coad, John (indentured servant), 137-138
Cole, George (merchant), 123
Colebeck, Colonel John: property owned by, 125
Collyer, Captain: land grants to, 125
Colwell, Captain George: trading route of, 97-98
Combmaker, 224
Commercial activity, 21, 85-105; illegal, 103-104
Common land, 127-129
Convoy system, 79
Cookleith, Robert, 20
Coopers, 224
Cope, Major John, 121-122
Cordwainers, 224
Cornwallis, Couba, 187
Council of Jamaica, 30, 79; support of privateering, 31, 32
Council of War, 35; responsibilities of, 67-68
Court-martial: of the crew of the *Norwich*, 78-79
Covenay, Peter, 18, 115
Coventry, John, 138-139
Coventry Papers, xiv

Cox, Jean and Oliver, 207, 213
Coxen, Captain John (buccaneer), 117
Coxshott, Abraham (cabinet-maker), 142
Craftsmen, 142-144, 207-208, 223-231
Craddock, Thomas, 160-161
Crane, William (merchant), 123
Crow, Francis, 140, 158
Cuba: mission to, 68-69 privateering attacks on, 34-35. *See also* Havana and Santiago de Cuba
Cundall, Frank, 200
Curaçao: privateering raid on, 32

Dacres, Vice-Admiral, 193
Dallyson, Captain William, 21
Dare, Captain Jeffrey: land grant to, 19, 20
Dayton, Mary (victualler), 119
Deakins, Joseph, 125
Defence. *See* Fortifications
Defence strategies, 156-157, 175, 186, 189-193
Demography, 136-140, 162n
Dewolf, Helen, 208
Diseases, 138-140
Dockyard. *See* Naval dockyard
Doctors, 142, 225
Downes, James (merchant), 148-149
D'Oyley's Journal, xiv, 10, 18, 20, 85, 219
D'Oyley, Governor Nicholas, 11, 12, 13, 14, 115, 125; support of privateers, 25-28
Ducasse: attack on Port Royal by, 177
Ducke, Thomas (member of Merchants' Royall Company), 136
Duperly, Adolphe, 199
Dutch: privateering raids against the, 32
Dwelling house: description of, 120
Dysentry, 138. *See also* Diseases

Earthquake: (1692), xiii, 4, 165-168, 175; (1771), 185; (1907), 194
Economic development: 85-105. *See also* Commercial activity
Edgegoose, Lieutenant: land grant to, 125, 139
Education, 157-158
Elletson, Roger: and religious freedom, 160

242 PORT ROYAL

Ellwood, George, 140
England: trade with Port Royal, 89-92, 94, 96-97
Englefield, Captain Epsley, 20, 118
Entertainment, 160
Essex, Captain (pirate), 69
Esquemeling, 35
Eustatia, 32
Exports, 85-86, 90-92

Fashion, 148-150
Fire, 170; (1815), 193
Fisher, Admiral Sir John, 198
Fishermen, 225
Fletcher, John: land owned by, 207
Food: availability and variety of, 140-141. See also Markets
Forge, 124
Fort Augusta, 186
Fort Carlisle, 52, 117, 205
Fort Charles; 16, 197, 205, 212, 215; earthquake damage, 166; expansion of, 49; land accretion adjacent to, 185; plan of 50; reconstruction of, 169; remodelling of 174, 179, 181, 194. See also Fort Cromwell
Fort Cromwell: construction of, 7-8, 14-16, 216; description of 9, 49
Fortifications: on the mainland, 11; in Port Royal 7-24, 49-55
Fort James, 51, 166, 203; archaeological investigations of, 204
Fort Morgan, 52, 166, 174
Fort Rupert, 51-52, 211; archaeological investigations at, 204; earthquake damage to, 166, 186, 203
Fort Walker, 174
Fort William, 169, 174, 186
Fox (shoemaker), 119
Francis, Peter, 212
Freeman, Humphrey: landholdings of, 19, 124
Freeman, Colonel Robert (judge), 155
French colonies: hostilities against, 189-191
French hostilities, 176-177
Furnishings, 145-147

Galdy, Lewis, 166, 212
Gallow's Point, 182, 198
Gauld, George (cartographer), 185-186
Gibb, Aaron (watchmaker), 205
Gifford, Sheila, 209
Glass artefacts, 205, 208
Glazier, 225
Gleed, Henry (merchant), 101
Goldsmiths, 225
Grammont (privateer), 71
Godfrey, Captain William, 9
Goodson, Vice-Admiral William, 8, 10
Gotelipe-Miller, Shirley: on pewter artefacts, 207
Governors of Jamaica, 12
Graves, Rear-Admiral Thomas, 190
Grasse, Admiral de, 190
Gun Cay, 50
Gunsmiths, 225

Hack, William: plan of Port Royal by, 118
Hall, Francis and William (merchants), 102, 149
Hailey, Tommy: on lead content in ceramic artefacts, 208, 209, 210
Hamilton, Professor, 207
Hanover line, 171, 180, 197, 212
Hanson, William (blacksmith), 125
Harrington, Captain (governor of Passage Fort), 11
Harrison, Marke, 123
Harvey, Bartholomew (brickmaker), 13
Hatmakers, 225
Havana, 67-69; capture of, 183. See also Cuba
Hay, John (merchant): property owned by, 126
Haynes, Jacob, 125
Heath, Dr. Emmanuel, 165, 166, 167
Hector, Admiral Charles (comte d'Estaing), 189
Herne, Captain Richard, 156
Heywood, Captain Peter, 75, 76; court-martial of, 78-79
Hicks, Daniel (merchant), 105
Hicks, Nicholas (merchant): property owned by, 125
Hill, Roger: land grants to, 126

Index 243

Historic Jamaica, 200
Hodgkins, Captain Thomas, 156
Holl, Edward (naval architect), 213
Holly (provost marshal), 155
Honeyman, Lieutenant Thomas, 115
Honourable Artillery Company, 157
Hopson, Vice-Admiral Edward, 182
Hosier, Vice-Admiral Francis, 182
Hospital (Greenwich), 185
Hospital (Port Royal). See Naval hospital
Housing, 13, 135, 145-147; in the 1650s
Howatt, Elizabeth (sole dealer), 124
Hudson, Thomas (merchant), 119, 156
Hughes, Captain, resident supervisor of Fort Cromwell, 9
Huie, Albert, 197
Hume, George, 124
Humphrey, Colonel, 8
Hurricanes, 171; (1722), 187; (1787), 186

Imports, 85, 88-89
Inchiquin, Governor, 142; and suppression of Catholics, 160
Indentured servants, 136-138
Infantry, 156
Ireland: trade with Port Royal, 90
Iron Bridge (Spanish Town), 213
Island Record Office, xiii, 86
Ivory artefacts, 144
Ivory Turners, 225
Ivy, Lieutenant-Colonel: land transactions, 17-18

Jacobs (privateer), 71
Jamaica Defence Force, 200, 218
Jamaica National Trust Commission, 205
James, Captain, 137
Jeffrey, Lieutenant B.: survey of sunken Port Royal by, 203
Jews, 129, 159
Jobling, Becky: on pipes, 208
Johnson, Dolly, 198
Judges, 155

Kampthorne, Captain Samuel: trading route of, 100
Keene, Nicholas (surveyor), 9, 13, 14, 111
Kerr, Captain William, 178

Keyes, Thomas (carpenter), 11
Kidd, J. B., 194
King's House, 12, 115-116, 124, 215, 216
King's Warehouse, 205
King, William, 124
Kingston: new seat of trade, 170-171
Kingston Act, 171
Knowles, Captain Charles, 183

Labourers, 224
Langford, Captain Abraham: land grant to, 18
Land accretion, 185
Land grants, 12, 13, 16-22, 115-130
Land reclamation, 109
Laurens (privateer), 71
Lawes, Sir Nicholas (governor), 171
Lawson, Phillip, 75, 76-77
Legal system, 155-156
Lewis, John, 124
Lewis, Samuel (merchant), 119
Letters of attorney, 86
Letters of marque, 74
Library of Congress, xii
Lilly, Christian: plan of Port Royal by, 174, 175
Limeburners, 225
Link expedition: artefacts recovered by, 127, 144, 204-205
Littleton, Commodore James, 178
Logwood: imports of, 101
Long, Edward, xiii
Lord, Captain William: trading route of, 101
Loving, John (merchant), 21, 119
Llanrumney, 39
Lloyd, Captain John, 27
Luke, John (pewterer), 144
Lumiere, Cornel, 204
Lynch, Sir Thomas (governor), 16, 30-31, 43, 116; on Heywood's court-martial, 78-79; inventory of possessions, 148; land owned by, 122, 146; resistance to privateering, 41; suppression of pirates, 69-70; survey by, 135
Lyssons, Nicholas, 231
Lyttleton, Sir Charles (deputy-governor), 30, 70

Lyttleton, James (London merchant): property owned by, 126

Man, John (surveyor-general), 14, 116, 119; property owned by, 127
Mansfield, Captain (privateer), 32
Marine surveys, 66, 203
Mariners, 225-226
Market conditions: in Port Royal, 101-103
Markets, 140-142
Marmaduke, 30
Marshallsea: prison for men, 117, 156
Marx, Robert: archaeological expedition of, 203, 205, 207, 209
Masons, 226
Mathews, Captain Thomas (merchant), 146-147
Maximilian, Archduke, 200
Maxwell (Anglican minister), 116
Mayes: archaeological excavations, 174, 204-207, 212
Mayne, John, 117
Maynard, Captain Francis, 175, 176
McClenaghan, Patricia: study of glass artefacts, 208
Merchant vessels, 87-88, 91; arrivals of, 92; owned by Port Royal merchants, 94, 99-102; trading routes of, 93, 96-102
Merchants, 20, 39, 86, 101, 105, 149, 223-231, 226-229
Migration: from Port Royal, 104
Mitchell, Captain, 71
Modyford, Sir Charles: arrest of, 40-41; revocation of the commission of, 37; support of the privateers by, 30-40
Modyford, Sir James, 34; property owned by, 126
Modyford, Sir Thomas (merchant), 86; property owned by, 126
Molesworth, Sir Hender (lieutenant-governor), 117, 119, 136-137; mercantile activities of, 86; suppression of piracy, 70-73
Monck, Colonel George, 85
Moone, John (merchant): property owned by, 126
Morgan, Lieutenant-Colonel Edward, 32

Morgan, Sir Henry, 209, 212; arrest of, 41, 150, 156; burial of, 139; comb cases of, 142; and fortifications, 51; leader of privateers, 34-45; rivalry with Lord Vaughan, 42-43, 61; support of piracy, 41
Morgan's Harbour, 205, 212
Morris, Quartermaster: land grant to, 16-17
Morris, Thomas (cooper): land grant to, 19
Mortality, 139-140; resulting from 1692 earthquake, 166
Murphy, Jeremiah: description of sunken Port Royal by, 203-204
Musgrave, Simon, 117; land owned by, 122
Myngs, Christopher, 14, 22, 28-29; raid of the Bay of Campeche by, 30

Napoleonic Wars, 171
National Gallery: turtle-shell artefacts, 142-144
Naval captains, 58, 176-184
Naval cemetery, 139, 211
Naval dockyard, xiv, 64, 217-218; construction of, 179-181; decline of, 198; expansion of, 184, 187, 193-198; plan of, 194
Naval hospital, 181, 185, 193-194, 213-214
Naval station, 173-200; careening operations, 173-174; (1692-1715), 173-181
Naval vessels, 59-61, 217-218, 220; Board of Survey, 65; careening of, 64-65, 173-174; defence strategies of, 68, 175, 182-183, 189-200; protection of commercial vessels by, 179; role in suppressing piracy, 69-74, 182; rotating system of, 177-178; route of, 61-62; salvaging operations by, 74; wartime role of, 69; watering of, 64
Navy, 57-84; expansion of fleets, 178-179
Navy office: responsibilities, 62-64
Nelson, Horatio, 188, 189, 190
Noell, Martin, 85
Norero, Elias (merchant): property owned by, 127
North America: trade with Port Royal, 89-90; War of Independence, 189

Index   245

Nugent, Lady, 193

Official receptions, 150-155
Ogle, Sir Chaloner, 179, 183
Old Gaol, 212-213
Orange, William of, 80

Palisadoes spit: geography of, 1-6, 128
Panama: privateering attacks on, 34-35, 36
Parker, Vice-Admiral Sir Hyde, 191
Parker, Sir Peter, 189
Parker, Lieutenant-Colonel William, 122
Passage Fort, 7, settlement of, 11
Peace of Paris, 173, 183, 189
Peace of Versailles, 191
Penhallow, Captain Charles, 156
Penn, 57
Pepys, Samuel, 58, 62, 78, 80
Pewter artefacts, 144, 207
Pewterers, 229
Phillips, Robert (sailmaker), 124
Pike, John, 159
Pinhorne, Edward, 29
Pipes, 144, 205, 208
Pipemakers, 229
Piracy, 41, 44, 54, 69-73
Pirates: punishment of, 67-73, 182, 198
Plan of Port Royal, 109-112, 114-115, 118, 121, 131, 174, 175
Plan of Spanish Town, 130-131
Plantations: establishment of, 104
Pocock, Admiral Sir George, 183
Police Training School, 200, 212
Polygon Battery, 197, 211
Pope, John (pipe-maker), 144
Population: description of, 135-139; overcrowding of, 109; relationship among, 188; statistics, 11, 88, 89, 135, 162n
Porcelain. *See* Chinese porcelain
Porters, 229
Port Henderson Hill, 186
Port Royal: physical description of, 7, 10, 16; standard of living in the 17th century, 209; sunken city of, 203-206; of today, 211-215
Port Royal Brotherhood, 200
Port Royal cay, 4

Port Royal Harbour: survey of, 185
Port Royal Point: fortifying of, 8
Porto Bello: capture of, 34-35; 182
Porto Principe, 34-35
Poulterer, 229
Posnansky, Merrick: study of silver artefacts, 208
Postal service, 157
Povey, Richard (island secretary and commissary), 18, 21, 22, 26, 85, 123
Powell, Rowland (island secretary), 52
Presbyterians, 130, 158
Priddy, Anthony, 207
Prince, Captain Job: trading pattern, 98-99
Prince, Captain Lawrence, 39
Prince William Henry's Polygon, 186
Prisoners, 137-138, 162n
Prisons, 117, 146, 156-157
Privateers, 25-47, 219; cooperation among, 71; decline of, 41, 43-44; definition of, 45n; economic base provided by, 38-40; French, 72; role in defence, 28. *See also* Pirates
Prize courts, 26-27
Property: subdivision of, 109-131. *See* Land grants
Probate inventories, 209
Provost marshal: responsibilities of, 155-156
Public buildings: construction of, 129-130
Public Record Office, xiii
Pugh, Peter, 20, 21
Pullin, Captain: trading route of, 99
Pym, Jonathan (gunsmith), 157

Quakers, 130, 158; and D'Oyley, 159

Rackham, Jack (pirate), 182
Read, Mary (pirate), 182
Religion, 130, 158; freedom of, 159-160
Rennie, John (engineer), 213
Rental arrangements, 145
Richardson, Samuel (bricklayer), 129
Rock Spring, 186
Rodney, Rear-Admiral Sir George (commander-in-chief), 185-186, 189
Rodney's Lookout, 186
Rodriquz de Leon, Jacob, 159

Ross, William (marshal), 137
Royal African Company, 73
Royal Society Library, xiv
Russell, Lady, 61

Saba, 32
Sailmakers, 229
St. Christopher, 32
St. Peter's Church, 212
Salvaging operations: role of navy in, 74; by vessels owned by Port Royal merchants, 94
Santiago de Cuba: attack of, 183
Sawkins, Captain (pirate), 69
Schoolmasters, 229
Scott, Norman, 205
Shipping. *See* Merchant vessels; Naval vessels
Ships: *Advice*, 176; *Alabama*, 200; *America Merchant*, 95; *Amphritrite*, 190; *Angell Gabriel*, 26; *Anglesey*, 177; *Arthur and Mary*, 95; *Assistance*, 17, 41, 58, 63, 67-68, 80, 81, 139, 154; *Beare*, 17, 19; *Blackmore*, 17; *Bonaventure*, 26; *Boneta*, xiv, 60, 64, 69-71, 73, 74; *Breda*, 177, 178; *Brothers Adventure*, 85; *Buzzard*, 199; Cadiz Merchant, 95; *Carlisle*, 58; *Centurion*, 28, 29, 30; *Cumber-land*, 199; *Devastation*, 19; *Diamond*, 26, 27, 57; *East India Merchant*, 17; *Expedition*, 178; *Experiment*, 176, 178; *Falcon*, 62, 154, 176; *Falmouth*, 17; *Foresight*, 61; *Francis and Thomas*, 85; *Friendship*, 92; *Generous Hanna*, 80; *Glorieux*, 191; *Gloucester*, 198; *Golden Faulcon*, 85; *Golden Fleece*, 65-66, 71-73; *Greatguest*, 49; *Griffin*, 29, 30; *Guernsey*, 74, 175-176; *Hampshire*, 176; *Hector*, 14, 15, 17, 57; *Hercule*, 192, 193; *Hinchin-brooke*, 190; *Hunter*, 52, 60, 62, 66-69, 74, 156; *Imaum*, 199; *Jamaica*, 26; *Jamaica Merchant*, 41, 61, 95; *James*, trading pattern, 98-99; *Jersey*, 60, 74; *John and Joseph*, salvage operations, 100; trading pattern, 100; *Katheryne*, trading pattern, 99; *Lambe*, 95, trading pattern, 97-98; *Lewis*, 173; *Lincoln*, 177; *Lodi*, 191; *Loyal*, 64; *Loyal Ivy*, 94; *Loyall Merchant*, 95; *Loyal Factor*, trading pattern, 100; *Marmaduke*, 9, 17; *Marston Moor*, 2; *Mary, William and Thomas*, 85-86; *Mordaunt*, 66-68, 75, 175; *New Garden of Flushing*, 26; *Niobe*, 200; *Norwich*, 75-79, 177; *Oxford*, 57-58; *Phoenix*, 61-62; *Rabba Bispa*, 26; *Racoon*, 191, 192; *Recovery*, 7; *Reserve*, 177; *Richard and Sarah*, 66, trading pattern, 96-97, 167; *Ruby*, 60, 69-70, 72, 177; *Sacrifice of Abraham*, 39; *Saint George*, 137; *San Josef* (Spanish ship), 178; *Sara and Abigail*, trading pattern, 99-100; *Sarah*, trading pattern, 101; *Sea Diver*, 205; *Seahorse*, 178; *Shark*, 191, 192; *Sphinx*, 190; *Success*, 74, 75; *Sunderland*, 178; *Swan*, 168, 175, 209; *Sweepstakes*, 65; *Torrington*, 8; *Valorous*, 205; *Ville de Paris*, 190-191; *Welcome*, 17, 41; *William*, 7; *William and Mary*, 96; *Windsor*, 178; *Wolverine*, 200
Shipwrights, 230
Sedgewick, 10
Semmes, Captain, 200
Settlement: of Passage Fort, 11; of Port Royal, 10-14, 16-22, 88, 215-216
Seven Years' War, 183
Silver artefacts, 208
Slaves, 88, 89, 135-136, 149; relationship with whites, 188
Slave trade, 92; illegal, 73-74
Sloane, Dr. Hans, 80; on diseases at Port Royal, 139
Smith, Lieutenant Thomas, 154
Snead, Robert (architect), 120
Society of Artillery, 117
Sonic High Accuracy Ranging and Positioning System (SHARPS), 207
Spain: threat of attack by, 25
Spanish American coins, 205
Spanish colonies: hostilities against, 189-193; illegal trade with Port Royal, 92; privateering raids against, 28, 30, 33-34, 36; trade with Port Royal, 90

Spanish galleons: naval attack on, 178
Spanish rule, 6, 130-131
Spanish Town: plan of, 130-131
Spragg, Captain, 72-73
Street plans. *See* Plan of Port Royal
Stubbs, Captain Thomas: trade route of, 96-97
Sturges, John, 213
Styles, John (planter): resistance to privateering by, 39-40
Sutton, Captain Robert Manners, 190
Sweeting, Henry (merchant), 116
Swymmer, Anthony (merchant), 39, 86; land owned by, 123, 126, 155, 156
Synagogue: location of, 129; 159

Tailors, 230
Taino Indians, 6, 215
Talbot, Captain Charles, 58
Tavern keepers, 230-231
Taverns, 20, 114, 118, 125-127, 147, 161, 232
Taylor, John, 216; plan of Port Royal by, 121
Taylor manuscript, 116, 118, 136-137, 140, 149, 156
Taylor, Thomas (tavern keeper), 147
Texas A & M University, 207
Thompson, Maurice (merchant), 85
Thornton, Diana, 209
Tilley, Thomas (merchant), 137
Tombstones (nineteenth century), 211. *See also* Naval cemetery
Tortuga, 25
Tosier, Captain Josiah, 58, 60, 67-69, 156
Towne, Arthur: land grant to, 17, 19, 124
Towne, Elizabeth: land transactions, 17
Trade in Port Royal. *See* Commercial activity
Trade routes, 93
Tradesmen. *See* Merchants
Transhipment trade, 92, 94
Trapham, Thomas (doctor), 231
Treaty of Madrid: 1667, 34; 1671, 37
Treaty of Ryswick, 177
Treaty of Utrecht, 178, 182
Treaty of Vienna, 189, 198

University of the West Indies Library, xiii
Urban Development Corporation, 212

Van Alphan, Captain Martin: resident supervisor of Fort Cromwell, 9
Vane, Captain Charles (pirate), 182
Vaughan, Lord: rivalry with Sir Henry Morgan, 42-43, 61, 150-151
Velasco, Don Luis de, 182
Venables, General Robert, 57; description of Port Royal by, 7, 8
Vernon, Admiral Edward, 64, 171, 181-183
Vice-Admiralty courts, 27, 29, 191
Victoria Battery, 197, 212
Victuallers, 230
Vintners, 230

Wager, Commodore Charles, 178
Wale, James (postmaster), 157
Walker, Rear-Admiral Hovenden, 178
Walker's Fort, 52-53
Waller, John (cordwainer), 142
Watermen, 230
Watermen's wharf, 123
Watkins, Moses (carpenter): property owned by, 127
Watson, Henry (goldsmith), 115
Watson, Thomas (merchant), 124
Watts, James (engineer), 213
Weatherbourn, Francis (pirate), 67-68, 69
Wells, John (merchant), 124
Wentworth, General, 183
Western Design, 7, 28, 85
Wheeler, Sir Francis, 177
Wherrymen, 230
Whitcombe, Benjamin, 119
White, John (churchwarden), 128, 165
Whitfield, Charles (merchant), 20
Willis, Edward (merchant): property owned by, 126
Wilgress, Captain John, 63
Wilson, Reginald (naval officer), 62-63, 128, 155, 156, 216
Williams, Captain Maurice (privateer), 26
Windsor, Baron of (governor), 26; policies of, 28-29; and religious freedom, 159-160

Wingar, William (craftsman), 141
Wivell, Francis, 75-76, 77
Wright, Captain Lawrence, 58, 80, 154
Women in Port Royal, 17, 117, 119, 124, 135, 144, 161, 182, 187-188, 198

Yabba ware. *See* Ceramics
Yankey (privateer), 71
Yeomans, Edward, 119-120
Younge, John (carpenter): land grant to, 19
Ysassi, Don Cristoval Arnaldo, 7; description of Port Royal by, 10, 215

www.ingramcontent.com/pod-product-compliance
Lightning Source LLC
Chambersburg PA
CBHW071227170426
43191CB00032B/1066